Island
of
Silence

FOURTH EDITION

by Carolyn Brimley Norris

P.O. Box 553, Eureka, CA 95502

ISLAND OF SILENCE was originally published in
paperback by Popular Library, a unit of CBS Publications,
the Consumer Publishing Division of CBS Inc.

Alinda Press
P.O. Box 553, Eureka, CA 95502
Phone (707) 442-6856

ISBN 0-933076-04-5
Library of Congress Number 83-071342

Printed in the United States of America

In memory of my father, Edward Hawley Brimley,
whose last decade was spent in silence,
and
for my friends at Gallaudet College,
Washington, D.C.

Carolyn Brimley Norris now lives in Finland where she teaches English at the University of Helsinki Language Centre. She taught at Gallaudet College and holds a Ph.D. degree in English. Deaf friends furnished material for this novel and for the companion novel, SIGNS UNSEEN, SOUNDS UNHEARD.

ISLAND OF SILENCE first appeared from Popular Library in New York in 1976. In 1978, it was put back into print by Alinda Press.

"People waste their lives crying when they could find something—there's always something, somehow—to laugh about."

I acted upon this as a child, when the landlord made me give away my Christmas puppy (dogs not allowed) and the electric company turned off our power in lieu of payment. I laughed; we all laughed, we three Fallons who had become four and then three again.

I was almost laughing now, hurtling southward down a streak of asphalt in the big bullet of a Greyhound bus. The aphorism about looking on the bright side was true. I wouldn't be heading for a summer in Florida, to do what my heart most desired, if tragedy hadn't hit us fourteen years ago.

The way Mother had put it was, "If life hands you a lemon, make yourself some lemonade." But two years after Cindy was born we found Cindy was a lemon. Shamefaced, we dropped Mother's saying. You can't call a pretty little two-year-old—even one with lemon-colored hair—a "lemon," as if she were a defective automobile.

As for me, my Florida summer promised to be as bright and sweet as lemonade. At twenty-one I was finally getting away from flat, smog- and corn-filled northern Ohio, heading to the palmy dreamland of Florida, to my first truly professional job, at a stupendous salary. I had been selected to try to salvage an injured young man and turn his family's tragedy into . . . into something that might include some happiness, if not laughter.

South through Atlanta I rode the bus, through pine forests, spiky palmettos, moss-hung swampland, and small Southern towns. I emerged from the great cylinder of iced smoke at the Florida border and found myself even at dawn wrapped in warmth like the fresh-baked towels that Mother used to dry me with (and that I had toasted for Cindy, bathing her at bedtime when Mother worked until ten). The air here was light, sweet, kind to the lungs, and always in motion.

In contrast to the neatly clipped, Germanic lawns of Ohio, here were front yards of foot-printed white sand, surrounded by discarded tires that cupped little gardens of bright zinnias. Washing machines wity yellowed wringers stood on front porches. Houses lacked the sterile uprightness I knew from Toledo; they were as random and varicolored as the riot of shrubs groaning under red, pink, yellow, and white blossoms—as insubstantial as the palms' rustling, stalactite fronds.

The bus station as Cross City was surrounded with pink and white periwinkles, ragamuffin flowers. Near here the west coast of Florida swung due west. My final destination lay under the right arm of the state, right on the Gulf—not a tourist-haunt, but a speck on the map called Okasassa.

In the station, when I asked directions, I was asked, in turn, incredulously, "What's a Yankee like you goin' to Okassassa fer?"

Good question. The precious want-ad lay in my pocket like a charm. I lifed my chin and replied, "I'm going to teach a wounded veteran who's been deafened."

"Why, that's mighty nice of you, Ma'am," the clerk said, and escorted me out to the corner, where he pointed along Tangerine Avenue. "Down a block, over by that Lucky Strike sign, is the bench where the jitney stops. Two o'clock, usually."

I had an hour's wait in the sun on that bench with nothing to look at but shoppers in bright clothes and no neckties, and two palms like cement columns with green satin tops. Below their fronds hung what looked like inverted bunches of wheat. I sat and pondered my dramatic reply to the bus-station clerk, the pride in my voice. This summer I was not only manufacturing lemonade, but also dispensing it. I was using our own family tragedy to rescue people worse off than the Fallons of Toledo.

Fourteen years ago, I had been a bubblegum-snapping, popsickle-sucking, scabby-kneed only child in what my sociology texts call an "upper lower-class family." That year Mother, with some aid from Father, gave me the most

2

wonderful gift ever, a baby sister, a live doll. She was supposed to be a brother, but Daddy said they'd try again. As for me, I preferred baby dolls to be girls.

She was so alert and happy an infant that I remember running all the way home from school daily to cuddle her and take her in a stroller over our uneven sidewalks to the swings, where I held her on my lap as she cooed and squealed.

My parents seemed happy, too; they were frugal people who made a bus driver's salary stretch further than the income of our impecunious neighbors. We were the "good" poor people of the textbooks—clean, hardworking, economical, and law-abiding. Cindy's and my toys were creations of retrievable junk that should have been in modern art museums. Mother converted worn dresses to child sizes; she made pillow slips from overage sheets, and washcloths from old towels. We always raised a lush garden—eight feet by five.

I was at home that Saturday twenty-seven months after Cindy came when it all started falling apart. Daddy stood in the kitchen beating on a pan—a new game, I thought, until I saw my parents' faces. My sister continued blithely stabbing fingers into the dough ball that was always given her to mold from the bread dough. She never turned her head.

Mother began to shriek louder than the clang of metal on metal that Cindy did not hear.

The rest of that day is fog, except I remember Cindy climbing cheerfully over Mother, trying to push the corners of Mom's mouth upward, just as she'd molded the dough that was the same color Mother's face had turned.

A year, then two years later, when Cindy was getting into everything and emitting uncouth noises instead of words, when she was being booted out of nursery schools and day-care centers, after she got run over (and lived), Mother saw less and less of Daddy. They fought more and more. Then he· said he could get better pay on the West Coast. He'd settle down and then he'd send for us, he said.

He never did. For a while he sent money, and then less and less of that. Mother took a waitress job. I didn't see Daddy again until I was in high school. Then he came

3

through Toledo with a new wife and two new babies—girls, again, but both of his new daughters could hear.

My textbooks in audiology class documented the high rate of divorce in families with any handicapped child. They also said that a bright deaf child could fool the family into thinking nothing was wrong for one or two years. Cindy beat that maximum by three months, but aside from that accomplishment, we were all normal; it said so in the book.

I'd changed very promptly from a movie-star- and horse-mad nine-year-old who ran with a gaggle of similar little gigglers into a solitary tigress who guarded an almost uncontrollable and unprotectable (but still smiling) tornado of a baby sister.

Worst of all, Cindy was unreachable. A series of ill-paid sitters penned her up during my school hours, and after school she exploded out of the house past me, a tiny whirlwind I had to direct, to channel, but mostly to run after—fending off bullies, tearing her away from the neighbors' flower-beds and kittens, trying, trying (by pantomime, show-and-tell, anything, any way) to get some idea across to her, any idea, just once.

When she was six, we sent her off to the deaf school and saw her only on occasional weekends. There she changed as totally as I had changed in order to pinch-hit as her part-time mother and father. She was still operating like a hearing child half her age, but she was turning into a human being. She'd learned something we'd never before heard of—the manual language called signs and finger-spelling. Words could spin like magic off one's hands.

"Hey! Stop! I'm going to Okasassa!"

I waved my purse at the jitney that threatened to leave me on my bench. I had to repeat myself to the wizened little driver before he understood me. He, like the first man, seemed disturbed by my destination.

"It's real isolated, Ma'am," he said. "Okasassa's just a dozen houses and a store. You sure you got the town right? Then Injun names're all spelled alike: Okasimee, Homasassa, Okechobee . . . ."

He put my one battered suitcase aboard, pivoted his small bus, and soon we left cement and asphalt roadways to

4

skid through powdery white sand slippery as snow. I was his only passenger.

When I told him the name of my new employer, he had one quick reply before he fell silent for the rest of the trip.

"Y'better ask folks around town, 'fore you get yo'self tied in with HIM! No nice young lady's got business around them Howells."

I made allowances for this, because Mr. Kenneth Howell, in the letters that followed my reply to his ad, explained that he lived "in red-neck country" among "real Florida crackers who hold all Yankees suspect."

In his last letter was a pitiful line I remembered well: "I'm just an old bachelor uncle trying to play parent (or two) and failing miserably."

Last fall Keegan Howell, his nephew, had quit the University of Florida to join the Army and be shipped over to Asia. Keegan was shipped back to America this Spring with both legs fractured by the explosion that had destroyed his hearing. Only twenty-one, my age, and he'd never hear another sound. Mr. Howell had described him as sullen and desperate, and between the lines I read "suicidal." I knew of several suicides among late-deafened people.

My jitney careened around a grassy-haired sand dune and slid to a halt in front of a long, rickety building perched on stilts. It had a deep, shady veranda. Bags of chicken feed leaned against the porch wall; a rusty gas pump guarded one end of the veranda; and the walls bore as decorations scores of colorful and too-familiar ads—beer to motor oil, cigarettes to Coke. In shadow sat several rattan chairs, unraveled almost to skeletons.

"Here we be, Miss," my driver said, and hopped up the steps to swing my suitcase onto the creaking porch. Tossing a bundle of newspapers to an aproned woman who emerged through a screen door, he jerked a thumb toward me.

"This 'yere young lady's headed to the Howell place, she says. To work fer THEM!"

By the time this was announced, five more people in faded denim and flowered house dresses were on the veranda staring at me, their faces not unfriendly but definitely

5

troubled.

Food boxes from the jitney disappeared into this grocery-post office-feedstore-gas station, and then my transportation made a U-turn on the hard-packed square of sand and headed with a farewell honk back toward Cross City.

My audience had been enlarged by four pre-schoolers in sandy underpants, a black woman, and a man in gaiters and a felt hat. That made a dozen. The sign for Okasassa had given the population as 116; I was now face-to-face with one tenth of the townspeople.

Mr. Howell had prepared me, but he hadn't explained why he chose to live here. He sounded quite sophisticated; his English had sent me running to the dictionary more than once, with his grimly witty letters in hand. Where did he find congenial company around here? He'd pay me seven hundred dollars a month and free room and board, yet he lived HERE?

"I'm a—" I decided to make it sound really good "—I'm a teacher of the deaf come from Ohio. . . come to tutor Keegan Howell. My name is Leslie Fallon."

"Mmmm," said all the lips, and the eyes passed a significant look, one to the next, all down the row of faces above me in the shade. I waited until a few smiles flickered to life.

"Where exactly is Okasassa House?"

I asked this while climbing the steps, eyeing three of the toddlers who were clambering, sober-faced, onto my suitcase. They sat in a row, fidgeting, like the monkeys who see, speak, and hear no evil. Keegan Howell could see and speak, but he would hear no evil . . . or good.

"Y'don't know where you're headin'?" said one incredulous voice.

"No. I just have the address as Okasassa. . . ."

"Ain't in this town. It's out on an island."

"ISLAND?"

Several tongues clicked in sympathy for my ignorance as I tried to remember letters I'd halfway memorized. "We're off Okasassa, Florida," Mr. Howell had said, but I'd missed that sly little preposition, "off." He also said I could begin working on June fifteenth.

"I came a day early, to get settled," I said. "He

6

expects me tomorrow."

"Well, they don't come over for mail and food more'n every ten days, and the last trip was four, five days ago. Ain't no way you can git out there," a woman said.

"I'll telephone Mr. Howell, then."

"Ain't no phone on the island."

"Oh. Well, a boat. Surely I can . . . pay someone to take me there."

"Ain't no way to land on that there island," an old man said, and spat. "Without gittin' lost in them mangroves or gittin' yer head shot off."

"Shot off?" I squeaked.

"Anybody comin' in on the beach, on the Gulf side, gits shot at. It's a mite discouragin', as you can imagine, which is how come nobody would take yer."

"You mean if . . . you mean I've got twenty-four hours to wait, and no other choice?"

"Yes, Ma'am."

"There IS a hotel in town, isn't there?"

The one man who laughed was cut off in mid-chuckle; the others took me very seriously.

"There's no ho-tel or mo-tel, Miss," a woman said, "but someone can find you a bed, fer sure. Sarah Quale's son's gone in Service, and she's got one."

The words "Southern hospitality" flitted through my mind as I looked hopefully from one broad-breasted broody hen in calico to another.

"I've a cot on mah sun porch you can use, Honey," said the tallest woman. "I'd be honored to have y'stay with me, if you're comin' to help young Keegan Howell." She wore a pink apron, and her grey hair was cropped severely short, not straggly like the other country coiffures.

"Do you know Keegan?"

"Sure do. He's the only one on that island who's decent, pore child. Went off to fight fer his country and came home deaf."

"Whatcha gonna larn him?" asked another.

I was still standing on the edge of the long veranda, my heels against the row of potted cactus plants, when the tall woman broke away from the firing-squad line, looped an arm around my shoulders and drew me over to the group of rattan chairs—apparently the town's social center.

7

Sit yerself down, Honey. I'm Araminta McElroy, widow of Joseph McElroy. Maybe we can give you a little helpful advice, and sometime you kin come back and tell us 'bout a few mysteries that's been bothrin' us."

Obediently I sat on the least skeletonized chair, and found myself holding an orange soda, freshly uncapped, that someone pushed into my travel-grimy hands. In this outdoor parlor, raised to catch the breeze, the afternoon heat was quite bearable.

"Whatcha gonna larn th' boy?" I heard again, and was more than happy to explain.

"He can't hear anymore, so he'll have to learn to lipread—" I began "—read words off people's lips. We call that speechreading."

"Like understandin' when the sound goes dead on the television?" Araminta asked.

"Yes, but it's hard. That's how I practice, using a TV with the sound turned off. But I'm a very poor speech-reader. It's sort of an inborn skill, and I hope Keegan will have it."

I was losing them, so I propped up my right hand and spelled the alphabet on my fingers, A to Z.

"See, these are the letters," I explained. "I can spell to Keegan, even though he can't hear me speak."

"Lookit that," a fat little squab of a woman grinned. "They's like the real letters, some of 'em!" She probably had caught the obvious ones like C, L, O, and Z.

"For whole words we make big signs, like this," and I signed "milk," tugging on a teat in my hand. Then I made the signs for "drink" and "eat," tipping an invisible glass and lifting food to my mouth. I ran through some animal-signs for the children, and had them rolling on the floor in merriment, imitating me quite accurately— flapping horse-ears and pulling cat-whiskers.

"That's mighty interstin'," Mrs. McElroy beamed.

"Y'see, we like the boy 'cause we got to know his paw before his paw died," A man said. "He warn't stuck up. Didn't prance around in no fancy clothes like that brother of his, young Keegan's uncle."

He was eyeing my homemade seersucker suit, which labeled me hardly more prosperous than these people. My aged suitcase hadn't escaped notice, either.

8

"Keegan's father died last fall, didn't he?" I asked.

"His paw took a long time a-dyin', pore man," said an elder townsman sitting with his sun-reddened forearms on his knees, cleaning his nails with a knife. "His lungs went bad on him. Coughed ever' minute. He came over to drink with us. He liked home-brew. He was so blasted proud of that uni-versity kid o' his! Lands, he lived for that boy! It's a good thing he died 'fore he saw the boy deaf like he is now."

"But he shouldn'ta died like he did, the paw. . . ."

"Does Keegan come here to town often?" I asked, remembering Mr. Howell had called his nephew a "recluse."

"Nope. We seen him come home in March, three months ago, hardly able to stagger and deaf as a post. The uncle took him out there to that island, and we ain't see the boy since, though the black folks say he's still there, and he don't limp no more."

"They've got black folks workin' fer them, but they ain't friendly like us folks here," the black woman put in. "They am bigger snobs than that uncle. It's yes, no, and hardly a thank you, and they be gone off, noses in the air."

"He use to come visit Mr. Brad Howell and Mrs. Howell, that uncle did, and he'd have a big, fancy camera strung 'round his neck. Now he's living there, stealin' Okasassa House from Keegan. That's how we see it. Got himself his own studio, and he takes pitchers that'd land him in jail if we tole," said an old man.

"But if you don't go to the island, how do you know he had a studio and takes pictures?" I asked.

"The Lord sees to it that the wicket git punished," said the gaitered man, who now held his hat upside down on his knees like a beggar's bowl. "We see what goes over to that island and what comes back. They dump trash on our town dump, and its full o' liquor bottles and of boxes and parts for pho-tography. Readin' a person's trash is like readin' his face. A man's sins is written on his face and left broken in his garbage."

During the respectful silence that followed, I remembered that "a man's character can be read by the books in his library." Books were an issue here, as well.

"I thought Keegan's father was in the rare-books

business," I offered.

"Oncet he were. But now it's pitchers, not books, a-comin' and goin' from there. Oncet that Mr. Kenneth Howell he sent a package out from here in a big hurry, and it come loose—the end come untaped. Before Mrs. Harvey could stick it back together again, as a nice favor to him, what yuh think come a-slitherin' out, like the serpent of Eden?"

I shook my head innocently.

"A pitcher of a woman . . . without no clothes on a-tall!"

I wasn't sure I could hold back a burst of laughter that beat on my pharynx.

"You see why we all o' us worry about any decent young lady teacher goin' out there, alone?"

No doubt they took my suffocated look for offended propriety. Mr. Howell had told me he was a free-lance photographer. He sometimes photographed nudes, of course.

"We hate to see you go out there, but if it means heppin' young Keegan . . . such a fine boy . . ." Mrs. McElroy sighed.

"You ain't no university teacher, are ye? At yer age?"

"No. I'm studying at a university, part-time, to teach deaf children. My sister was born deaf; she's fourteen. She can't hear or talk."

"Land sakes!" cried Mrs. McElroy. "Then you've got you a sister like pore ole Barney, who lived here thirty years and never said a word?"

"Deaf-mute, Barney was . . . the nicest, most helpful boy."

"Colored," another woman qualified.

"You mean to say Keegan Howell's gonna quit talkin'? He's gonna git like Barney?" a man gaped.

"No. He won't become mute," I said, trying always to quash the myths surrounding the deaf. "And actually, you know, deaf people aren't mute; they can yell. Keegan went deaf so late that he's different from my Cindy and your Barney. He can already talk and read and write. His problems will be emotional—I mean, how he feels, losing so much, so suddenly."

I could have itemized his losses: voices, telephone, radio, television, music, movies, traffic-sounds, animals, machines, but most of all voices. The blind lose things; the deaf lose people. I was willing to lecture them all afternoon, but gossip resurfaced.

"Seems like somebody ought to get young Keegan off that island. It ain't no place fer him. They're doin' evil things, maybe even keepin' his mother a prisoner."

"Prisoner?" Mr. Howell had told me Keegan's mother "vanished," and I told the townspeople that.

"She ain't been seen since jist after Keegan went in the service last September. Fust off her mister died, not like anybody expected, but real violent. Then that crooked uncle was there. Then Miz Howell she jist disappeared. We ain't seen no letters of hers come in or out, though they don't send much mail outta here no more, not since we found out what pitchers he was sendin' to New York, and big money comin' in fer worthless ole books. . .

"How do you know about money for books?"

"Some folks use awful thin envelopes. I don't reckon you'll get mail very often?"

"Well . . . " I thought of my mother honeymooning in New England, remarried and beginning a new life of her own.

"As we said, the island people come across the water no more'n ever' ten days, so if you need anythin', you'd best stock up. Like cigarettes—a person'd hafta take a big supply of cigarettes over."

"I don't smoke."

"Somethin' else—did we say there's a mean old man with a beard livin' out there, too, doin' somethin' with the books? Keeps his car in the Potters' garage and don't pay 'em enough to do so. You know them bearded kinds."

"And they's always been a ghost out there, ever since Miz Bayless died."

"Hush up, or you'll have the chile runnin' right back to Ohio," said Mrs. McElroy.

Her warning did not succeed. The dam had been breeched.

"The ghost, yeah. Wasn't never any good come outta that place. The house was built fer smugglin', and lotsa folks died out there. . . ."

"Ain't no way through them mangroves, 'less you get taken in and out in their boat. . ."

"And him takin' pitchers of our coast," added another

11

voice, ominously. "Some thinks he's a Commie spy, sellin' them pitchers to Cuba, to tell 'em how to invade us."

My tall friend rose and faced down even the pious man with the hat. "That's a mouthful of garbage! Who's to hep Keegan if Miss Fallon don't? Come along home with me, Honey, and I'll let you get some peace and quiet and good cookin'."

She shot a last, baleful look over the assemblage. "You folks love gossip more'n good sense."

Araminta McElroy, widowed mother of five girls, made up a cot for me on a sun porch not much wider than the cot itself, shucked me out of my suit jacket, and sat me down in her kitchen. She fed me my very first okra and the best fried chicken I'd ever tasted outside a Colonel Sanders. She seemed delighted to have me to herself to pump while she washed dishes. I was not to help; I was to consume my first mango, a messy fruit that slipped through my fingers and stuck in my teeth and was delicious, except for its faint flavor of kerosene.

"Yer sister was born deaf?" she asked over her shoulder. "How'd you all talk to her?"

"We took her to a clinic, and experts worked for years just to make her say 'Maaa' and 'Baaa.' Finally she made those sounds, but she didn't know what they meant. We just pointed and gestured. It was impossible."

"Our Barney tried to talk on his hands like you showed us, but they was made-up signs, and I was the only one that could sometimes figger 'em out," she said.

"I know; you try and try and sometimes you go half crazy with guessing. And nobody tells you that hearing people can learn to talk on their hands, too. That's what makes me furious," I confided. "For six years Cindy couldn't ask us a single question, and we couldn't have answered her if she did. She didn't learn anything. I had to protect her, and people thought she was a moron!"

"Like I stood up fer Barney."

"And Cindy's got a higher I.Q. than I have."

"Barney was our yard-boy, and slept out behind in his own little shack, doin' odd jobs fer people. But them ignorant ones, they threw things at him and teased him somethin' terrible," she said.

"And I bet Barney never learned to read or write."

"Lan' sakes no, Honey! But since half of them here can't read n' write, the older ones, it wasn't so strange. The worst of it was the awful noises he'd make—'cause he couldn't hear himself, pore boy!"

"I know. Deaf people who can talk often don't talk, because people stare at them and think they must be not deaf, but retarded."

"But you look at that Helen Keller from Alabama. She wrote and traveled and was smart, and she was blind, too!"

"Helen Keller is Cindy's idol," I smiled. "She knows Helen's life like boys know their baseball heroes. But Helen had two years of sight and hearing before—"

"Why isn't yer sister down here with you? I'd feel a lot better ifn' it was two girls goin' out there, not just one alone."

"She's spending the summer with a deaf family," I said. "The parents and kids are all deaf, and they sign faster than we talk. They were signing to each other when the kids were only six months old!"

"Fancy that!" Little babies!"

"Words like 'milk' and 'mother' are much easier to say with your hand than with your mouth."

Araminta sat down opposite me, drying her soapy fingers one by one. "How'd you learn 'bout these Howells, anyway?"

"Mr. Howell put an ad in a national magazine," I replied. "He asked for an 'unattached young lady to teach communications methods to a deaf veteran,'"

"Humph" Unattached, indeed! Now why'd he say that, 'less he means no good? You got a boyfriend?" she demanded.

"Nope. I had a fiance, but he ran off with his new secretary." (I could laugh about it now—what progress since those bitter tears of last October!)

"He's got a habit of takin' pretty women out on that island, some younger'n you, and they don't come back fer days!"

"Is it a big island?"

"It's a big house—three stories high—but the island's nothin' but a narrer doughnut shape with no clear land fer a garden or anythin'—just jungles around a lake, I hear. I never been out there. Wouldn't go if I was in-vited."

She wiped the table clean for the third time. "Kenneth

Howell's a bachelor twenty years past when he oughta been one. I think they call his kind a . . . a lecher."

"Oh."

"'Course, I know things are changin'. My ideas are more modern than them that Okasassa usually cottons to, but a girl pretty as you with them big eyes and nice womanly figger. . . ."

"I'll be careful."

George had been too old for me—thirty. Mother claimed that I saw in him a father-figure. I was well rid of George. He had seemed terrified of ever being alone with Cindy, with whom he couldn't communicate. My life sure never was dull. Now I'd have a "lecher" of forty or fifty as my boss!

Araminta cast a dark look my way. "Don't you have nothing' to do with any dirty pitchers, y'hear? If that's what he's up to, he belongs in prison!"

My lips trembled with suppressed amusement, so I lowered my voice to sound suitably grave. "I won't even let Mr. Howell know I spent twenty-four hours in Okasassa, how about that? Shall I pretend that I arrived here just before he picks me up, tomorrow? You'll take me to meet his boat . . ."

She liked that idea. Leslie Fallon—Secret Agent for Okasassa—could serve as a pipeline of information to these honest, righteous, desperately curious townsfolk. I didn't promise to snoop and carry tales, but I'd let them think I was in league with them against sin.

Sin? One doesn't reach twenty-one, without some people trying to help themselves to one's "womanly figure." I feared I was much more "modern" than even Mrs. McElroy—bless her soul!

That night, my first-ever scorpion appeared right above my cot, and I woke in the blackest hours to what I was certain was the roaring of a lion. I slept restlessly after that, wondering which of their tales just might be true. Then I worried about my crusading attitude toward Keegan Howell. I had to be sure to treat him as a young man with no hearing. He was not just a pair of deaf ears riding around on the head of a young man, though his deafness occupied so much of my attention. Deafness must not blot out everything else about him.

14

My guess about hearing a lion in the night was wrong. It was a bull alligator two miles north in a swamp. Mrs. McElroy was as protective of him ("Old Bill," she called him) as she'd been of Barney, the deaf man. I seconded her hope that Old Bill would never leap for the poacher's bait, the dead goat with a stake through it. (Hearing that description, I almost gagged on my grits.)

I slipped a couple of dollars and a manual-alphabet card under Araminta's sugar bowl before we left her cottage. We walked through town, filling our shoes with sand and tugging each other off balance as we carried my suitcase. Down a lane we wobbled, to a ramshackle dock thrust out over lapping green water. Shoreline trees stilted in the shallows, their shiny, leathery leaves deflecting light upwards.

"Mangroves," Amanita responded to my question. "Remember, now," she cautioned, obviously reluctant either to leave or to stay, "You teach Keegan good, so he can get off that island. You let us know if there's anythin' the sheriff should know. There'd be no weepin' in this town if that uncle landed where we figger he belongs—in jail."

"Where is the island . . .in what direction?" I asked blithely.

"Off to th' left, there, 'round the head."

"Are they Southerners? Floridians?"

"Sakes, no! They's New Yorkers! From up where the Maw-fia comes from!"

"Oh, really?"

"You'll know his boat. It's the only one on our coast with paint on it." She patted my shoulder. "You be careful now, y'hear?"

Waves sucked at the pilings, and a hound barked up in the town. A crook-necked black sea bird came winging to the dock, saw me just in time, screeched indignantly, and wheeled away. I dangled my feet just above the green water, dreaming of rewards of satisfaction greater far than the monetary recompense I had been promised—though the pay in itself was ample reward. My salary would let me go to school full time next fall and give up my dime-store clerking job.

I leaned sideways to exchange glances with a long fish in the transparent shallows. No decent store, theatre, or

15

restaurant was in Okasassa. I sighed. I'd brought with me some cash for "real Florida" clothes, a gift from my new stepfather, the chef. Where could I buy clothes around here? And how is a tutor supposed to dress? Victorian governesses wore sweeping black gowns of bombazine, whatever that was. Their high lace collars were fastened with brooches. . .hair parted down the center, like mine, but tied back in a bun (my hair flowed). I remembered Jane Eyre and her Mr. Rochester. A threatening Mr. Rochester was who the townspeople thought Mr. Howell was—the mysterious, immoral master of the mansion. But Jane, the governess, had tutored a girl child, not a young man her own age. Jane had had no one to fall in love with but Mr. Rochester. Keegan would occupy my mind . . . and maybe my affections, too. . . .

I was picking up tiny pastel pink and violet snails from the piling and letting them trail silver paths across my palm. No telephone on the island; I wondered if the house had TV, electricity, and indoor plumbing? Did it depend on gaslights and flickering candles down eerie long corridors? Trespassers were shot. The strait was like a moat; was it full of sharks and crocodiles? How did one distinguish between the beloved Old Bill and a man-eating croc?

Did the coast have hurricanes? Cindy would like that. I'd even convinced her that Ohio tornadoes were fun, so any storm she felt in her bones made a hit with her. To Cindy the stars crackled (as in "Twinkle, twinkle, little star"), but she couldn't hear our rusty apartment toilets flush themselves for hours, though I'd taught her to fix them. She had to watch for the teakettle's steam, while I endured the earsplitting whistle two rooms away. I wished she could see Florida, if not hear it.

A shiny little cabin-cruiser came coasting around the mangrove-lined headland before the breeze brought me its sound. It banked sharply, like a racer on a curve, its white paint dazzling in the afternoon sun, contrasting with the dark wood of the deck. It flaunted the name SIGFORD, and I felt smug that when someone misspelled "Siegfried," I knew it—from studying World Literature I!

A fat, middle-aged man leaned over the side, riveting his gaze on me. I groaned in disappointment. No Mr.

Rochester this! The opposite of tall, dark, and mysterious, he was short, pallid, and bald. At the wheel would be the black employee, I supposed. But when the boat pivoted up to the dock, rocking in the swells, the wheelsman turned out not to be black; he was tan, with long sideburns graying down his jawline. He was wearing a knit shirt and yachting cap. This man was fortyish, husky, and plenty handsome.

"Leslie Fallon?" he asked.

It had to be him.

"I'm Ken Howell." He confirmed my guess. "This is Baker Johnson, whom I'm bringing back to civilization, if you can call it that!" He tossed a loop of rope around my piling, pulling near enough for the fat man to clamber, gasping, onto the dock.

"You can get to town unescorted, can't you, Baker? It's a nice walk. Try jogging; it would do wonders for your figure!" He chuckled.

Trying not to slip from the precariously tipped, rotting boards, I was now eye-to-eye with Baker Johnson, and the closer view did not do anything to improve my first impression. He mumbled a greeting and turned back to the boat.

"She's damn young," he drawled. "I thought she was a teacher."

"I told you her age. Youth is what I wanted."

I noted both the accent—New York but not the Bronx— as well as the peculiar implications of his words.

"You gonna live there all summer?" Johnson demanded of me.

Tired of such challenges, I was almost as rude as my new boss. "Certainly," I snapped. "What's wrong with that?"

If he was surprised at my tone, he hid it. Ken Howell grinned, his eyes dancing, showing white teeth. He reached up for my suitcase and me, jumping me down into the boat with sinewy brown arms. He put me onto the padded seat in the stern.

I looked back at the retreating waddle of Baker Johnson and was startled when I turned around. My employer was leaning over me, affording me a closeup of his brown face and dark eyes. I almost thought he was going to kiss me, but he made L-shaped hands to frame my face and gazed at me.

"Who would've expected it? You're perfect! Absolutely perfect, every inch of you!"

He hadn't come near to seeing every inch of me, and never would. I gathered my garments about me defensively, trying to smile like a sophisticate.

As I stared at his uncle, a picture of Keegan Howell began to form in my mind. I assumed I'd be meeting the deaf young man in only a few minutes—but most of my assumptions that day were wrong. Ken Howell was not tall. Of medium height, very well put together, supple at the joints and beaded with muscle, Mr. Howell turned the wheel, squinting at the sun that blinded him from beyond the island, murmuring, "Dark, long hair, those eyes . . . why, I couldn't have done better if I'd asked for your photo." He added, "There were nineteen other applicants for this job, Leslie."

"Thank you for choosing me," I stammered.

"You'll be great. I know you will!"

"Hope so," I chirped, from among piles of waterproof flowered cushions, thinking uneasily, "be great" at what? At teaching Keegan? Or posing for his uncle's camera?

Or what?

You'd think a fast trip across a quarter mile of water would be uneventful, but not for me. A black shadow on the waves was cast by no cloud. Mr. Howell responded to my shakily pointing finger, my weak exclamation.

"A manta ray. A nice big one." He smiled.

Eight feet across, a shadow was flying through the water, just below the surface, flapping a little at the edges. My stomach dropped. Who would dare swim here?

"Rays are harmless, really," he soothed me. "Impressive fella, though."

Close to the island now, I found that the trees weren't five feet tall, as I first calculated, but three times that height. No break showed in their dense foliage. Between glossy leaves and the lemon-colored shallows over black muck was a tangle of grey trunks, water-stained. Big trees up to their knees in water vaguely disturbed me.

"Over here, or you'll get hurt," he shouted, spinning the wheel abruptly.

I obeyed, lunging forward under the awning, huddling against him to avoid branches and leaves that suddenly came aboard, filling the boat and slapping at us. We were in a narrow channel in the mangroves, if it were a channel at all. We slipped into the trees like a magician's two rabbits, and my eyes were slow to adjust to the dark. I hung onto the ledge above the cabin door as the boat began to zigzag.

"How can you see anything?" I exclaimed.

"If I misjudge, we'll be right up a tree!" He laughed.

Ice-breakers plow ice; we plowed branches. Then we burst into sunshine again, and he cut the motor to let us coast across the mirror-sheen of what appeared to be a lake, actually a lagoon, the center of the doughnut of the island. Everywhere mangroves walled us in except dead ahead, where Okasassa Hosue reared itself three stories high, its paintless wood a silver, satiny grey. It was a tall, narrow house with tall, narrow windows reflecting gold from the late afternoon sun.

On a dark, misty day it might look forbidding, but now it was a silver and gold house set in a necklace of jade trees over an emerald lake, which mirrored the arc of trees and house until we erased the image with our prow.

"Surprised, Leslie?"

"Very!" I didn't tell him its beauty was less a surprise than the existence of the island. I leaned straight-armed on the rail of the SIGFORD, over limeade water that revealed a sandy bottom far below.

"The lagoon, of course, isn't natural. It was dredged years ago. Makes for security. Anyone but us gets lost trying to climb through the mangroves, and a boat needs to be guided in. We like that," he added.

"We do?" I tried to smile. "Sounds rather cloak-and-daggerish."

"The house dates from Prohibition days, long, long before your birth. This island did a lot of business."

"Smuggling?"

"Chiefly Caribbean rum was once landed and hidden here, and then smuggled onto the mainland. Quite a colorful—and grisly—past our house boasts." He was grinning.

"Oh?" I hoped he'd shove far into the past anything grisly about the island. It began to dawn on me that I would be, in effect, a prisoner here, ringed by impassable jungles and unswimmable bodies of water containing sea-monsters, without even a telephone to summon help. . . which of course could not come, for fear of getting lost or shot.

We reached the freshly painted, sturdy dock before our momentum was spent, and I was lifted from the boat as easily as I had been lifted in, feeling smaller every minute in comparison with Mr. Howell's quick strength, the mansion's glory, and the wealth I sensed around me. He unloaded my suitcase, looking with interest at the corroded latches and frayed bindings.

Beside the pebbled path to the house were bushes of pink and white flowers, like lesser gardenias. Their leaves, I later learned, were so poisonous that murderous wives were known to grind them into their husbands' coffee with no one the wiser. Over the great front porch climbed vines bearing little paper tents, purple bougainvillea, bright as if lit from within. Potted palms decorated the sand-lawn that sported not one blade of grass.

"It's lovely," I said, "and the house is really magnificent."

"We don't use half of it. I made myself a studio adjoining my bedroom—see the plate glass windows on the second floor, there? If I continue to bring people here, though . . . " His voice trailed off.

"Pretty flowers, too."

"You're certainly the prettiest addition to the place in a long time, Leslie."

My attention swung from the horticulture to the host, and I blurted, "Does your nephew know I'm coming?"

He did not meet my ingenuous gaze.

"Can you tell me how to get a simple fact like 'a young lady is coming here to tutor you' across to a kid who's closed to all communication?" Ken Howell asked. "Keegan can't hear a word, he scorns note-writing, and he refuses to lip-read."

"Maybe he cannot lip-read. I'm terrible at it, myself. Does he scorn everyone's notes?"

"The emphasis I put on "everyone" was a shot in the dark that hit live flesh. His dancing eyes and mobile mouth both drooped.

"He's especially closed to me. It has a long history, nothing to do with his deafness. It isn't the kid's fault, but don't be surprised at anything he says to me."

"He does talk to you?"

"Oh, Keegan hasn't suffered any loss of voice, rest assured! He expresses himself with great fluency. It's a monologue, though, no feedback; no one can reply to him."

No loss of voice? I let that pass. Without speech-therapy, in a few years, Keegan's unmonitored, unheard voice would blur, become inaccurate, and his advantage over so-called "mutes" would narrow. This was no time to pile troubles on troubles for these people, though. Not yet.

The long porch was up six wide steps. At one end was a wooden porch swing, and at the other dangled a net-like hammock. It seemed a hybrid between a Midwestern farmhouse and a Spanish hacienda.

My host lugged my suitcase into spacious coolness. Braided rugs lay on the highly polished hardwood floor; the furniture was scanty, which added to the impression of airiness. In the dimness I saw no young man, but a black woman materialized. My nerves unwound with what I recognized as relief. Mr. Howell was extremely attractive, but he was too much aware of that fact.

I had been warned that Keegan might treat Ken with disrespect; I wasn't prepared for the coldness in the woman's voice.

"This child is the teacher?" she cried.

Watching her glare pitchfork into him, I winced, even though she smiled at me, laying her protective palms on my shoulders, brushing back my long hair. "Why, yer just a girl, Miss . . ."

"Fallon. Leslie Fallon," he said. "This is Mrs. Dean, our household supervisor. She's run the place for seven years with great efficiency."

His flattery didn't impress.

"My name's Margaret, and I'm the housekeeper. How old are you, Miss Fallon?"

"Twenty-one. I . . . you can call me Leslie."

"I'll fix you suppah and show you to yer room when Mr. Howell here says I can, Honey."

Her icy formality toward him contrasted with her warmth toward me. I wondered what she felt toward Keegan.

"I'll get you a drink and show you something of the house," my host said. "Then you might have a light supper in your room. We went ahead with dinner before Mr. Johnson departed. You can't keep a fat man waiting long for his feedbag."

Mrs. Dean—Margaret—blended back into the shadows, muttering ". . . suppah and a glass of warm milk, which is better fer a girl than hard liquor!"

I followed Mr. Howell and his martini up the curving, regal staircase to the next floor. The living room below us could accommodate a ball—at least a small one. It contained breezes, this wind-tunnel big enough to swallow up our cramped city apartment. But the house seemed unused, unlived-in, a shell, waiting.

I was impatient to meet Keegan Howell. His uncle was

interesting, as light on his feet as a boy, and I wondered
why he was a bachelor. Mrs. Dean would be a needed friend
to me, but Keegan . . .?

"We can talk more privately in my studio—" The man's
hand delicately guided me around a corner in the long,
polished hall, dark except for the white sheen from its
waxed floor. "—That is, if you don't mind a bevy of
nudes!"

Here we go, I thought, prickles chasing up my spine to
the roots of my hair.

On the high white walls of his studio were nudes, all
right, acres of them, but art, not pornography. Among them
hung striking action photographs, much enlarged, of
athletes leaping and straining, sailboats swinging in the
wind, storm-dashed waves and trees. He was good, very
good. He admitted his work was widely published. He
flipped open issues of famous slick magazines to prove it.

I sank down on the low, red corduroy couch where he
indicated, weak with relief. He was "legit," then. Score:
Howell, one; Okasassa, zero. He read my mind uncannily.

"Imagine the local sheriff walking in here? Or one of
the pillars of Okasassa society? I'd land in the local
hoose-gow on a morals charge."

I tried not to stare at all the long svelt limbs and
swollen globes around us. The working half of the room was
full of tilted drawing tables and geometric tools, all
apparently in heavy use. Papers and books were strewn
about.

"In there is my darkroom," he gestured. "My bedroom is
off thataway. You see the advantage of this location. I
get sun almost year-round, and my windows face north."

"Can you do all your photography from here?"

"I've turned down most assignments since Brad died," he
said. "And since Keegan came home in March, I've been gone
only three weeks in all—to Toronto and Los Angeles. I
don't want to leave him alone, here."

I nodded, gripping my sweating glass of fruity vodka.
This chatter was preliminary to something serious. I
presumed to ask a question—the question.

"Where is Keegan?"

"Leslie," he said, "I scarcely recall what I've told
you in my letters. You know what when Brad died, Keegan

23

joined the Army instead of going back to school last fall. Keegan's mother went off with her grief, God knows where. The island and the bookselling business and the house were willed not to Sigrid but to Keegan. This doesn't mean Brad cut his widow out of his estate. There was a reason for writing his will that way . . . a personal reason. Besides, Keegan being a model son, Brad knew he'd take good care of Sigrid.

"Brad's estate is in a financial snarl—mortgages, a suit to settle, that sort of thing. Brad bought thousands of books and hated to part with any. Those he sold he didn't show much profit on. So the estate's tied up and will be for a month more. Keegan gets disability from the Army, which he squirrels away. I've been shelling out for taxes, keeping the place going, and paying the help, but it's quite a drain. . . ." He looked wistfully at me.

"What I'm trying to say, Leslie, is that a helluva lot depends on the kid's getting back to normal. But I've no idea what's possible for Keegan. Can he hold a decent job, or maybe finish college? The only deaf men I've seen were peddling deaf-alphabet cards or begging."

". . . and other deaf people are setting print for newspapers, programming compulters, doing biological research or library work or—"

"How did they learn those fields?" he interrupted. "Not by rejecting help, I'll bet! Not by tearing up people's notes and cursing. . ." He caught himself. "Listen to this. When I met the poor kid's plane in Atlanta, I took him to a hotel for the night. When I started phoning firends in the city, Keegan got right out of bed and tore the telephone cord out of the wall. Why would he want to do that?"

"For the same reason a deaf man got furious when I climbed over him to turn up the sound on our TV set. . . which he couldn't hear. Put yourself in his place."

"How does Cindy act? Don't you ever get so angry at her you could ki— hit her?"

"No! Never," I said. "I absolutely adore her."

I didn't like the droop to those powerful shoulders. "Look," I said, "Sure, Keegan acts strange, but he's awfully lucky in some ways. Many of the very successful deaf can't talk understandably. He can. He's had twenty years in the hearing world, handling English. Yes, he can go back to college, maybe he'll choose Gallaudet, in Washington, D. C., the famous college for the deaf. Mr. Howell—"

"Call me Ken." He was recovering from his anguish. I'm not quite old enough to be your . . . grandfather."

"Your housekeeper won't stand for first names, I notice."

"That's one sore point between us. It goes against her grain to be treated with dignity. She's old enough to be my mother, but she must be 'Margaret,' while I'm 'Mister.' Do you prefer to be called 'Miss Fallon'?"

"'Leslie' is fine."

He looked at me for a long time, until I shifted uneasily. I wanted to stroll to the window to see if the town was visible from the upper floors. But from two cushions away on the couch, he stretched out his arm and laid his hand upon mine.

"Leslie, then. Leslie, you've already seen what a big job you've got. You've cheered me up already, and I'm gambling that a sweet young girl will get through to Keegan. With your face—"

He didn't finish. I attributed this obsession to his photographer's point of view. I did photograph well—big eyes, a small nose that didn't case inconvenient shadows, and an olive complexion above an hourglass figure.

"You certainly could twist me around your little finger," he said emphatically.

Immediately I extricated my hand from beneath his warm palm and gulped the last of my cool drink. He was moving close to the thin line between flattering and worrying me. I wanted to back off but not appear childish. So I stayed put and fired a question at him.

"Tell me exactly what kind of person Keegan was . . . is. Was he a good student?"

"Oh, tops! Always. And with little effort. Not a grind, just a phenomenal memory. That's what's hit him hardest. He's always been gregarious and popular, but now he's cut off completely. He won't contact any of his friends, let them know . . . how he is. He was on the swimming team, he loved to dance, was planning to get two or three degrees in biology and teach it. . . ."

"But sociable, well-balanced people bounce back quickly from tragedy, I've always found. Why is he—?"

"He's got all this other . . . well, this family problem on his back. Wondering where his mother is, losing his father so suddenly, not at all wanting me here—but who's going to look after the legal mess if I don't? He can't negotiate with lawyers—no way! And now that he's deaf, he thinks no girl would have him. He was engaged to be married before he went overseas."

"He was?"

Ken Howell let silence balloon around us, then asked, "Whom do deaf folks marry?"

"Other deaf folks," I said grimly, knowing I was less accurate—in Keegan's case—than cruel.

"I . . . see," he murmured. "Do you think Cindy should have come down here with you?"

"She's too young for Keegan!" I cried. But he might not mean that. "Well, she'd do him some good, perhaps," I admitted, "but remember, she can't hear him, and she's not much of a speech-reader, either. At least I can hear Keegan."

I rose and strolled over to the tall picture windows. A bit of the coast was visible to the right, beyond the strait, but no houses. Ken was suddenly beside me, talking about their home in upstate New York, the cruel Syracuse snows they'd fled for the swimming and sunshine here. He described Keegan's collections of crabs and other seashore wonders, the skin-diving, the boating. . . .

He talked fast, depicting a family of three now blasted by death, the son's flight, then the mother's desertion, and then deafness. The setting was incongruous—this tropical Eden.

But Eden had a snake. I shuddered.

"Brad wasn't strong," Ken continued. "He was nervous and sickly, a three-pack-a-day smoker. He always anticipated dying young, and he died at forty-three. He was only a year older than I. He improved a little in this climate. He could sell books from any isolated spot, by mail-order. He was never one for society and travel, like me. Keegan went away to a good school in Atlanta, then to Gainesville where he could come home from the University on weekends. Sigrid loved the outdoors, like her son.

26

She's Norwegian, you know. She ran the SIGFORD all over, had Keegan's pals home to stay for weeks on end. Now it's ghastly quiet here, and lonely as hell. . . ."

"Lonelier, and much quieter, for Keegan."

My words seemed to shock him, but he managed to mutter, "Don't I know it!"

"The boat's named for her?"

"Yes, Sigrid plus Bradford."

His face twitched when he said that, and I was learning to watch his face closely, the way Cindy watched faces. He was a man of the world, my first real one in a life where such characters were the creations of romantic novelists. These Howells lived tragic lives in Technicolor.

"Do you know where his mother is?" I couldn't forget that Okasassa had used the word 'prisoner' for the widow.

"No," he said, and stared glumly out the window.

"She could be a comfort to her son, if she came back."

"But coming back to him as he is—wouldn't that tear her to pieces? Seeing his life ruined at age twenty-one? I don't know if he wants the book business, or if he could handle it. The bibliographer is assessing the value of over six thousand books, right now. You have to appraise everything to get an estate through probate."

"What does Keegan do with his time? Read?"

"He was a terrific reader before, but since he came back he doesn't seem to be reading much. He wanders around the island, swims, sleeps . . . he's got good use of his legs again, though I'm afraid he's no longer swimming-team caliber. He sulks. Does Cindy read a lot?"

"Do you read a lot in French or in Spanish?" I asked, "or in German?"

"I studied French and German at Cornell, but it's a struggle to translate the odd paragraph I meet. Why?"

"English is as tedious for Cindy as foreign languages for us," I said. "She's fourteen and reading third-grade books. We learn English automatically. Look how much a child understands before it can talk. But she started at six to study queer marks on paper." I had slid into my schoolteacher voice, because he was so attentive.

"Of course, you can't judge Keegan by Cindy. He'll get most of his information the rest of his life through reading, but for her it's laborious and confusing—the

27

word 'right,' for instance, has dozens of different meanings she has to memorize. Even a newspaper is a chore."

"But you said she had a language, sign language."

"Her American Sign Language is a language all its own with its own patterns—its own grammar. It's based on hand-shapes, positions, and motion, not on sound and spelling. Cindy's trying to become bilingual in both English and ASL."

"American Sign Language?"

"You catch on fast."

"I've a lot to learn, Leslie, and it intrigues me."

I handed him my glass to indicate I was ready to move on. The man's loneliness was so palpable that it made me nervous. He leaned slightly toward me, never relaxing.

He next said, "Relax, my dear. No one's going to attack you!"

"Could I see my room?" I tried to match his smile.

"Your room! Yes. I've given you the nicest one in the house. Hope you don't mind climbing to the third floor, but the view is terrific. Hollywood sunsets, the moon over the Gulf . . . it even has a private bath."

I followed him up a second flight of stairs.

My windows did overlook the Gulf; from here I could see the far side of the island which wore a beach on its edge. There lay my very first Florida beach, with breakers rolling white upon it. The sun, now touching the horizon, was as big around as a truck tire and blood red.

I contemplated the high four-poster bed under a dotted Swiss canopy. A girl's dream bed.

Did Keegan have a sister? No. He was an only child. I blurted out, "I wish Cindy could see my bed!"

"Perhaps that can be arranged," said Ken Howell.

There were two chiffoniers plus a desk for teacher, and the adjoining bath contained an ancient tub on lion-claw legs, immaculate white but chipped. Old. In the bedroom color shimmered from the deep rug of peacock blue. Slatted wooden roll-up blinds on the windows looked oriental. It was a lovely, peaceful room, and Ken knew my opinion from my face.

"I wish we could have both of you Fallon girls here," he said. "The job may require two. You'll see. The war, the jungle-fighting, the gruesome killings . . . all of that hurt Keegan emotionally. I feel as if I'm tossing you a live grenade, Leslie."

"But you forget I'm used to deaf people. Members of the Toledo Deaf Club taught me to sign. I'll work with the deaf all my life . . . I hope."

"Margaret Dean will soon be trudging upstairs with your supper." he said. "Here's your closet, with sufficient hangers, I hope. Inconvenient that hot water takes about four minutes to ascend the pipes, but I hope the view will please you . . . and the bed!"

He was backing toward the door when I asked my question again.

"But where is Keegan?"

"I don't know. I really don't. I'm not hiding the kid from you. He keeps out of sight, nursing his wounds. Ask Mrs. Dean. Tomorrow he'll surely appear."

I stood silently, disappointed, while he left. No Keegan tonight, then. I slipped out of my painful shoes and had just made a leap for the fine, high old bed, when steps sounded in the hall outside. Sitting spraddle-legged on the down comforter, looking out through the filmy curtains gathered and tied to each bedpost, I wondered if it might be Ken with Keegan in tow. I struggled down off the bed and padded to the door.

Margaret stood in the hall with a tray in her hands and towels over her arm. Before I managed a word of welcome, she started shaking her head.

"The man's a devil! A plain devil! Find a chile fer a teacher who looks like you, and bring her here!" She added in a grieving voice, "Honey, you got troubles ahead you don't know nothin' 'bout!"

After an introduction like that, what could I do but grit my teeth under a dead smile? Mrs. Dean set the tray on my desk. She straightened her matronly loaf-of-bread figure, smoothed her apron, and shuffled her plastic scuffs, trying to delay her departure. She had laid the clean towels and wash cloths on the bureau. Now she picked them up again.

I yielded, asking in desperation, "What do you mean?"

"You'll find out, soon enough. Ain't my way to gossip." She sighed mightily, unfolding and folding the towels and washcloths she'd brought, not meeting my eyes.

"Honey, if you'd lived here seven years and seen all I seen—" She went into the bathroom, hung the towels, and returned. "I just don' want to see nobody hurt. And anything . . . or anyONE bringing any more hate into this house. . . ."

"I haven't come to hate," I said incredulously. "I don't understand. I've just come to teach Keegan."

"Now, what exactly t'teach him?"

"He must learn to read people's lips, to grasp the language of . . . of hands, so he can come back into society, at least join deaf society."

"He was such a good, sweet chile," she breathed. "Up till last September, he was so happy . . . then the Devil rose up and destroyed this household and all that was within it."

"Destroyed it?"

She shook her head. "Keegan's grieving so bad, and you ain't gonna help, with that face of yours!"

"Whatever is wrong with this face of mine?" I demanded, "Both of you harp on it. What on earth is going on around here, anyway?"

My insistence ended Mrs. Dean's revelations. She took the covers off a bowl of soup and off plates containing a hot sandwich and a big piece of pie. She lifted the saucer from off my milk glass. Her lips stayed tightly compressed.

"What are you fearful of?" I persisted. "Please let me know."

"You be as sweet as you can to Keegan. You stay far 'way as you can from Mr. Kenneth Howell. Stay out of his rooms. Study what he says before you go believin' it. Your mama know you're fixin' to live here?"

"Yes, but she just got married again, and she's off honeymooning. . ."

"That figgers!"

"Who else lives here?" I demanded. "Tell me."

"Just my own mister, Rufus Dean, and that book-man. But I never can tell who's gonna show up—that fat man, his women. . . you. . ." She shook her head.

Mother taught me never to judge anyone on hearsay, and if there was any fear in me of Ken Howell, it was mixed with pleasure at being so evidently admired by him.

"The house and island are so lovely," I ventured, trying to smile.

"There ain't no way of gettin' off this island without you get his permission. And this house is haunted."

Without another word, Margaret Dean departed.

It took me a few minutes to recover. Trapped in a haunted house? That was a little much—like the blurb for some romantic thriller. My appetite daunted not one whit, I ate the vegetable soup, Welsh rarebit, and pecan pie. Excellent. I caught myself chuckling: "I'm surprised she didn't suggest the food might be poisoned!" So much for scare-tactics.

I put the tray outside my door, as I understand you do in a hotel. Now to unpack. Pausing every so often to watch the fading sunset's golds and purples, I flitted from suitcase to closet to bureaus, stocking-footed in the deep rug.

Stowing the empty suitcase far back in the closet, I discovered something. A square, metal can. I dragged the heavy thing out of the closet. It bore no label, but from the smell when uncapped I knew that the fluid inside was gasoline.

Probably Margaret used it for cleaning—my room was

31

spotless—so I shoved it even further back in the closet and put my suitcase in front of it. No good for someone to kick it over; and if it met up with a lighted cigarette? How can one get out of a third-floor room without a fire escape or even a handy tree limb? No ladder-truck could come cruising across the strait, and the sand was a long way down.

But here I was thinking like the heroine of some thriller—ah, captive princess in the tower! Let down your hair, Rapunzel, and so forth. I let down my hair and brushed it vigorously, counting fifty strokes.

My books numbered only four. One covered speechreading, with pictures of fractional lip-movements and lots of drills: "May, bay, say, ray; mat, bat, sat, rat." One was my audiology textbook, explaining degrees of deafness, but it wasn't much use without metering equipment. Two were sign language books, manual manuals, with sketches of flying hands. I also brought two issues of THE DEAF AMERICAN, a magazine by and for the deaf. There hadn't been room for a bigger library.

I shed both skirt and blouse. My day had begun at seven a.m., so I was willing to roost with the chickens tonight, lulled by the hum of the generator that gave us light. There was after all, electricity, not candles and gaslights. After I'd bathed in the long, high-sided tub, I slid into a costume worthy of the cover of a novel—a full-length blue nylon chiffon gown with bell sleeves and a low neck. It was from the dimestore counter where I worked, on sale at $7.99, but with careful laundering it might last the summer.

Turning off the bedside lamp with its rosy parchment shade, I thought for a moment about Ken Howell's nudes. I wondered who they were and when they posed for him. The townspeople were fixated upon the topic of his nudes, and here I was dressed like a princess or a bride in this bridal bed, staring up at the ceiling, stained red with sunset. The sheets were sun-dried; they smelled of sun and salt, and crackled—expensive sheets, ironed.

I turned over in my lace, burrowed into the splendid sheets, and fell contentedly asleep.

When awakened out of a deep sleep, one is supposed to "sit bolt-upright" and scream. Lacking that sort of courage (or foolhardiness), I froze, stiff on my back, the covers convulsively jerked tight from my toes up to my nose.

After a shockingly loud, rasping turn of my doorknob, someone opened my door and invaded my bedroom.

I dared not even turn my head, but my eyes stayed painfully wide. The door, moonlit, was closing behind a figure who proceeded to walk right in. I couldn't believe it. I was fully awake and sane, and there was a man walking boldly into my room—not quietly, either. All Margaret's and Okasassa's warnings rang in my ears, but this was not the stocky, weight-lifter's body of Ken Howell.

Walking through moonlight toward the windows, passing my bed, this man was no taller than Ken, but was slender, youthfully narrow-hipped and broad-shouldered, his clothes tight-fitting. He came to rest propped on outstretched arms, leaning on the window frame, staring out at the Gulf of Mexico, breathing raggedly.

Because I could hear him breathe, I knew he was not hearing himself breathing. He was deaf.

Panic hit me, and cold rationality would not put it down. Keegan obviously didn't know I was in this bed. As long as he faced away from me, and I didn't vibrate the floor beneath his feet, he wouldn't know it. I could flee, but where? He stood between me and the closet where my quilted robe hung, and one thing I didn't plan to do was gallop downstairs to Ken's room in a gown like this—which was not quite transparent, but which I, Miss Modesty Schoolmarm, filled to overflowing.

Should I call for help? Keegan wouldn't hear me. I rustled the sheet. Any hearing person would have spun around; he didn't.

The Deans were probably on the first floor, the book-man with the beard slept somewhere else, with dozens of empty rooms between. I had so little time to ponder.

Keegan rested his forehead on the glass pane now. I very slowly left my bed. Behind him, in his shadow, I eased my bare feet along the rug. His hair glistened; he must be blond. His hair hung half over his ears and to his collar, but he was clean-shaven.

Should I approach him in this get-up? I couldn't touch

33

him and startle him right through the window; I'd have to
glide into his side vision. But what to say? Then, tardily
I remembered. He could talk; I could not. He wouldn't know
why I was there to witness his agonized, chest-racking
breathing that was almost like sobs. He didn't know who I
was.

What made me move toward Keegan, not toward the door,
was the memory of Ken's dire predictions. I couldn't have
Keegan reject me, and if appearing in moonlight in a
diaphanous gown would help, I'd risk it. I could always
scream. Later.

I floated across the rug, my hair cascading down,
uncombed. I stood beside him. His knuckles were white with
the strain of his grip on the window frame; his eyes were
shut tight as if in prayer; lines on his lean jaw
twitched. It was a hard, youthful profile with a slightly
uptilted nose.

Before his eyes opened, I saw the shock of another
body's warmth hit him; he jerked around to face me in a
wrestler's stance, feet braced, knees flexed, hands out
and clenched into claws.

"God!" he gasped. "Oh my God! YOU! HERE!"

Before I could back away or shake my head, he pounced,
pulling me hard against him, burying his face in my hair.

Pity overcame fear, as they say.

I didn't struggle. Ropes of muscles in his back moved
under my hands. He held me strained up on tiptoe against
his heaving chest, then—one hand cupping my head, the
other locking my waist against his—he kissed me fiercely
on my closed lips. I did not respond, but it was painful
to endure that kiss.

He pulled away from me a few inches, looking into my
face, brushing back my hair, tilting my chin higher. I was
shaking my head no.

But he didn't release me. He gripped me by the upper
arms, keeping us almost nose to nose.

"You're HIS! Why, you're just another one of his sexy
models! But you look like HER! And he dared put you here,
in my mother's room, in my mother's own bed!"

He shook me, my arms flapping like fins at my sides, my
feet nearly flying off the floor.

He's trying to drive . . . me . . . crazy!"

Then Keegan let go, and I almost fell. Shaking my head, blinking back tears and locks of hair, I retreated, my hand moving toward the desk behind me. I'd show him a sign language book. I was afraid of him now, of what he was feeling—both before the mis-identification and after.

When I seized the book, he must have thought I was going to strike him with it. Still a jungle-fighter, he sprang at me and twisted my arm. The book hit the floor.

No communication; no appeal. My knees grazed the rug, and then I was jerked upright again and whirled to face him. He secured both arms behind me.

He bit off words, his eyes pale and glittering.

"I know what you are! The Big Man's woman. Another dual-purpose model! Don't shake your head at me. You don't scream because he told you I'm deaf, so it won't scare me off, eh? You know how he's using you? Why he brought you here, put you in this room? So I won't forget what he did to Mary Ann . . . and to my mother . . . and to his brother—my father!"

I tried to pull away, but he was frighteningly strong. He arched my back in his grip, his jeering words twisting his boyish features.

"Being what you are, delectable little morsel, all gift-wrapped, you deserve anything you get. He's not visiting you tonight, or is he done with you already? He wanted me to find you here, eh? He followed me and knew I came up here to think." His voice dropped lower, "Oh, how I'd like to— But I wouldn't stoop . . . so . . . low!"

This creature was the man—this slender but powerful and furious deaf man—that I was supposed to salvage from despair? This was the "sweet chile" Margaret knew, before war and tragedy and Lord knows what else worked him over? We hung near a chasm, but I would not bring up a knee and try to hurt him. I just stared back at a face in which desire and loathing battled, and tried to extricate my right hand from his gripping fingers.

I managed to succeed. I dragged my hand up between our bodies so he could see it, and I commenced to spell rapidly on my fingers.

He wouldn't understand. It didn't matter what I spelled—The Lord's Prayer would serve as well as just the manual alphabet. I gazed beseechingly at him, spelling

35

away, while his brain-cells feverishly worked.

I spelled to show him I could communicate soundlessly with him. But he was as ignorant as the rest. His lips parted. His eyes narrowed under the dark, arching brows.

"YOU are deaf, too! You're a DEAF girl!" He released me instantly.

Let the mistake stand, for his sake and my safety. I nodded, and signed, "I am deaf." I pointed to my ear—to both ears for clarity—then added the sign for "closed." "Ears closed." Deaf. Nodding.

Lying.

"But you can understand what I say?" he marveled. "How can you understand?"

I put my fingertips delicately on his lips, signed "see" with V-fingers from my eyes to his lips.

"You lip-read? You lip-read that well? I try and try, but I can't lip-read a single sentence!"

No deaf girl could have lip-read his words in pale moonlight. At best, an expert speech-reader can catch one quarter of the words and guess the rest. Anything more was myth, and he believed the myth, as most hearing people did, and was frozen in awe and hope.

I backed away to a safe distance. My arms aching, I backed toward the door.

"Who are you? Why do you look like her? How could Ken plan that, too? How on earth? You're deaf. . ! Oh my God."

I had to capture the moment, give him hope by letting him read a word or two off my lips, in such very bad light.

But the easiest line to read I dared not say: "I love you."

"Please go. Good-bye," I said, my hands on his chest, urging him gently toward the door, my face tilted toward the moonlight.

He understood me. I saw surprise in his face. My body-English gave him enough clues to guess the words I said.

"You're deaf," he breathed, not moving. "But no one would ever know it. No one! You are not cut off!"

My eyes swam in tears. If I were deaf I wouldn't understand his words. The shock to hit Keegan when he knew I could hear—was one of "them," the "hearing

36

world"—would be greater than the shock of my mysteriously familiar face or my sleeping in his mother's bed.

"What . . . is . . . your . . . name?" he persisted, starting to slow and exaggerate his words to "help" me lip-read, which would not help at all.

This had to end. I'd break down completely, and he'd want to stay to comfort me. "Leslie" was two tongue-flips no one could lip-read, or it was six finger-shapes, two repeated, worse than Greek letters.

"Why are you crying?" With exquisite gentleness, he touched my wet cheek. He pulled out a handkerchief, which initialed a real torrent. While my face was bent into the white cotton square, I felt Keegan's hand begin to stroke my hair, the way one strokes a valuable and unpredictable pedigreed kitten.

"I need so badly to talk with someone," he said. "It's worse at night, when I can't see."

He forgot that my eyes were buried in the handkerchief.

"I'm sorry I shook you . . . I'm so very sorry!"

The more he wanted to touch me and hang on every word I communicated to him, the worse his horror tomorrow. Even now he ought to realize I was hearing him without looking at him, but he was so naive that he thought that if I finger-spelled I had to be a deaf girl.

I managed a forgiving smile. "Good-bye," I repeated. The wet handkerchief back to him, my hands were signing him toward the door. "Please go."

He went out with reluctance, deferring to maidenly hysteria, backing through the door, letting me close it quietly in his wondering, marveling young face. There was no lock.

I leaned my back against the door, listening to his footsteps retreat. Tears again began streaming down my face. The poor, poor guy! His image was indelible on my retinas—thick, smooth, fair hair over his forehead, deep-set eyes shooting fire, his crisp white shirt against my lace bodice, the grace of his violence, . . . all in the weird white moonglow.

He'd retain my image, too, but he'd remember best my spelling fingers and my eyes on his lips. He'd forget all the misunderstandings, and remember that I was deaf.

But I was not a deaf girl.

I awoke bruised and swollen, afraid it had not been a nightmare. It hadn't, and I'd now have to pay the price for lying to Keegan. My arms ached, and one wrist felt broken. My big, yellow sign language book still lay on the rug, a family happily signing together on the cover. After the long wait for hot water to climb the pipes, I took a slow, deep, hot bath. Would the two of them talk about me before I got downstairs, Ken and Keegan Howell?

Drying myself in the biggest towel I'd ever seen off a beach, I returned to Sigrid Howell's bedroom which now was mine. All four of them were Howells—including the dead man, Bradford Howell, Keegan's dad. Keegan said that Ken had single-handedly hurt them all—himself, someone named Mary Ann, and Sigrid and Bradford. Margaret detested Ken, as did the townspeople. Yet Ken himself had said I could twist him around my little finger!

The only twisting I'd done was with the truth, and that must be remedied. Quickly. But I dreaded the long march down those two flights of slippery stairs.

How childishly innocent I'd been only sixteen hours ago, the do-gooder with her standard texts in hand, quizzing Ken about the Howell family. This was turning out to be a nest of snakes . . . serpents. There was evil here, but I didn't know where it lay. I'd never been in more physical danger than I was last night, but I couldn't blame Keegan. Keegan blamed Ken, but what I'd seen thus far of Ken was kindliness.

In a blue denim dress with a sailor collar, I checked my looks in a freckled antique mirror too foggy to reflect my bruises, then descended the stairs. I found Ken at the foot of the stairs, welcoming me with a big bright smile.

"I was going to send Margaret up to rouse you at nine," he said. "Eight-thirty and you're ready for work already! How energetic! It's going to be a cool day, for once.

Thanks for bringing us a few blessed clouds, Leslie."

Then he looked more closely at me.

"How did you hurt yourself? Let me see your. . ."

He turned me around and inspected the backs of my arms.

I drew away, shoulders hunched; where I covered each arm, the skin smarted.

"Leslie, it almost looks like finger-marks on your arms. On both of them. As if someone . . ." His face underwent a scary slide into certainty. "Did you have those bruises when you arrived, yesterday?"

No lie occurred to me. Besides, I had to stop lying. I said firmly and pointedly, "I'm very hungry, Mr. Howell. Is breakfast ready?"

He respected my reticence, but his smile was gone for the morning. In the bay window a round table was set for four. Ken seated me, saying, "Keegan seldom eats with me. I destroy his appetite. He usually dines with the Deans in their rooms."

Margaret fed us well; her bacon deserved to be featured in an ad; her eggs were scrambled with cheese. I watched her move grimly around the table and shuddered to think of her sharp eyes spotting my bruises. But to run upstairs for a cardigan would really draw their attention.

"What do you plan for today?" I asked, sliding the toast down my throat with a gulp of mint tea. I didn't ask after Keegan, which probably alerted Ken even further.

"You'll first have to size up Keegan, " he said tentatively, and paused.

I did not raise my eyes. I said, "Margaret tells me the house is haunted."

"By whom?" was his retort.

"She didn't say. Has anyone died here?"

"You're too well educated for any haunted-house nonsense, aren't you?" But Ken's face belied his casual tone. "Any house this age has seen plenty of deaths. Rumors get started. This part of the country is full of ignorant, superstitious people and Margaret, for all her city ways, is a very emotional woman."

"Have you seen any ghosts?" I persisted, picturing Keegan gliding like a noisy specter across my bedroom.

"No. And I don't want to."

He didn't say he didn't expect to, which surprised me.

"Neither do I."

"If anything ever happened to disturb you, anything at all . . . you'd come to me, wouldn't you, Leslie? I must believe that."

Back to the bruises, eh? I rose. "I'll clear the table. Must start earning my pay." I picked up our empty plates.

"No! Margaret does that! Sit down," he commanded. "Leslie, whatever is the matter? Have I said something wrong?"

I disobeyed his command with a noncommittal little shrug and headed fast for the kitchen, carrying plates.

Beyond the swinging door, Margaret intercepted the dishes, clucking disapproval of my maid-duty.

Past her shoulder, I saw—sitting on a stool by the kitchen counter—Keegan Howell.

The blindingly white sweatshirt and socks, faded blue jeans, sun-bleached hair lighter than his tan—all of it was real. He was no ghost or nightmare. At the sight of me, his face again lit up with radiant wonder. He slid off the stool and came toward me slowly, hand extended, face wreathed in false hope and happiness. He'd never frighten or hurt me again, his eyes promised, in a face made for smiling, elfin and boyish.

"Good morning," the fine, wide mouth said carefully.

"Good morning." I couldn't think of another phrase he could easily read off my lips.

"I'm Keegan Howell," he said so slowly and precisely that he would've been hard to speechread. "What. . . is your . . . name?"

Arched brows up, gaze glued to my lips, he waited.

I stood stock-still, drinking in his charm, listening to Margaret mutter, "You tole him you was deaf, and he don' understand me that you are lyin'!"

I'd have only a few seconds more of this admiring, smiling Keegan.

Behind me I heard Ken's voice heartily noting, "Ah, here's Keegan!"

I didn't turn toward the voices, but Keegan stared at my face—sudden understanding darkening his complexion.

"Let me try to introduce you two," Ken went on, blithely unaware. He pulled out a pad and pen (a hearing man carrying the deaf person's equipment) and began to

40

write.

"You hear him! You can HEAR, you dirty little liar!"

"What's that?" Ken said.

"So she IS just another of your little nudies . . . and she sure has the figure for it! You got yourself a girl like Mary Ann this time, and put her in my mother's bed, and put her up to wiggling her fingers at me; tease the deafie, eh? That's your filthiest trick yet!"

"Keegan? No! That's not so!" Ken cried uselessly. "You don't understand!"

Then Ken did some rapid understanding himself.

"Leslie, you two have met, already? And he hurt you!"

This easy communication enraged Keegan. With a twist of his body, he snatched up a knife from the ruins of our breakfast grapefruit, and brought his wars, Asian and otherwise, to Margaret's clean kitchen.

"Put that knife down!" Ken snapped, unheard. The scribbled note for Keegan still dangled in his fingers; he could no more hand it to Keegan than stuff it down an erupting volcano.

And Keegan did erupt: "This house is mine! Get out! Get out and take your women with you! Get her out of here, the brutal little tease!"

To me, he added, "You could hear me! You said you were lipreading, but you heard every word! Oh, God, what a shameless . . . sadistic little liar!"

I gaped like a fish drowning in air, looking from nephew to uncle and back. The knife was too close, though it twitched at Ken, not at me.

Ken thrust out a hand to stop Keegan. Words had no effect. Margaret had vanished.

"I'll fire the house!" Keegan shouted. "I warned you! You won't get a thing, if it burns down. Get out! Get her out of here, before I make her sorry—"

"Leslie has a deaf sister. She's come to teach you signs," Ken said, fluttering the note he'd written past the knife pointed at him.

"You think you'll drive me nuts, don't you? You torture me, destroy my mother, murder my father—" he was shouting now—"you drove off Mary Ann after terrifying her . . . fraud after fraud, till I can't . . . take any more!"

"Keegan, that's all lies!" Ken cried.

41

"I don't want the house or the books, but they were Dad's, so I'll make sure YOU won't get them. They'll all burn first!"

I gazed wretchedly at him as a second door into the kitchen, a door behind Keegan, creaked opoen. A man entered, a tall and heavy man with a white mustache and goatee.

Keegan had now turned to me. "Very clever girl, here. Go on, show how you wiggle your fingers. Show him!"

Of course Keegan had heard nothing, and I knew that to look over his shoulder would warn him. Ken was staring at the knife to keep from betraying the presence of that fourth person. Now, behind the big, white-haired stranger, Margaret hovered, craning her neck to see Keegan.

With a grunt, the old man lunged and grabbed Keegan's knife-wielding arm. Ken burst past me. The two of them pinned Keegan between them, the knife drawing someone's blood before landing with a clatter on the linoleum. Ken kicked it across the kitchen. Then he and the white-haired man jumped back from Keegan's struggling torso and let him go.

Paralyzed, as if I were watching a stage drama, I saw the violence play itself out: Keegan's blazing blue eyes, hot with impotent rage . . . Ken's forearm oozing blood that dripped off his fingers . . . the old man sidling around behind Margaret . . . the black woman reaching out a hand to Keegan . . . Keegan shying away from her touch.

"Crazy kid! He doesn't understand anything," Ken cried, breaking the silence. "Thanks, Geoff!"

The large old man panted, "He's gone too far. He's got to be restrained!"

"What's driving Keegan crazy?" I begged to know. "What happened to his family. Who is—?"

They ignored me.

"I'm not hurt badly," Ken said, gripping the pressure-point above his elbow. "It's all over, now."

"I don't mean your cut," the stranger retorted. "I mean his threats. You expect me to live in this God-forsaken place with a murderous, arsonist punk? He could've killed you, and he could burn us all alive in our beds!"

Glowering in wary, desperate anger, Keegan leaned his back against the counter, his chest heaving. He had to watch our mouths move, and our eyes flash to each other's faces.

"I can't lock him up, Geoff; he's my own nephew, and he inherits everything."

"The books in this house are priceless, and lives are at stake!" this man called Geoff replied.

"Use good sense. This is a family quarrel, and it's decades old. He won't do anything. He never has," Ken protested. "He's bluffing. How could he burn the house down?"

"How does anyone burn a house? With flammables— kerosene, gasoline."

"What would you have me do—lock him up? He'd go right out a window. He did as a boy, and the Army certainly taught him more along that line. Would you have him committed, sent away? He's as sane as you or I."

"He needs either jail or a psychiatrist," the old man persisted.

"And how would a psychiatrist talk to him?"

"Easier than the police will, when he sticks someone less tolerant than you, Kenneth. If he touches me, I'll have him in jail the same day."

Through it all Keegan had to stand there between them, his face tight with shame, watching mouths snarl vapors back and forth. He was no longer a person. They debated his future as if he were a pet dog turned vicious.

To my horror, the bearded man suddenly caught Keegan by the neck of his sweatshirt and roughly wheeled him around, shouting in his face, "You just TRY to set a fire! You endanger ME, you young animal, and see what I do to you!"

He shook Keegan hard, savagely, sputtering through his mustache. . . which effectively veiled both his lips.

Ken and I watched Keegan pull his fist back. Neither of us was about to stop him. Then his face contorted with disgust, and he let his arm fall. He tore free of the man, and lunged between Ken and me on his way to go slamming out the back door.

"You're lucky he has some self-control, Rauenbauer," Ken said to the old man's retreating back. "Don't you ever touch that kid again!"

Rauenbauer did not reply. Margaret followed him out of the kitchen, and Ken, still holding his arm and dripping

43

blood, struggled to pull open drawer after drawer. I took over his search, found a roll of tape, and rinsed the blood off his muscular brown forearm. I stretched short pieces of tape tightly across the wound, overlapping them.

"You need stitches."

"I'll be okay. Look, Leslie, I'm sick that you had to witness all that."

Busy playing nurse, brooding about gasoline and murder, I didn't make a reply through my tightly pressed lips.

"So Keegan put those bruises on you," Ken rumbled. "Did he come find you? When? This morning? Last night? And you wouldn't tell me?"

"Why did you put me in Keegan's mother's room?"

"Because it's the nicest bedroom in the house. Why should it stand empty? I certainly wouldn't use it, and I never put any other guest there, but a young woman who's willing to come tackle—"

"Keegan goes up there to be alone to think. He walked in on me."

"In the night?"

"In the night. I was asleep."

"Good God! He didn't—what did he do? How long did he—?"

"He just grabbed me . . . and yelled at me. He said the same things he just said to you, that you destroyed his family, that I was a model, your girlfriend. To get loose, I had to pretend I was deaf. It was an awful mistake. I finger-spelled to him. Stupid, but I did it."

"I think you had to. Yes. When you think what might have happened!"

"But I've got to know what's going on. I must know everything, right now."

"He won't touch you again, Leslie."

"He won't listen to me, either! I mean, he won't cooperate with me, not now. Now he hates the sight of me, and I can't blame him. Tell me, who's Mary Ann?"

"His former fiancee. She abandoned him because he came back from the war deafened. She was too immature to accept a deaf husband, and she was cruel enough to admit it to him. She as much as said he wasn't good enough for her anymore."

"But he said you did something to her. You drove her

away?"

"I didn't do anything to that shallow little creature. I wanted them married."

The bloody knife lay in the corner under a window full of marigolds. I took my eyes off it. "Mr. Howell—" I tried again— "why does Keegan hate you so?"

"I told you. Keegan doesn't understand what's going on. He's in the dark; he's cut off so totally, that his imagination runs wild. You see what he thought you were. He's just as mistaken about me."

"But before he was deaf? You yourself said that it all started back when Keegan could hear. Trouble started decades ago, you said."

That gave him pause. I'd paid more heed to his words than Ken perhaps wanted me to.

"Trust me. Don't pry, Leslie. You'll find out all you really need to know, in time." His voice mellowed. "You came here to help the kid, and you'll get your chance to."

"If it kills you?"

"If it kills me—which it won't. He won't," Ken said.

"I'm not used to knife-fights," I said, "but you almost got killed, just as I almost got. . . ." I swallowed the word. "And, you know, it IS easy to burn a house down, if you have . . . gasoline."

"He hasn't any gasoline. He's been on the island since March, and there's no—"

"You have to have gasoline to run a boat."

"Sure, but the gas tank's got a lock, and so does the shed for the gasoline cans. Don't worry, I thought of that."

"May I go up to my room? This has been . . . rather harrowing."

"Certainly. I'll go up with you. A lock for your door is one precaution required."

I didn't want him to accompany me up the stairs—until we reached the second floor. Then I was glad he was there, to step between me and the white goatee thrust out at us.

"That is precisely why I changed from teaching into bibliographic studies," the old man began, without preface. "To escape wild hippies who throw bombs, knife people, and burn up buildings and precious books!"

Ken sent him a scornful glance. "I'd better introduce

you two, at last. Geoffrey Rauenbauer from Virginia, meet Leslie Fallon from Ohio. He's appraising Brad's books. She's going to teach Keegan to communicate."

"He communicates very effectively already, the vicious young animal!"

I choked with indignation. Hippie indeed—and animal, to boot!

Cindy had been called an animal, and here was the word again, applied this time to Keegan, an articulate, well-educated college man. Anyone who could call him that was heartless as well as stupid. My dislike of Rauenbauer doubled. If Keegan was dangerous in his frenzy, this Geoffrey Rauenbauer, with all his faculties intact, was disgustingly cruel.

Seeing no sympathy in our faces, he darted back into his room like a heavy weasel into its hole,.

"I didn't pick him out for the job," Ken explained to me. "I don't like the man, but he's a hard worker. He prefers books to people; that's his hang-up."

My next request was, 'Will you please explain this Mary Ann look-alike business?"

"Come up to my studio, Leslie. All I can do is let you judge for yourself."

In his studio, he pulled out a drawer full of glossy photographs, all 8 x 10.

"Find her," he said.

I picked up the photos, one by one—slick surfaces, black on white and every gradation between. Teenagers, older people . . . there was Margaret, shelling peas into a pan, squinting resentfully at the camera. Keegan, I recognized, clothes wind-blown against him, braced barefoot on the bow of the SIGFORD, or suspended in the middle of a dive off the dock. Next, he was bending to pull a girl out of the water.

Here was a slender, lined man who looked like Ken with all the vigor worn off him—this must be Brad Howell. A tall black man—Mr. Dean? None of them were posing; the camera caught them with emotions fresh on their faces, poised like dancers.

Several pretty girls appeared, one a blonde in pigtails, another with her arm looped affectionately around Keegan's neck. She had long, dark hair half over her cheeks . . . yes.

"Here's Mary Ann," I said.

Ken nodded. "Right. Now, I ask you, without meeting you or seeing a picture of you, how could I pick you for your looks? Sure, there's a resemblance; it startled me, too. But a lot of gals wear their hair parted in the middle, long and straight. Mary Ann was big-eyed, like you. Keegan loved her. I can't help how you look, or how he felt, either one."

"Mistaking me for his love really hurt him."

"He's been hurt so many times in the past year. . . ."

It didn't occur to me until later that someone was missing from the photographs—the mother, Sigrid the Norwegian. I gathered up handfuls of prints, Keegan with Mary Ann, playing, leaping through surf, studying with her, walking hand in hand. No wonder Ken took pictures of them—they were an extremely photogenic couple. These 8 x 10's were more effective, I thought, than his enlarged studies of nudes (though Mary Ann in a bikini was almost in that category).

"When I was summoned here, again and again, to bail Brad out of his financial catastrophes," Ken went on, "I had to do something for relaxation. This is both my profession and my hobby."

"They're beautiful pictures," I admitted, looking at a shot of the thin man smiling into the camera and Keegan, behind him, scowling.

It was strange to have a glimpse into a past, very different life for Keegan. It felt like dreaming someone else's dreams, or finding a peekhole backwards in time.

"A year ago, that one. Before . . . before everything blew apart," Ken remarked.

"Thank you for showing me."

I didn't give back two of the pictures, as beautiful as expensive greeting cards for lovers. In one, Keegan, wearing a bulky sweater, his back to the camera, stood by the Gulf with his hands in his pockets, his winsome profile superimposed on mountainous waves. A chill, wintery picture, lit only by the breaking surf, the foam around his ankles, and his pale, blowing hair.

The other photo showed Mary Ann resting her sleek head in Keegan's lap, gazing up at him as his fingers combed through her hair. He bent over her, dark lashes lowered, poised on the brink of a kiss. Beautiful. It must have been snapped with neither of them aware. I looked questioningly at Ken.

"Okay, I admit it. It was taken through a telephoto lens. What price beauty—could I turn my back on the chance to crystalize beauty beyond reach, Leslie? It's kind of like stealing your neighbors' flowers to bring home for your own pleasure."

His words touched and surprised me, but why wouldn't a skilled photographer talk like a paint-and-canvas artist? When I put these two photographs aside to carry with me back to my room, he made no move to retrieve them.

He continued speaking of Keegan. "He rows across the lake and burrows into the mangroves to where he's apparently got himself a camp. After this morning he'll be gone Lord knows how long, licking his wounds."

He dropped his gaze. "Anyway, don't expect to see him for a while. I hope you've got a lot of patience."

"But when he reappears, what do I do? How do I say what I want to do for him?"

"Use Margaret. She's his greatest fan, and always was. She'll do anything for him, like give him food to last him for days in his hideaway. She also believes every word he utters. If you can make a hit with Margaret. . . ."

"I don't find Margaret any more frank with me than you are."

"Because you aren't a member of this unfortunate family," he said. "Some things are better kept in the family. They're too personal. Don't play spy, little lady."

"There've been no crimes in this house . . . lately?" I ventured to inquire.

"Leslie, don't probe! I warn you." A gentle voice for ungentle words.

"I've already been informed—without spying—about a ghost, a murderer, and a devil. How can I ignore things like that? I'm not nosy; I'm uneasy."

"There's no more a ghost than there was a murder."

That was his concluding sentence, as I marched off down the hall, my mind darting back to the problem of the gasoline can. I'd hide it from everyone, including—or especially—Keegan. I'd hide it far under my bed, with something draped over it.

In my room, I jerked open the closet, moved my suitcase aside, and almost screamed.

The gasoline can was gone.

I flopped down abruptly in a chair to recover. Had
Keegan grabbed his gasoline while I ate breakfast? Or did
someone else know about it? Margaret hadn't been up here,
yet, since my damp towel still hung awry in the bathroom,
and my bed was made up to my own imperfect standards.

Who else slept on the third floor of this house? Ken
and the petulant bibliographer roomed below me. Did Keegan
sleep up here in lordly isolation—when he deigned to
sleep indoors?

The mangroves were darkening outside. One of the clouds
Ken had credited to my account was overhead, and there was
a bigger one on the horizon of the pond-smooth Gulf. The
Florida air blew sweet and clean through my window, the
threat of rain bringing no chill or smell of metal as it
would at home. Warmth flowed in. It occurred to me
suddenly that I might need a raincoat in Florida. Yes, and
some more things, like shampoo and a bathing cap. I'd want
to swim in the lagoon when the water again was green,
instead of its present shark-color.

I rested for an hour, nestled in the rocking chair by
the window, the two beautiful photo-portraits in my lap.

Somewhere between the murderous look Keegan last turned
on me and the adoring gaze that Mary Ann enjoyed was what
I needed from him: the receptivity of a student. Otherwise
I couldn't teach him, and I was here for nothing. Useless
to begin by introducing Ken or Margaret to sign language,
because Keegan wouldn't learn it from Ken, and Margaret
was no longer friendly.

The tapping at my door was Margaret's. Again she was
carrying fresh towels over her arm as she presented me
with a dinner tray. Her face gave me grief. She was
staring at me as fiercely as Keegan had.

"Mr. Howell, he say lunch won't be served today. This
here's a snack for you when you get hungry. This here's an
envel-ope for you, too."

50

What service! So I'd be fed in my suite at alternate meals? Well, I was safer up here in my bedroom, perhaps, at least in the daytime.

"Thank you," I said stiffly, miserable around any person who is cold to me. "Thank you for climbing all those stairs, Margaret." (Be ingratiating, Leslie.)

"I won't need clean towels every day, though, and you won't have to make my bed. I'd be happy to do that."

"You goin' t'stay on, here?"

The same defiance filled me, as when people asked—re: Cindy—"You gonna send the deaf-mute to an institution?"

"Certainly, Margaret!" I retorted. "I'm not beaten yet! I was hired to do a job, and I'm not quitting."

"You're not afeared to be burnt up in your bed?"

I had no reply but the blankest face I could manufacture.

"He might think burnin' is what a person deserves for foolin' a pore deaf boy . . . and foolin' around with a man twicet her age!"

"Margaret!"

She made a circuit of room and bath, touching surfaces for dust, aligning a chair with the desk, rinsing out the sink. She'd apparently done the same things for Keegan's mother, starting seven years ago when Keegan would've been only fourteen. Watching her, still appalled by her words, I tore open the envelope she'd brought me.

Labeled "For Miss Fallon," it held two big green and black capsules wrapped in a note which said, "Pills to help you relax." The words were neatly printed. It was signed "Ken."

"I never take tranquilizers," I said aloud.

"What tranquilizers?"

"Uh . . . Mr. Howell wants me to relax. Is he too busy to eat a sit-down lunch today, then?"

"Mr. Howell done gone to town for a tetanus shot."

Odd. I'd heard no boat's engine, but my windows faced away from the lagoon.

"I'm glad he's being careful," I said. "Has Keegan ever before . . . ever taken after him like that, before?"

"Ask Mr. Howell. You already got you a friend in this house. You shore don't need t'ask ME!"

"Oh, Margaret!" I groaned. "You don't believe what

51

Keegan believes?"

"I'm not sayin' what you are, Miss Fallon. Actions speak louder'n words." She indicated the pair of photos on the desk. "You take an interest in his pitchers, I see. Fancy him sneakin' 'round takin' pitchers of young folk. They's a name for his sort: Dirty Ole Man."

"He's an artist! It's his work, Margaret, the way he makes his living!"

"Work don' have to be naked women and people's personal lifes or takin' pitchers out of windows thet nobody knows is bein' took."

I sighed. She was a pillar of righteousness, devoid of hypocrisy. I had to try another tack.

"How did Keegan's father die?"

"Sui-cide!" she blurted, nostrils flaring. She headed for the door.

I cut off her escape. "Why does Keegan say murder, then? Why do the townspeople imply that he died of some lung-disease?"

"You want somebody dead bad enough, you can MAKE a sui-cide. Nobody ever gonna do hisself to death . . .THAT way!" she responded.

"So you think it was murder?" I gasped. "But you said 'suicide.'"

"I'm followin' orders!"—again the bitter sarcasm, and a little curtsy to go with it. She got a firm hold on the doorknob, as if I'd drag her back into my room.

"Margaret, what about Keegan's mother? Where is she?"

"Dead, for all I know!"

"Murdered?"

"You really do pry, don't you, Miss Fallon? Ask yo' close friend that!"

I hung onto Margaret's nearer arm while I shot a last question at her.

"Mary Ann—the girl I look like—did she go to Keegan's University? What's her last name?"

"Let loose of me! Yes, she did. And she was a Monahan. No more questions. I got work waitin', and you kin ask yo' friend with the cameras!"

I was left with my lunch and my pills, all by myself.

It was noon, but I still couldn't eat. I wasn't about to swallow the pills sent with the neatly printed note—

52

even its signature printed.

Resolutely, I took out a packet of stationery. Time for psychological therapy; write two Pollyanna letters—that would help. Make myself believe the words I wrote to my mother and my sister, my inventory of the good things at Okasassa House. There were many: the beauty of the island and its climate, the good food, this lovely room. Ken's attempts at kindness, his wizardry with cameras. I told them Keegan was a very attractive man, but that's all I could honestly say about him.

I made Cindy's letter simple, using short, subject-verb-object sentences and an elementary school vocabulary. Cindy would love it here. Swimming, beachcombing, and other vigorous activities were great for a child lacking easy access to books, TV, or hearing playmates.

Folding the two letters into their envelopes, one directed to Maine, one to Youngstown, Ohio, I prepared my mind for writing a third, very different, epistle.

I hated resorting to communication in writing; there were much better means, which I'd come here to teach Keegan. But I'd lost more respect than I knew how to regain. Leslie Fallon—who even in her teens was more wrapped up in her sister and in deafness than in boys— had been taken for a temptress. What a laugh. Jane Eyre never had this to face!

The first draft of my letter to Keegan sounded as if a Founding Father had written it: It was a: "Whereas I have long been involved with the deaf and find nothing more rewarding than to teach them . . ." sort of thing. The second draft sounded more human—and humane.

I folded the note and shoved it into my pocket, then lay down as bidden. Too alert to drowse, I tried to unknot my muscles one by one, thinking over and over, "What next?"

Next, I dozed off . . . I must have, for I was only vaguely aware that someone had quietly eased my bedroom door open without knocking. I said, lazily, "I haven't eaten, yet, Margaret," protecting my lunch from being whisked away. The door quietly closed.

Well! Not one word in reply? Weird. I got up and padded to the door. I peered down the hall in both directions. Margaret never moved fast, but she was nowhere in sight.

53

Perhaps the person who sent me the capsules was checking to see if I was getting a good snooze. "The person"? Come now, Leslie! Ken Howell had sent them, Ken the activist, who liked secret picture-taking and surprise tutors. I knew one person who had NOT quietly opened my door: Keegan. A totally deaf person can seldom do things totally silently.

It was one p.m. when I finished my lunch and descended the stairs. I needed voices; it was too silent for too long in that house, even for a person wary of violence.

The first creature I saw was the bibliographer, loaded with books, sliding into a room lined with book-loaded shelves. I followed, finding Ken in there, too, flipping through a mildewed volume that was molting on him.

"That is an 1821 first edition," Rauenbauer was saying. "Do you have any notion of the value of that? It's been out of print for nearly a century!"

Ken didn't guess at the book's value. He shoved it at Rauenbauer, saying to me, "Leslie, welcome back! All rested and recovered?"

Rauenbauer, however, wasn't to be shunted aside for a mere female. "Let me dust it off," he said, wiping the book tenderly with a piece of chamois cloth. "I shall need to use the reference room again. I think that I'll drive over to the library the day after tomorrow."

"Sure. Suit yourself," Ken said, off-handedly, not taking his eyes off me. "Leslie, this is only one of the six rooms Brad filled with books. They piled up, sitting unexamined, not bringing in cash for his family to live on."

"Where do they all come from?"

"Usually from estates. A scholar or a collector dies, and the heirs sell them off. Book-collecting has a bit of the vulture about it."

"Vulture, indeed!" Our resident vulture's feathers were rumpled. Goatee wagging, he cried, "I'd think you would appreciate the value of my work, Kenneth, even if you don't appreciate my saving your life this morning!"

It took till then for Rauenbauer's travel proposal to hit me. The nearest big library would be at the University of Florida in Gainesville, Keegan's school.

"Are you going to Gainesville day after tomorrow? May I

come along?" I burst out, quite aware of Ken's displeased surprise.

"Leslie, I'll take you to the city; you needn't catch a ride with—"

Probably to spite Ken, Rauenbauer agreed to take me.

"I need to shop for some things," I explained. "I can't get them in Okasassa, and there's no need to inconvenience you, Mr. How—Ken." I smiled endearingly (I hoped) at both of them. Ken would sure be better company on a long drive, but I didn't want him dogging my footsteps in Gainesville. I had more than shopping to do.

"I plan, as usual, an overnight trip, Miss Faulkner."

"Fallon. I'd be happy to stay over, in a motel. By myself, I mean."

"I'm aware of what you mean." He cast a jaundiced eye at me.

Oh, heavens! Not Rauenbauer, too, deciding that if a girl is pretty, she must have nothing on her mind but men, men of all ages.

"I'd rather take you there myself," Ken complained, "but it's too late to go today, and I can't make a trip that overlaps Geoff's and leaves Keegan here, alone."

"No, you dare not leave that boy alone with the Negroes in this treasure-house," Rauenbauer snapped. "It will be acceptable to me, Miss Fallon, if you can be ready to depart at eight o'clock sharp Friday morning, not a moment later. You decide."

"I'm just afraid you won't come back, Leslie," Ken admitted. "You'll take a bus from Gainesville straight back to Toledo."

"Not a chance. I shall return. I promise."

"After all this violence?"

His words reminded me. "Did you get your tetanus shot?"

"What shot?"

"I thought you were having a shot . . . because of the knife." My voice diminished to a whisper. Had Margaret lied?

"No, Margaret keeps the cutlery so clean that I hardly think any tetanus bacilli could survive her scouring. No, I've been helping Geoff transfer books from room to room all day."

I changed the subject, wondering again about that

printed signature. I said, "I wrote Keegan a letter. That indicates how desperate I am!"

He took it quickly from my fingers and read it. "Good. Sounds good. I asked Margaret how much she'd told—I mean wrote down for Keegan about who you are, and she gave me a very evasive answer. She's getting to be a problem, but she's been here so long that I can't bring myself to pull rank on her." He smiled wistfully.

"Where shall I start looking for Keegan?"

"Try the lagoon."

"Swimming? It looks like rain."

"Well, that didn't faze Beryl . . . but, then, Beryl never even wore a bathing suit—"

"What? Who?"

He declined to tell me. "Go stroll along the lagoon, Leslie. But if Keegan lays one finger on you, or even acts rude, I want you to scream your head off for me, you understand? Keegan won't hear a thing."

When I got outdoors, the sky was not dark, merely devoid of color; both foliage and sand had lost their shine. I strolled beside the now-opaque water where the SIGFORD bounced, tied to her dock. I surveyed the near side of the lagoon from one mangrove boundary to the other, and sat down on the cool, damp sand, not far from the house. The sand was of ideal consistency for castle-building.

At my age? Once in my dim past, when we'd had a house with a father in it, I'd played in a sandbox with tiny tin cars and plastic soldiers. Now as I sat idle, my fingers doodled with. the sand, and slowly a castle grew, fistful by fistful. Why not? People considered me a loose woman; let's confuse them with a Leslie playing in the sand like a baby. Like the person named Beryl? Imagine! I had never dreamed of going swimming in the nude! Who was Beryl?

Lifting my eyes for the hundredth time, I saw, beyond the crenelated towers of my castle, a person standing on the surface of the lagoon—golden-haired Keegan Howell.

Then I realized that his feet were in a skiff so flat it was almost a raft. He was propelling himself slowly toward me with one long-handled paddle. So he wasn't going to avoid me or lurk in the mangroves for several days? Wonderful! He beached his craft, and I arose. Then, in a triumph of aloofness, his eyes focused far beyond me, he walked right past.

This was worse than feeling his eyes rake over me in rage. He dared to add blindness to his deafness and icy silence! I sprang into his path before he could out-distance me, and, without smiling, I thrust on him my carefully written note.

He took it without glancing at it and shredded it. Pink confetti sprinkled down. Then, unwilling to litter, he dug the specks of my stationery into the sand with one bare brown foot.

"Oh, Keegan!" Like Ken, I demanded his ears hear me. "Keegan! Don't be so stupid!"

He didn't say a word. He walked past me and up the flight of rickety back-steps to the kitchen door.

He hadn't even acknowledged me as a human being! I pounded my fists on my thighs. After almost kicking over my ornate sand castle, I scuffed my way up to the front door of the house.

Cindy could be difficult, but only out of ignorance, exuberance, and devilment. Keegan had calculated from the moment he spotted me how he would treat me. I ought to urge his uncle to knock Keegan over the head, package him up, and deliver him to Gallaudet College. Yeah, set him down among kids his age far worse off than he—students born deaf, ones who couldn't see, or who suffered cerebral palsy or paraplegia plus deafness. Wouldn't Keegan's stubborn pride be shamed right out of him!

But when Ken proposed a lesser tactic, to rewrite my note and put it in Keegan's room, on his bed, unsigned, so he'd have to read it to know its author, I objected. How dare he go into his nephew's room without permission? Did Keegan invade Ken's rooms? Ken said maybe Keegan did. So what? The door was never locked.

"Please don't plot more surprises for the poor guy," I cried. It isn't fair, and it isn't wise. Keegan's deaf; he's not a child or a pet puppy dog."

"Okay, okay!" He waved me off. "I never thought of it that way, never having had a kid of my own. When stymied, I'll try anything. I always err by doing too much, not too little. I'm too aggressive, and I suffer from it. People either love or hate me; nothing in between."

At supper, which was a huge Brunswick stew followed by lemon meringue pie, there were only Ken Howell, Geoffrey Rauenbauer, and I, evenly spaced around the table. I hated to have Keegan miss that great food, but perhaps he didn't.

Ken told Margaret she'd never cooked a better meal, and she snorted.

"I mean it," he persisted. He lowered his voice. "Come off it, Margaret! We need your help very badly."

". . . last Fall," was the end of a sentence I missed. She set Ken's coffee cup down hard in front of him, and said something else, of which I caught only one word.

". . . poisoned!"

The prospect of ascending the stairs and heading to bed my second night at Okassasa House was not a pleasant one. My knees shook. Every person who'd been mentioned seemed to be missing, destroyed, murdered, or at least suspect. Though deaf people don't seek pity, I'd gotten over my anger, and I now pitied Keegan intensely. I had some pity left over for Margaret or Ken, but I didn't know which one of the two of them deserved it.

I wandered around the big living room, looking through doorways at towering cliffs of books. I stood on the porch in the dark, breathing in salt air. I went into Margaret's kitchen and had my offer of help curtly rejected.

Ken followed me with his eyes over the edge of the NATIONAL GEOGRAPHIC magazine he was holding.

A practice trip upstairs at nine, to test my courage, showed me a streak of light under one third-floor door not my own. I stood outside that room for a while, biting my lips. No sound. What did I expect? Well, if I heard a radio or stereo, that would tell me whose room it wasn't.

In my own room down the hall, I flipped on the light instantly and looked into the closet and the bathroom. No one. I picked up a DEAF AMERICAN magazine before I descended to the living room again.

"Does Keegan room on the second floor or third?"

"The third," said Ken, "on the lake side."

We stared silently at one another, thinking our own thoughts.

"Keegan won't go into your room again; I'm sure of that. He's been burned," Ken reassured me. "What I fear is that you'll get awfully lonely if you can't start accomplishing something right away. You ought to have your sister here with you for company."

I contemplated that idea. Let Keegan meet a real deaf girl? Let my innocent little sister meet a charming accused murderer, an emotionally damaged war-veteran, a

resentful housekeeper, a nasty-tempered book-appraiser
. . .and a GHOST? Great!

I stood in front of Ken Howell and pondered my problem.

"Well . . . I just don't know. Cindy? I doubt it. But I
can't imagine what to do next. If he won't listen to you,
or to me, or read notes, and if Margaret won't serve as a
go-between, well . . ." I ran out of words.

"Poor Leslie."

"I did bring along a copy of the magazine published by
the National Association of the Deaf . . ."

"You mean 'for' the deaf?"

"Oh, no! 'Of.' It's their own organization, not a
charity; their magazine is produced by deaf people. I
could leave it lying out, in hopes Keegan might get
curious enough to leaf through it."

"Good thinking!" Ken took the magazine from me and
started flipping pages. "You mean these athletes,
teachers, and actors in the photos are all deaf?"

I nodded. "Lots of them excel. Some born-deaf people
get graduate degrees and have fine careers . . . and not
because they can talk or lip-read well, either." I felt as
proud to say that as if I had six children born deaf who'd
become lawyers and physicists.

"That fact would surely impress Keegan."

"If he'd even pick up the magazine." I shrugged.
"Beyond that, I'm lost."

"I'm sorry." He put down the magazine. "I'm depressed
and lonely, too. If you knew how much I miss a social
life—bright lights, good restaurants, the theatre,
expeditions for pictures . . . this house is so deadly
silent and so isolated."

We stared sadly at each other.

"Leslie, have you ever been to Europe?"

He might as well ask if I'd ever been to the moon. My
negative started him on a fascinating tale of his own
travels to South America, Australia, Scandinavia, and all
points between. He told me about movie stars and
politicians he'd photographed and said I could come up any
time to see more of his pictures. I didn't rise to the
bait.

At least our boredom dissolved in the rush of his
eloquence.

When Ken looked at his watch, his brows went up. Already eleven-forty. Time for bed?"

"Yep. And I can manage without any sleeping pills or tranquilizers," I said pointedly.

Ken's face betrayed nothing. "Lucky you," he grinned. "Moreover, you probably sleep the dreamless sleep of the just—while I dream of lovely ladies . . ."

"Without bathing suits?" I astonished myself by asking, "Who was Beryl?"

"Okay. I'll tell you about Keegan's experiences with my models."

I plopped back down again, all ears.

"There've been three female visitors here since April, not counting Mary Ann's visit in March. The first of the models I hired was only three years older than Keegan, but she stroked his hair and nearly cried with pity over him. You can imagine how he reacted; he practically cursed her out."

"I'm not surprised."

"The second woman acted exactly opposite."

"I can guess. She was afraid of him?"

"Right. She wouldn't look at Keegan. She talked only to me and didn't half listen to him for fear she'd be called on to communicate. I don't know which one was worse."

"For Cindy, the second would be worse; she loves to be cuddled. But fountain-of-pity types must infuriate a man."

"Okay, two beautiful girls fly down from New York, and of course Keegan assumes they're here for work and for my pleasure, too. I have no way to remind him that some models are very married women, and others are so staid and businesslike you can't lay a finger on them, unless you keep your camera in the other hand.

"Here's Keegan all alone, refusing to contact any of his university friends, having no young people he knows in Okasassa, so I tried something."

I winced in advance. "Uh oh!"

"Keegan and Mary Ann had been engaged, and at it, hot and heavy, the summer before. A kid his age needs . . ."

"Tell me something about Mary Ann, first."

"She wasn't much for conversation. She wasn't a very interesting person. She'd have made a boring wife. A woman needs a career or craft of her own to be a complete

61

person, but Keegan's easily satisfied, and he's loyal. Mary Ann, however, was not loyal."

"She left him?"

"Did she ever! She and I had such a scene—it almost came to blows. She's one of those I told you about—one who hated me right from the first."

"What did you and she fight about?"

"About her leaving Keegan, leaving a badly injured, depressed, pitiful kid who could scarcely hobble around and who couldn't hear a word we said. Oh, hell, let's get back to Beryl. I was desperate to do something to cheer Keegan, so I picked up a little hitch-hiker outside Cross City one day, a hippie kid, and brought her home."

"Oh, no!" I groaned.

"I hope she was eighteen, but I never got an age or a last name out of her. I told her Keegan's problem, and she was intrigued. Okay, I admit to fraud. I pretended Beryl was here for a picture-story I was doing on the hippie culture. She waltzed in with her ragged jeans, frizzy hair and guitar (the guitar wasn't a good idea, but I couldn't separate her from the thing). She rummaged in Margaret's kitchen for food organic enough to eat; and she skinny-dipped in the lake as well as in the Gulf. She rolled her own joints, right in front of everyone.

"Her virtue was that she treated Keegan as if he were still normal—casually, with teasing good humor. I even saw her act out jokes about his deafness. She made him understand her—and even laugh!"

"Golly!"

"Yeah. He was her first deaf friend, but she didn't freak out. She had a plastic enough face, and she threw herself into communicating with him. She was the touchie-feelie type, which was good; he has a very affectionate nature, though you'd never guess it, now.

"For two weeks they went off together and wrestled around like a pair of puppies, and Keegan lost a few of the premature lines on his face. Then she blew it."

"How?"

"She decided to 'let it all hang out.' She told Keegan that it was a setup, that there was no picture-story at all. That I'd brought her home as a gift to him."

"Oh, how COULD she?"

62

"She was being honest, she said. She wrote it all out for Keegan, and he threw the paper in my face and called me a p-. . . you can guess."

"Why would she do that to him if she liked him?"

"Maybe he was too square for her, too much like me. She called me a hypocritical, game-playing, materialistic Male Chauvinist Boar WASP. I'd requested she wear some clothes around the house, and hide the grass in front of the Deans and Rauenbauer. Keegan told her he'd seen enough of grass in the Army, and he laughed at her diet and her Tarot cards."

"Then what happened?"

"She went out of here, jet-propelled—propelled by Keegan's rage. I whisked her back to Cross City, paid her fifty bucks (which she violated her principles to take, I'm sure), and left her and her silent guitar on the same street corner.

"Then Keegan disappeared for so long I thought . . .I feared he'd done away with himself."

"Oh, poor Keegan. Everything turns out so rotten!"

"I know it. I tell myself at least he had two happy weeks with a kid who accepted his deafness and showed him he was still an attractive male. But the episode sure didn't improve his opinion of me."

I didn't comment. The conversation died away.

When I was so sleepy that I just had to go to bed, Ken was my escort up both flights of stairs. His nearness made me pull in my elbows, hairs prickling on the back of my neck. Without touching me, he made me very aware of his longing.

"Please. No farther."

On the third floor I brought him to a halt with just those three words. He stood and watched me go to my room and shut myself in. It didn't yet occur to me to brace a chair under my doorknob.

It was very warm up here under the roof, and the wind had died on this cloudy night. I rolled up the slatted blinds to bring in any breeze that happened by, later that night. I'd not be coward enough to sleep with a lamp on, but tonight I dug out of the bureau my Mother Hubbard gown to replace the confection Keegan had seen me wearing.

Then I went promptly to sleep and dreamed I was a

hippie in a long dress who ran off with Ken, and Mr. Rauenbauer rescued Ken from me.

I am no believer in the supernatural. Ghosts, spirits, demons and that sort of paraphernalia turns me off. By necessity a hard-minded sister-raiser, I didn't for a moment believe spooky things existed. "Missouri mule," George once called me. "Always it's 'Show me, show me.' "

I didn't ask to be shown the Howell ghost, that night.

Not that night, right above my head, in blazing color! I couldn't scream, because my fist was rammed into my mouth. With the other hand I ripped back the sheet. There was no moon, but my dark room was glowing with blue light. My gaze swung toward the ceiling, and there it was, right above me.

It was acid blue, and it was a face, grinning.

I shot my feet onto the rug and snatched up my robe under one arm as I half-ran, half-crawled toward the door. The image swam, blue and quivering, above me.

I was more angry than frightened. That someone would go to the trouble of inflicting THIS upon me on night number two was infuriating. I bolted into the hall, shut the thing up behind me, and put on my robe. I was too disoriented to remember which door must be Keegan's, so I felt along one wall until I found the stairs. Then I backtracked to the most likely door. I pounded with the heels of my hands and stamped my feet, the way one summoned Cindy—with vibrations, not sounds. I listened. Bedsprings creaked—in the next room over. I transferred myself to that door. Keegan opened it.

He stood there in lamplight, groggy, wearing low-slung jeans, his skin so brown he didn't look half naked. My face must have been a sight, for he stepped back and let me in, saying, "What did he do to you?" There was curiosity in his voice, but no sympathy.

While I caught my breath, he waited, narrow-eyed. My fingers jerked, as they do with any deaf person, and I cast a glance around the room for paper and pencil. Keegan's feet were bare, his hair and bed were both mussed. I had surely awakened him. Therefore, he had not been creating that face—that blue, mirthless cadaver-grin on my ceiling.

I waited for terror to set in. Once, in a deserted

rest-room, a man had jumped out of a toilet-stall and tried to grab me. Furious, I'd shouted, "Act your age!" as I fled. Five minutes later I'd been catatonic.

It was good distraction to be able to explain the ghost to someone. "Ghost," I said, and outlined the thing. Scowling, he handed me one notecard, three by five, and a pencil stub.

I wrote, a bit shakily, "I saw a ghost."

He read those words, holding the card well away from him as if very far-sighted. He wss careful to seem uninterested.

Surely he knew the ghost rumor, since my informant was Margaret, his sole confidante.

"A ghost, huh?"

I nodded my head rapidly up and down.

"Another lie for me? Leslie's one lie per night, huh?"

Any pity I felt for him congealed into an impulse to slap his handsome, jeering face . . . hard.

I snatched back the card. "In my room was something," I scribbled. "I don't believe in ghosts, either. But this horror show has to stop."

"Why don't you leave?" was his response, "Instead of waking me up in the middle of the night?"

"YOU woke ME up last night!" I cried so emphatically that he showed by a humorless smile how well my retort communicated.

"You worry about a stupid ghost when you're in the house with a murderer? A poisoner?" said Keegan.

I grabbed at my throat, then grabbed my card back, flipped it over, and wrote, "I was given some peculiar capsules, yesterday."

"You didn't take them, did you?"

I shook my head.

"No, you didn't, because you're still alive. You just see visions—without the help of any drugs."

"What'll I do?" I said, raising my shoulders and palms along with my brows. There was no more space on the card.

"Get out," Keegan said. "Go away and leave us to kill each other off."

I motioned for more paper, which he reluctantly furnished—one more measly index card. "Didn't Margaret tell you about a ghost?" I wrote.

65

"Margaret? She's not that silly," he snapped. Then he reconsidered. "Unless 'g-o-s-e' is her spelling for ghost. I didn't understand her notes about a 'blue gose.' I thought she meant 'goose.'"

"It was blue," I wrote. "A huge blue face, grinning." Then, below the words, I drew the face. It was very easy to outline.

Expecting another superior male laugh from Keegan, I drew back, tensed. Instead, his tight mouth opened, and his athlete's chest swelled with an intaken breath.

"A blue . . . face? Grinning?"

I outlined it with both hands, toward his ceiling.

He put a hand to his face and stared at me through his spread fingers. I'd have given a year off my life to read Keegan's mind. No more mention of my foolishness, no sneers, no commands to leave. If HE believed in a ghost— he, a biologist—would I have to believe in it, too?

He let his hand drop, turned me around, and pushed me out of his room, not speaking. I hung back, and he jerked me with him down the hall. We plunged into my room.

No blue light. We were in darkness.

"It's gone," he whispered.

"So you believe in ghosts?" I said to the back of his head, in the dark room, forgetting he was deaf.

He put on the light, then closed and locked all my windows, jerking down the blinds, one after another.

"Go to bed," he ordered. "If you see anything else, you pound on the wall. I'll hear it and come." He glared at me in my bulky, quilted robe as I sat meekly on the side of my bed, fists in my lap.

"Put a chair under the doorknob when I go out," he said curtly, and without another word, he was gone. Of course I couldn't make any understandable reply to his commands.

At least the ghost—or ghastly practical joke—had done some good. Keegan talked to me, however grimly and laconically. He'd read my notes and also grasped replies I'd mimed. Even if I didn't understand his response to the blue face, we had communicated.

I lay awake in the heat behind my barricaded windows, expecting anything. I fell asleep at last, and only slits of brilliant sunshine and smothering heat could awaken me.

Okay. Today I'd communicate with Keegan again. And

today I'd make friends with him and start his instruction. No man could imagine I was a girlfriend of Ken's after seeing me in last night's frumpish outfit.

But that day Keegan was gone without a trace; Margaret was no longer discussing ghosts; and Ken—after I reported the night's adventures to him—looked actually ill, chalky beneath his tan. He didn't have anything to say except, "This is serious, Leslie. This is very, very serious."

I knew how serious things had become when I went outdoors and saw my poor sand castle.

It was intact, turrets and battlements white and shimmery as sugar against the green water, but a hefty piece of wood was sticking out of it. I pulled it free. It was an axe.

An axe, embedded deep in my castle—very funny. Grisly. Yes, I was getting the message, now. Somebody's message!

At the beginning of that long Thursday, finding no one communicative, I put on my bathing suit and went out into the hot sun for a swim.

On the way, I kicked down my sand castle, demolishing it and smoothing the sand until no trace was left of my violated creation. The rusty-bladed axe I carried up to the house and dropped with a crash on the front porch, muttering, "Here it is back, Whoever likes me so much!"

The lagoon, situated below the house so that three tiers of windows rose close above it, suddenly turned me off. I took the food I'd collected from the kitchen under Margaret's sour gaze—fruit, cookies, and a bottle of Pepsi—and hunted for a path to the Gulf beach. Ken had said there was a path.

I finally found the way, and after hiking through shoulder-high grasses, prickly bushes, and the sensuous windings of mangrove trunks, I found the beach and marked the path with a broken branch planted like a flagpole, on which I hung my bathrobe. I wondered if Ken was skulking in the leaves with a camera to photograph my provocative white suit on my already scorching white body. A girl-friend had given me the suit, and though it was one-piece, with a high neckline, the back was cut low, and circles the size of dinner plates were cut out of each side at the waist. It was a bit startling, but it was the only suit I owned.

I splashed into the calm, bathtub-warm water, yellowish green and lovely. No more sixty-degree water to force myself to enter; the Gulf must be eighty, and I loved it. Not a fish or a faraway boat invaded the great lonely expanse of sky and sea. Okasassa House was barely visible above the trees, only its roof and third-floor windows showing. I almost dozed, floating in the ebb and push of the shallows, resting on my elbows and letting the whole Gulf of Mexico caress me. I got a nice sunburn.

That night I shut all my windows and blinds, wedged the chair under my doorknob, and slept toasted and bone-tired, grateful for the bottle of anti-pain sunburn cream I'd found right outside my door when I came up from the beach. Ken admitted putting it there, and I did apply it, hating the habit I was developing of suspecting everyone's every action.

Early the next morning, when Ken Howell, Mr. Rauenbauer and I were ready to board the SIGFORD to go to the mainland, Ken drew me aside. He seemed very uneasy. He expressed concern over all the sunburned skin visible on me, while I stood watching the contortions of the scholar who was trying to cross the six-inch space from dock to boat. Ken tried to pay me my first week's salary—in cash.

I refused. I'd done nothing to earn it, and I feared I might never earn it. I ended by having a fifty dollar bill rammed into my pocket. He said, "If I can't furnish you a shop nearby, I can at least cover your motel bill and food in Gainesville; you mustn't pay for all that."

I remembered Beryl's fifty bucks, and what she'd done to earn it. Along with the bill, Ken handed me a matchbook cover from a Gainesville motel called The Four Palms.

"This is a nice, clean place within walking distance of department stores," Ken explained. "Geoff always stays at the Inn on the east side of town, but en route he'll pass right by this one. If you stay there, he can also pick you up easily tomorrow morning—and I'll know exactly where you are. Four Palms Motel, Geoff. Third and Live Oak Streets."

Methought the gentleman protested and described and explained too much, but I liked the idea of separate motels for Geoff and me. The less I saw of Rauenbauer the better, and if Ken wanted to know where I was, well, more credit to his sense of responsibility. I knew what it was like to be responsible for someone younger than oneself, twenty-four hours a day.

I soon was climbing out of the SIGFORD onto that rickety wharf so different from the Howell's spruce little dock. Ken Howell gently restrained me by my less sunburned arm.

"Come back tomorrow, Leslie."

"I will."

"I can't lose you; Keegan's whole future may rest in your hands."

"In every sense," I said to myself.

Hurrying up the slippery, sandy path after Rauenbauer, I knew Ken was watching us from the boat. I didn't look back or speak to my unpleasant companion.

At the garage where he stashed his car, he muttered something about "poor white trash and nigras," while he examined his Buick's hubcaps, tires, and battery. There was no tampering. He was probably disappointed to find no excuse to skin someone. As soon as he'd backed out of the garage, he started in on Keegan.

"Selfish, egocentric hippie," he said. "He acts as if he's the only one wounded in the war . . . in all wars. Suppose he'd lost his sight, instead?"

All I trusted myself to verbalize was a question. "Were you in World War Two?"

"No. I was . . .uh, exempted." Unabashed, he continued, "But I could lose my hearing completely and get along fine. I'd not miss it particularly. If he were blind, he'd have some reason to whine, but deaf? Ridiculous!"

"Helen Keller said if she had her choice, she'd rather have her hearing back than her sight."

"What does SHE know?" he snapped, too quickly. When he realized what he'd said, he fell silent for a few miles.

He hadn't forgotten Keegan, however. He verbalized his thoughts.

"The boy went into service voluntarily, too. He wasn't drafted. Now look at him. A good-for-nothing. A burden on overburdened taxpayers."

At last I knew what "seeing red" really meant. I locked my jaw shut.

"Don't you agree?" he prodded, driving very slowly, even though we had now reached the asphalt paving. No wonder he needed an overnight stay, with his driving habits.

"I don't know Keegan well enough," I said, wary of angering this creep at the very outset of our forced association.

"Take me, for example. I have arteriosclerosis, but you don't hear me complaining. I don't have a family to look after me. I've always been alone. I could die at any

70

moment, but I don't run off into the woods and let other people manage all my affairs."

"How long have you been on the island?" I asked him.

We were edging past a mule-drawn wagon.

"Five and a half weeks. I've nearly finished the appraisal. There are a great many books worth a great deal of money."

"Did Keegan communicate with you? Ever?"

We were easing slowly back into the right-hand lane.

"Yes. Upon my arrival, I wrote down who I was and what I was doing on the island. He read that. The boy actually can read, though you'd never guess it. Then he turned on me and started handing back anything I wrote, unread, with that unbearable insolence. He wouldn't give me a modicum of respect."

"Did he ever read Ken's notes?"

"You call him 'Ken,' already?" Rauenbauer peered at me sideways over his spectacles. "Yes, I suppose you would; he gets along very well with members of your sex, I notice."

When that didn't get a rise out of me, he went on, "Read his uncle's notes? Of course not. The boy won't pay any heed to his elders."

"Except Mrs. Dean."

"Margaret, the black maid?" he retorted. "Why, she's practically illiterate! I've seen him trying to decipher her patois—that means her uneducated language. What a person to choose as the source for all one's information! Of course, he's not so jealous of her. It's jealousy that makes him hate us and threaten to burn the house down. There's no earthly excuse for such uncouth behavior."

My black look stopped him short.

I had to grant him one point, though. Margaret's spelling of "ghost" had indeed misled Keegan. But "gose" was how Margaret heard the word, a problem Cindy never had. My sister's vocabulary was infinitesimal compared to Margaret's, but each word was always spelled absolutely correctly, on paper or on her fingers.

"I can sympathize with Keegan," I said. "My little sister is—"

He had no interest in my little sister. "You children all stick together, don't you? Thank heavens I got out of

71

teaching and never married and had children. Books don't talk back to you."

We rode in painful silence for the next hour, through flatlands and swamps toward the ascending, scorching ball of the sun. He never went over thirty, and other cars angrily passed us, honking. Rauenbauer glared at them, his insecurity too obvious.

This man who never complained now launched into a list of his afflictions: gout, arthritis in his left thumb, diabetes. He said that the damp Virginia winters were endangering his health. On and on went his "I, I , I."

As for me, I almost dozed, but he didn't notice. He never asked if I went to school or what I hoped to do for Keegan. He never learned a thing about Cindy, which was a preferable, because criticism of my little sister would have turned me into a screaming maniac.

At last came clusters of houses and stores. We'd reached the city. I showed him my matchbook cover and started looking for four palms. I found three palms and a stump. Though Rauenbauer said no one would check me into a motel this early, I got a royal welcome.

"Nine o'clock tomorrow morning, no later," he scolded, before he drove away and left me blessedly alone.

I spread out my city map, compliments of the motel manager, on the plaid bedspread to find the campus of the University of Florida. Within half an hour I'd left the motel, leaving behind the borrowed overnight case that belonged to Sigrid Halsingven Howell, the little suitcase Ken urged me to take along, with the "S.H.H." embossed upon it.

If I met Rauenbauer on campus, so what? But for safety's sake I did make one purchase, and stuck the bright paper bag under my arm.

I passed the library where my chauffeur-scholar would be deep in the stacks, his long nose in books. The administration building was what I wanted. I strolled along, admiring bushes with speckled leaves like paint-splatters. 1 passed couples walking hand-in-hand and couples lolling on the grass. I breathed Florida-fresh air, kept my chin high, and tried not to notice their embracing, thinking of a moment high up in a dark mansion when a total stranger had whipped my body against him to

72

kiss me so hungrily that if I'd for a moment relaxed—

I dared not imagine anything further. We weren't even friends, Keegan and I. It was Mary Ann Monahan he had been kissing, the girl whom I sought on this campus.

Too soon I was at the Records Office stammering out her name. The tanned, smiling secretary disappeared, then returned with a file folder pressed to her shirt-front. She asked, "Your sister? You sure look like her photo."

"No. Mary Ann's a friend of mine I've come down south to find."

Finding her wouldn't be easy. Classes were over for the term. She'd completed her junior year and had left for the summer. I wrote down Mary Ann's home address and phone number on the inside of the Four Palms Motel matchbook cover. Then the friendly secretary gave me a short course in Florida geography. Mary Ann lived in Starke, fifty miles northeast of here, up towards Jacksonville.

It was now eleven thirty-five, and long-distance phoning was not what I'd had in mind. For forty-eight hours I'd been preparing myself to find and face Mary Ann Monahan. To grill her. In person.

I had no car. I also had no change, no coins for a telephone call.

So I strolled off campus toward a nearby drugstore. Did I have the nerve? Having the nerve, did I know the right words? Ken and Margaret had told me only tantalizing snippets. Keegan had dropped ugly hints. Rauenbauer knew even less than I. There was only one person to clarify everything for me, a girl about my age who lived fifty miles away.

As I received my handful of change for the shampoo and the mascara, my gaze went to the prescription counter of the store. Faint nausea bothered me—from mental, not physical causes. I dug into my purse to find a certain carefully folded square of tissue. If someone gives you a couple of big, fat capsules under odd circumstances, an expert opinion is certainly called for.

I presented my capsules to the young pharmacist at the counter, pleased with these unrushed, cordial, smiling Floridians.

"Can you tell me what's in these capsules, please?"

He looked me up and down without appearing to ogle,

then frowned at the capsules. "They don't look familiar. I can tell you in a minute."

"I was supposed to take them, but I wasn't sure I should, not knowing . . ."

"These were prescribed for someone else? You should never take someone else's medications, Miss."

"I know that. I wasn't tempted to take them, but I want to know what they are. I think they're probably some kind of tranquilizer. I was . . . nervous."

He grinned down from the high pharmacy counter at me. "Very interesting tranquilizers." His hand ran across shelved bottles, row after row.

"Well, I'm not nervous anymore," I added, wondering how many hypochondriacs he met every work-day.

He took a bottle from the shelf behind him and held it out to me. "You can start bein' nervous, again, Honey. These are strong medicine."

"What are they?"

"Powerful sedatives. You'd need enormous tolerance. If an average healthy person ingested these . . . wow! Each one would equal a dozen mild tranquilizers."

"They'd make me ill?"

"Someone your size? Both of these? You'd have been practically comatose. Or worse."

My knees went gelatinous, leaving me hanging on the edge of the counter like the little "Kilroy was here" figure, my nose almost on the glass surface.

"You're lucky you checked them out. No one should take anybody else's prescriptions," he sternly reiterated. "Who gave you these?"

"I'm really not sure. they were sorta sent to me. By mistake."

"Come back behind the counter here and sit a spell, Honey," he suggested. "You look pretty shook."

I decided to do just that. Easier to sit down, while my throat kept spasmodically swallowing air. . . better air, than poison packaged in gelatin. I sat.

"I want them back," I said.

Obediently, he slid the capsules into a small vial, capped it, and then crouched down in front of my bench.

"I'm Duane Gunlock," he said, in a lovely mush-mouthed drawl I preferred to Midwesterners' nasal twang. "Who're you?"

"Leslie Fallon," I said. "I'm from Toledo. I'm living on an island off the coast—"

"Glad you came in and checked these things. You can't play around with sedatives. How about eatin' something to put the color back in your face, Leslie? Had lunch yet?"

I considered his invitation. Duane fitted his name; he had a long-jawed cowboy face, squinty brown eyes and crisp brown curls. Curls even emerged from his shirt cuffs onto the backs of his hands. He wore his hair shorter than Keegan did, and looked very competent and professsional in his long white coat.

"Yes, I would like lunch," I said wryly, "if I can manage to eat!"

Seeing my suspicions confirmed, I became more angry than frightened. The ghost-thing must be a patently ridiculous hoax; drugs were something else. Not drugs. Poison.

"Great!" said Duane, and offered his hand to pull me to my feet. "Across the street they grill really fine hamburgers."

In a plastic booth behind a window draped with fish net and dyed starfish, I sat looking at this young man's yellow shirt, polka-dot tie, and capable hairy hands.

"What're you gonna do with your pills?" he drawled.

"Find out why I got them, and from whom," I said, before I could shut up.

I told Duane that I'd been hired to teach a deaf fellow, but I didn't give him any names or details.

Duane was a graduate of the local University, he said. After studying pharmacy in North Carolina, he came back here to work near campus—for the atmosphere, said he, and for the girls. He was twenty-four. His family lived in Tampa.

As we crossed the street after lunch, I peered into a familiar looking, hearse-like car sitting at the stoplight. Yep, there was my own Mr. Rauenbauer waiting for the green. He had another man with him.

I couldn't be sure, but in shadow and seated, his companion resembled Baker Johnson, the fat man I'd met at the Okasassa dock a few days ago. I didn't stop to stare. Neither man saw me, I thought. Their heads were nodding in

75

earnest conversation.

So what? Rauenbauer worked for Ken Howell; Ken knew Johnson. Rauenbauer and Johnson must've met on the island. Why shouldn't three acquaintances meet in pairs? I mustn't let myself be waltzed into paranoia.

Back in Duane's drugstore, I determined to telephone Mary Ann Monahan. I balanced a row of coins on the tiny ledge under the phone and dialed the operator. Waiting for my call to go through, I watched Duane at work, jollying up old ladies and handing out medicine. He was always smiling. I tried to smile, too.

I didn't reach Mary Ann. She was out shopping until four, her mother said, and then she had a date.

"Mary Ann keeps very busy, since her wedding is just next week."

I was so startled that I abruptly hung up.

Wedding? She'd been Keegan's fiancee a few months ago, in March. How fickle could a person be?

I didn't leave the store without thanking Duane Gunlock for insuring my continued health. Then I was loath to say adieu to my one friend in Gainesville.

I ventured to say, "Though it's an awfully big school, did you ever meet a student at the University of Florida named Keegan Howell?"

"Sure, I remember that name," Duane amazed me by responding. "He was a freshman—he took beginning biology with me. I was his lab instructor my last year here. A blond guy, right? Real nice-looking, and got straight A's, right?"

"Right! You think he'd remember you?" My heart pounded.

"He'd be more likely to remember me than I was to remember him. Old Gunlock the Fierce, with those deadly lab exams. He'd remember. He used to stay after lab to shoot the bull. He was from Atlanta, wasn't he? A prep school kid, really well prepared. I urged him to go on through to the Masters and the Ph.D., but he was getting more and more tempted by med school."

"Med school!"

Merely using a stethoscope would be impossible for a man who couldn't hear. He couldn't even listen to his patients' complaints. I didn't know of any deaf people entering med school. How could Keegan become a physician, now he was deafened?

"Keegan jointed the Army," I heard myself whisper.

"He did? That's surprising," Duane said. "He was so eager to finish school and either practice medicine or teach. I'd never guess he'd join up. He wasn't draftable, not with his grades and his potential."

Duane frowned, adding, "I thought the only distractions HE'd have to worry about were the swimmin' team . . . and the girls!"

I let the subject drop, beginning to understand clearly why Keegan kept his deafness secret from friends.

Within two hours I finished shopping and made up my mind what to do next. I'd stick my packages in my motel room, and then— On my way past the office, I got stopped by the motel manager.

"Miss Fallon? A man called, asking about you. He wanted to know if you'd gotten here all right. Called just a few minutes ago. I said you'd checked in and then left again."

"Did he leave a number? Say who he was?"

"Nope. Sure didn't."

"Did he . . . did he have a Southern accent?" inquired Leslie-the-Detective.

"Yeah, he did. 'Bout like mine," the man grinned, not giving the answer I'd expected to my unpremeditated shot in the dark.

"It wasn't long distance?"

"Didn't sound like it, and no operator came on the line."

I thanked him and went to my room. Only two people knew where I was staying, but it was neither Ken nor Rauenbauer who'd called. Neither one had a southern accent. It couldn't have been Keegan, of course. Rufus?

As I sat on the foot of my bed, staring at the blank, cold face of the TV set, the phone rang, and I threw myself at it.

"Hello? Hello? Who is it?"

Only silence, and after a moment, someone hung up. The dial tone began. I shivered. Watching me or watching over me, which?

It didn't occur to me that a Southern accent could be faked.

77

You clench your teeth, fists, and eyes shut to dive into cold water. I had to clench all my muscles for nerve enough to climb into the Greyhound bus bound for Starke, Florida.

Taking action sure was preferable, though, to sitting in my motel room watching soap operas and waiting for the phone to ring again. I dressed in a brown knit skirt and a white pullover, and tied a bandanna around my hair. I picked up my purse and the lovely portrait of Keegan and Mary Ann. That would prove my identity . . . as what? Not as Keegan's friend or his teacher. As Ken's employee, I supposed.

With stops, the Greyhound required an hour and a half to reach Starke. Before I boarded, I made sure when it was to return. It wouldn't do to end up stranded in a town where I had no right to be.

Leaning back in the familiar mustiness, listening to mellow Negro voices, I smiled at the cocksure amateur who less than a week ago had ridden another Greyhound bus South, almost singing with glee. I'd expected a grateful welcome from Keegan, but I earned his rage. Ken, overly grateful, was labeled a poisoner, and evidence against him was piling up. I feared this trip would be useless. Mary Ann would be just as shallow as Ken described her. She'd know nothing, or would say nothing.

I dwelt for a few pleasant moments on Duane Gunlock, who knew his job well enough to rescue me. I might, by now, have felt like gulping both my "tranquilizers."

The bus driver finally called Starke, and I was out on the sidewalk downtown, gripping my leather purse by its strap and looking wildly around. At four o'clock Mary Ann was due home. Then she had a date scheduled tonight with Keegan's replacement fiance. I had no choice but to hike to Haynes Road and face her on her home turf. This prospect felt too much like my visits in the past to homes of children Cindy had offended, to explain her problem to angry parents.

To fortify myself, I downed a mucilaginous milkshake, and it was five before my courage and my cab got me to Haynes Road, well outside town. I had the driver drop me at the corner nearest 1124. The house turned out to be white and nondescript, with pink plastic flamingoes on the lawn behind a row of red "high biscuits" (as I'd heard the hibiscus plant called.)

Her mother let me through the screen door, and suddenly a broad-faced young man in chinos stood up. Mom introduced me to Randy Parker. His future mother-in-law burbled over "their comin' wedding just four days from now," and Randy resumed his seat without stepping off the newspaper that had been spread to catch the red clay shed from his boots.

I met Mr. Monahan with his round bald head, round low belly and strong handshake, and a younger female Monahan in a ponytail. Then Mary Ann herself came rushing out and showed me she was a college girl by how cleverly she read my grim face.

"You're at the University?" she asked, tucking in her blouse nervously.

"I've come through Gainesville, yes," I hedged, very conscious of five pairs of eyes watching me. I added, "I need to talk to you about a student who went to school with you, Mary Ann."

"Like we had someone asking about Mark Poteet, once, remember, Mama?" her father said. "Checkin' up on him, 'cause he applied for some job with the feds. Are you from the University or the federal government?"

"Neither," I said. "It's not an FBI check or anything like that. Don't worry."

But Mary Ann was worried already, and Randy reached over to catch hold of her hand protectively.

"You a social worker?" he asked in his pleasant drawl.

"No. Well, yes, sort of. I'll have to speak to Mary Ann alone, please."

She blinked. "Alone? But this is just my family, and Randy's going to be my husband. I don't understand this, Miss—"

"Fallon," her mother reminded her.

I was grateful that no one commented upon our similar looks. Mary Ann had her hair skinned back in a ponytail like her sister's, and one of her eyes was made up with blue eyeshadow. That lessened our similarity a lot.

"It won't take long," I said. "I see you're very busy. At. . . this season."

She led me out of the living room and down a narrow hall, her dark head bent. We passed a towel-laden pink bathroom, a master bedroom, and a "God is Love" plaque on the wall. I caught up with her at her bedroom door.

"May we go inside?"

Mary Ann, Keegan's ex-beloved, frowned as if she smelled something. In her bedroom, with travel posters, stuffed animals, cosmetics, play programs, menus, and photos covering every surface, I made a big mistake. Before she even got the door completely shut behind us, I pulled from my purse the beautiful photograph of her with her head resting in Keegan Howell's lap.

She shrieked. Before I motioned her to silence, she shrieked, "Who took that picture? HE took that? What're you here for? Don't let anyone see that picture!"

Randy came thundering down the hall, murder in his eye.

"Whatsamatter, Honey?"

Her mother was right behind Randy, so was her sister, and I could hear her father at the far turn.

Mary Ann stuck the photograph back into my purse, where I was only too happy to hide it.

"I can't tell her anything," she wailed to Randy. "I'm not involved in anything she's. . .investigating."

"Some crime's been committed?" Randy wanted to know.

"Why'd you scream, baby?" her mother asked.

Mary Ann stood close against her current fiance, shooting warning looks at me. I knew she'd retreat with him like a Siamese twin if I didn't think fast. I did.

"There's a girl who's having difficulties," I said, "really life or death trouble; but nothing incriminates Mary Ann. I just need her to tell me how the girl was acting a year ago, back when she was in normal emotional health."

Mary Ann did not miss a word, or the gender-change. I'd guessed by now that no one knew about Keegan. Probably her parents no more than Randy knew about a Yankee lover in a mansion off Florida's west coast.

"Do you wanna talk to her, Honey?" Randy asked the girl tucked under his big left arm. He had a blond mustache and short hair, and he looked at Mary Ann as if he could absorb her right through the dual ducts of his eyes.

Mary Ann considered me gravely, eyes enormous.

"You don't want a friend of yours to be hurt," I said very softly. "She's possibly suicidal. I just have to know a few things about her family."

This ploy succeeded. She wriggled free of Randy and returned to her bedroom with me. I shut the door and waited until all the footsteps faded into silence.

"Suicide? Keegan?" she asked, leaning on the wall beside the open window. "Talk. Get it over with."

I felt old enough to be her grandmother, standing there on the other side of the window, listening to mockingbirds singing their hearts out in the back yard where clothes flapped on the line.

"I've come to Florida to help Keegan Howell," I began. "I have a little deaf sister. I'm studying to be a teacher of the deaf."

"His uncle sent you," she said dully. "That man's so despicable."

I shook my head vigorously. "Wrong. Ken Howell doesn't know I'm came here, and I would never tell him. I came to find you because he won't tell me what's going on, what's driving Keegan half mad."

Mary Ann's face crumpled into misery. "Keegan's still suffering?"

"He can walk normally, now, but he's permanently deaf. I can't help him until other things get resolved. His resentment of Ken is—"

"But it's deserved!" she broke in. "Ken took that photo when we had no idea. The filthy, sneaking . . . what else does he have pictures of—to blackmail me with?"

"There's no blackmail involved. You heard me protect your secret. Keegan IS being kept a secret, isn't he?"

"Everyone's had their hearts set on Randy since we were kids. The boy next door, you know. I wasn't supposed to be out on some island. They thought I was spending weekends with a girlfriend."

"I understand. My mother doesn't know everything I get involved in, either," I admitted. "Mary Ann, please tell me what Ken has done. Margaret and Keegan hate him, and you hate him too, but he's my employer, the man I work for. I have to know how the hatred started."

"If Keegan KILLED Ken Howell it would only be his just deserts!" she hissed. "Okay, I did leave Keegan. You know that. I couldn't deal with his deafness, or with his being half-crazy because of . . . other things. I couldn't even talk to him. He talked, and I listened—and watched him suffer. I couldn't bear it; I'm not a strong enough person. Ken made me come see him, but he didn't tell me Keegan was deaf—he said 'shrapnel wounds.' And he never told Keegan I was coming. It was a horrible scene.

"Ken had me walk right up to Keegan, unaware. Keegan didn't understand me. I thought his brain was gone. It was hideous. I went into hysterics right in front of Keegan. Ken was yelling, 'He's just deaf! He's just deaf!'

"JUST deaf! Imagine!"

I had no trouble imagining it. I could understand Ken's not being able to tell Keegan that Mary Ann was coming. But to leave Mary Ann ignorant was unforgivably cruel to them both. "Just deaf!" How can people be so stupid? Smart, well-educated people! "He's just deaf, like Grandpa."

"Now I'm over it, and I'm happy, again," Mary Ann said. "I love Randy. I want Keegan to be happy, but I can't help him. I won't go back there."

"I'm not asking you to go back. I'm there, now."

She looked at me hard. "Keegan's still the same? All of them are there, just like in March? Nothing's changed?"

"They're trying to settle the estate, appraise the books. And I'm supposed to—"

"If Keegan fell in love with you, it would help him. Would you ever. . . accept him?"

"As . . . as what?"

"As a lover . . . even as a husband? Could you? Could any girl?"

"I'd be a better bet than any other hearing girl I know." Color seeped into my cheeks, and she saw it. "But that's not the issue, Mary Ann. If I'm not to abandon him, too, I have to have the facts. For instance, someone is playing around with a hoax. A blue face was shining on the ceiling of my room. Margaret saw it, too, and called it a ghost. When I told Keegan about it, he just went wild."

The blue face also drove Mary Ann wild.

"Oh NO!" she screamed out. "Nothing so AWFUL . . ."

"You okay, Honey?" Randy called. His words, down the hall, echoed like a voice inside a milk bottle.

She cracked the door open and reassured him, then came back into the bedroom.

"Please tell me," I begged. "That specter has some connection with a death. I've guessed that much. Keegan's father's death?"

"Must I tell you? Won't you just go away?"

"I might stoop so low as to threaten to show Randy the photo of you with Keegan."

"But you'd prefer to be more civilized? What's in this for you, Leslie? Money? How much is dear Uncle Ken paying you anyway?"

"I'd help Keegan for free," I said, "now that I've met him."

"Okay." She filled her lungs, and out it all came, as fast as she could talk, fast enough to daze me.

"They think . . . the coroner and sheriff believe that Keegan's father killed himself. He didn't. Brad Howell was a strange, sickly man who leaned on Keegan just maddeningly, but Keegan looked after him and maybe loved him. No father would kill himself like that. Do what he did in front of his only son . . . and all of us."

"Do what? Tell me!"

"The . . . the autopsy said he was dying of emphysema. Smoking did that. His lungs were wrecked. But he died by poisoning."

"Poisoning!"

"Cyanide."

That one word told me volumes. Why hadn't I thought of cyanide, after all the mysteries I'd read? Cyanosis is blueness from cyanide.

A blue face.

I was visiting the island last Fall," Mary Ann went on. "My folks didn't know. I was only seventeen when we met, and it went so fast . . . Keegan is so— I didn't have permission to go out there, and you must never let on.

83

Anyway, last September, just before school started, I managed to plan a weekend on the island.

"We got there about three in the afternoon. We went swimming, Keegan and I, and supper was at seven. We all sat down . . . all of us: Keegan and I, Keegan's dad, Sigrid—his mother, and Uncle Ken. Margaret was serving, and Rufus stayed close by.

"Mr. Howell wanted a sort of formal dinnerparty, to celebrate the end of summer, he said, and Keegan's going back for his senior year. He had this dream of Keegan's becoming a great scientist or doctor, and he wanted Keegan and me to get married. He . . . he . . ."

I came over and put my arm around her, tight. She was already trembling;

"He . . . Keegan's father proposed a toast. All of us were to drink our wine—they kept very expensive wine, though Keegan's dad could only drink water. He offered his toast in water, lifting his goblet.

"He was a very dramatic man. He looked like he'd suffered a lot, mental pain too. Well, before we drank, while we were still holding our goblets, he went off on this tirade, saying his brother Ken ought by now to forgive him for taking . . . taking Keegan's mother away from him. Then he got even more excited, and said he knew Ken wished he'd hurry up and die from one of his illnesses. Then Ken could marry Sigrid, his widow.

"I remember every word, because of what happened next."

I tightened my grip on Mary Ann; our bent foreheads were almost touching.

"We drank our wine. Keegan's father smiled up and down the table. Then he gulped down his water. He immediately clutched his throat and gasped, 'You poisoned me! You did it!'

"I thought it was real tasteless, Leslie, and just an act, until he dropped his glass. He fell into convulsions, right there in his chair. He jerked and choked. For what seemed like forever, no one could move. Then Keegan leaped up and ran to him. Sigrid screamed and screamed. Keegan held him in his chair . . . his face got all gray . . . almost blue . . . with the lips drawn back. He was dead, and he turned blue. Blue! Grinning and blue!"

My stomach was turning, rising so forcibly against the

underside of my heart that I was all one big throb. The room tilted. But getting it out was good for Mary Ann. Her voice moderated, and she stopped trembling.

"It's too awful to think about, Leslie. I shouldn't have told you, if Keegan wouldn't!"

"Keegan won't tell anyone anything. Now I know why. You are a saint to tell me."

"The coroner said the water left in his goblet contained cyanide. There was cyanide in the dark room where his brother developed his pictures—potassium cyanide. They got the can, and because it had Keegan's father's fingerprints on it, along with Ken's, they decided at the inquest it was suicide. But the poor man died at his own table, in front of his whole family. And he accused Ken. He said his brother wanted him dead, said 'you poisoned me,'"

"When he said, 'you poisoned me,' who, exactly, was Keegan's father looking at?" I felt cold and shrewd, asking that.

"He was looking straight down the table at Ken."

"Oh."

"Keegan tried to get his mother to bring charges against his uncle, but she refused. She said his father had been nearly insane, that it really was a suicide. Keegan didn't buy that. He said their finances were getting better, that his father wanted to see our wedding, and then he wanted to see Keegan graduate from college. There was every reason not to die that day—or that way!

She caught her breath and went on. "Ken and Brad had been enemies since they were our age. Keegan told me that, after his dad died. They fought over Sigrid. He said his dad took Sigrid away from Ken. Both brothers wanted to marry her, and his dad won, but Ken couldn't stay away from her."

"And Ken's still a bachelor," I muttered. "What kind of woman was . . . is Sigrid?"

"She waited on her husband like an angel. She didn't ever seem to pay much attention to Ken, except to break up fights between Ken and Keegan or Ken and Brad."

"Then after the mur- . . . the death, Keegan ran off to the Army. I can begin to see why. Do you think he'll now try to bring charges against Ken?"

"He said he would. For murder. But he needs more evidence. And now he's handicapped. What can he do, stuck out there with Ken? What about Sigrid? Has she come back?

"Nope. Do you think she's dead, too?"

"Maybe. And I liked her. She'd have made me a great mother-in-law. You should see the one I'm getting! Randy's mom is—"

"Can you actually suspect that Ken killed Sigrid? You said he still loved her."

"Think about it. She is—or was—the key person who could send him to prison, if she changed her mind and talked to the sheriff."

"I see." It was really getting complicated. "Did Ken leave the island when Keegan did, last Fall?"

"If Ken left, he was back a few weeks afterwards. I know because he wrote me a letter from Okasassa, apologizing for what I'd had to witness. Imagine! I get a sickeningly sweet letter from the murderer, apologizing for the horrible murder-scene! He asked if I had any idea where Sigrid was. Fancy that! He said he needed her to help settle the estate. He was still there in March, and now—"

"He's still there, and no Sigrid, and the townspeople sure are suspicious," I reported. "Ken admits importing models to the island. He even tried once to get Keegan another girlfriend. Then Keegan mistook me for you, the first time we met." I traded her secrets for secrets.

"Do we look alike?" she studied my face. "Ken Howell's sure a skirt-chaser. You must know that by now. And what a manipulator! Look at the photos he takes."

"Did Ken ever make a pass at you?" I inquired.

"He flirts automatically. But no, we just yelled at each other."

"Keegan assumes I'm a girlfriend of Ken's," I said.

Her eyes widened. "That would infuriate Keegan."

"It sure has. Okay, anything else you can tell me about Keegan?"

"Well, I wrote to Keegan after I got off the island. In March, back at school, I wrote him a letter saying I was weak and immature, not strong enough to live with a deaf husband. You won't believe what happened.

"His blasted uncle intercepted my letter, read it,

found it 'hurtful,' he said, and sent it back to me. Ken told me not to write to Keegan unless I changed my mind or made up a story about falling for another man. He said deafness alone was not a excuse Keegan could bear. His words."

"Ken will pull anything, won't he?" I marveled. Still, I remembered instances when I'd fooled Cindy almost as brazenly, to keep brutal truth at bay.

"Do you still feel . . . anything for Keegan?" I asked against both better judgment and mercy.

"I love Randy. Always have, sort of. I want to be his wife and have kids with him. Keegan . . . was like that photograph. Lovely and new . . . and young. Romantic. He was my first love . . . and a very fine one, too. We had it good, for awhile. Keegan's a marvelous swimmer and dancer and tennis player—" She sighed, then snuffed out the glow in her eyes, lit by memories. "And Keegan will never, never dance again!"

"Not necessarily true, but Mary Ann did not get my standard lecture, Myths about the Deaf. She'd closed the Keegan chapter of her life.

As the fragrance of dinner cooking seeped in through the door, she said, "Will you promise?"

"Promise what?"

"You forgive me for leaving Keegan, don't you? I'm not smart enough for him, anyhow. I'm Randy's speed. You won't let anything slip, will you?"

"I won't. I promise."

"Then stay and have supper with us."

The upshot was that I gorged on roast ham and banana cream pie, scorched my lips on black coffee, and stayed so far away from the topic of Keegan that Mary Ann's eyes radiated gratitude. We did discuss deafness, however, because her parents pried out of me what my occupation was.

I talked about Cindy and sign language, and Mary Ann drank it all in, knowing that they'd never guess the truth about me, because they didn't know Keegan Howell was deafened. They didn't even know Keegan Howell existed.

Mary Ann and Randy took me back to the local bus station, to a glaringly lit waiting room with a few other rumpled passengers reading and dozing among the candy and cigarette machines. They dropped me off, because they were headed to the nine o'clock picture show. I was headed back to Gainesville and to Okasassa House.

"Hate to leave you alone till the bus comes," Randy worried, so much like Duane Gunlock. I assured them I was fine, not realizing until after they left that the bus I thought reached Gainesville at eleven p.m. actually left Starke at eleven and arrived by a circuitous route well after midnight.

I had the inconvenience of a long wait in the bus station; however, I received an unexpected gift from my friend Mary Ann Monahan. A letter.

She'd slipped the letter to me before we left her house, but I had no chance to read it until now. I opened it out and found that the signature was "Sigrid." No date on it, and no salutation except "My Dear." I hand-ironed it flat on my skirt to read it.

> My Dear,
> Your coming to the island has been
> wonderful. I hope the day won't be too
> far in the future when you come live at
> Okasassa House as Keegan's bride. I'm
> sorry there has been so much family
> strife, but it won't last forever. Keegan
> has good taste in girls, and if a mother
> may say so, you've made a wise choice, too.
> Keegan has been a better son than any of
> us deserves, and will make a dear and
> a loving husband. God bless you.
> Sigrid

I, too, found myself liking Sigrid. Where was she now? This note was probably the last souvenir Mary Ann had from the Keegan-days. I pictured Mary Ann, long before now, making a bonfire of any love letters Keegan wrote.

More bad luck. The bus to Gainesville due at eleven was forty minutes late. It came limping into the station with engine trouble. Half an hour more for repairs, and I finally arrived back in Gainesville at one-thirty in the morning.

The walk to the bus station in daylight had been short

and unremarkable. After midnight the district scared me; I hadn't Cindy with me to be brave for. But no one staggered out of a bar or a seedy hotel to impede my hasty steps. Not until a block from my motel did anyone approach me.

I remember in the vivid neon of the Four Palms Motel sign his lean red face, the unironed blue shirt, and the intent dark eyes.

"Got a dime fer a poor man, Miss?"

My purse was tight up under my arm, clamped against me. I ignored him and walked fast toward safety, eyes straight ahead. He stepped in front of me.

"Please, jist a dime. You sure can spare thet!"

Maybe the truth of his words, the Southern accent, or his hungry look made me acquiesce. I unslung my purse, seized the plastic bar on my precious motel room key, and then took out my coin purse.

I glimpsed motion toward me. I pivoted, my purse clutched against my bosom. He'd grabbed only the strap, and my motion tore it from his grip. I ran on wobbly legs toward the motel door, more desperate to save Sigrid's note and Ken's photograph than to save my cash.

I'd escaped his hands, but not his voice.

"You better go home, gal! You'll die on thet island! You'll die on thet island!"

I locked myself into room 17 before I realized what he'd yelled. How did a beggarman in Gainesville know I was living on an island, and that my home was elsewhere?

The question was whether to report an attempted purse-snatching. Should I just forget it? I'd be gone early tomorrow. It was already tomorrow. At nine a.m., Rauenbauer would pick me up.

I might even have misunderstood the beggar's words. Did he really say, "You'll die alone," or something like that?

From the safety of my room I dialed the police station, described the man in detail and said where I'd met him. I declined to give my name. The exasperated officer had my sympathy when he called me "uncooperative," but I couldn't stay in town to try to identify the man among their next batch of vagrants. I had to go back to the island when Rauenbauer came by for me, seven hours from now.

To go to sleep I had much to forget, from the hideous poisoning last Fall to the poisonous capsules still in my

89

purse. Asleep at last, I had another too-realistic dream, this time of myself stumbling up a long incline, my legs aching, dragging Cindy behind me, Cindy who wanted to stop and play because she couldn't hear the goblins and other monsters pursuing us. I knew I could let her go of her and save myself, but I would not. In the pre-dawn cool I awoke with a dry mouth and a bad conscience over the rage I felt toward my blameless little deaf sister.

Yes, the idea did enter my mind. I could return to the bus station and take a bus North. But I didn't have the cash to get very far, and Keegan didn't need another desertion.

I got up, dressed, and drank coffee from a foil packet beside an electric pot. I stacked my purchases and Sigrid's suitcase by the door and started making the bed, until I remembered not to. I wasn't very familiar with motel-living.

This was Saturday, and the streets were full of traffic. I went outside and paced the patio, keeping an eye on my wristwatch. Nine-thirty. Rauenbauer, late? The later he was, the more eager I was to see him. At ten, I would have crawled very gratefully into his Buick, and at eleven I was starving and yearning for any kind of transport back to the island. He wasn't coming!

The motel manager came to tell me that the same man had phoned me again, last night at midnight. Someone knew, then, that I'd been out late. I could keep my trip to Starke secret by saying I'd been to the last showing of a movie. That was believable.

"He called again at one-thirty, a.m. The same man. Got me out of bed," he complained. "You're sure a popular girl."

Now I was caught. But by whom?

I phoned the Inn and found Rauenbauer had checked out at nine. At eleven-thirty, I walked out of the motel with my suitcase, totally perplexed. The weird phone calls and then that beggar— Should I take a bus north as far as I could go on my unspent cash, and then wire Mother for money to reach Toledo? No, Youngstown; that was closer. Go to Cindy. I missed her.

Food was my first need, but bacon and eggs had no appeal. What did weary, anxious soldiers eat? Chocolate bars. It was not wholly coincidencal that I chose to buy my candy bar at Duane Gunlock's drugstore.

"Did you telephone my motel last night?" I asked him, feeling foolish. I did not say how late the calls had been.

"No, but I wish I had. I'd of liked to take you to a show last night. I didn't think of you stayin' alone in a motel the whole evenin'."

Stalwart and open-faced, a protector of women like Mary Ann's big fiance, he came out of the pharmacy. He looked down on me so sympathetically that I admitted I was stranded there.

"Delighted to hear it! I'm off work at noon today, and I'd just love to drive you over to the coast."

I knew he meant it. Also I knew I'd never accept such a big favor if my life weren't complicated by threats and horrors. In fact, Duane might help Keegan. The fact he'd known Keegan cinched it. I'd act like Ken. If Keegan refused to leave the island, we'd fetch him friends from the mainland. Ken had brought him a girlfriend; and me? I'd reunite him with his old lab instructor.

The only awkwardness came in admitting to Duane that Keegan and the deaf man I hoped to tutor were the same person. He didn't demand an explanation of my deception, and I volunteered nothing about my trip to Starke. He still assumed I spent the evening in the motel.

Over a meal of red snapper in Trenton on the way west, Duane questioned me in detail about deafness and Keegan. How could they communicate?

"Use simple sentences. Pantomine. He'll want to see YOU, and that's a big plus. I could make some signs, ones so representational that he'd have to catch on. That is, if we can find him. He's emotionally labile."

Duane murmured, "It's a pretty day. You aren't in a great rush to get home, are you?"

I wasn't. Let them worry. Let Rauenbauer reach home without me and suffer Ken's wrath.

Duane swung the car onto an intersecting highway and took me to a tropical garden, a tourist spot called Poinsiana Gardens, where he led me along paths between palms upon swards of green grass, and across tiny wooden bridges over hyacinth-crowded pools. Under a flutter of narrow leaves I spotted the indisputable knobby stalks of bamboo and asked if they were lacquered to that shiny perfection. The whole place looked like a Hollywood set.

Quite an oasis that was, flowering in the palmetto scrub, and I appreciated Duane, who lacked the scary dazzle of Ken and Keegan's tragic volatility and was very restful company, a comfortable old bedroom slipper. He kept a hand under my elbow and brushed his lips across my brow when I thanked him for the sightseeing, but he was not a man I was longing to kiss, at least not that day.

We rolled into Okasassa town at five, and I made a beeline to Araminta's dark little cottage under its canopy of flame-vine. Asking for a rowboat to rent, I gave ambiguous replies to her eager questions, whispering, talking fast. I admitted almost nothing of what happened to me, not in front of Duane.

The rowboat owner's warnings made Duane laugh.

"The Howells sure must have a reputation 'round here," Duane remarked. "The old codger acted as if we were goin' into a dragon's lair!"

Rowing across the strait was harrowing. The SIGFORD was too big to leap from wave to wave among the whitecaps as the rowboat did. Duane rowed energetically, panting while he described his love for boating and fishing. It was not until we were up against the mangroves that I realized I could not find the tunnel through them. Leaves closed its entrance. My confidence had been overweening, and already the old boat was sloshing with water.

"I'll row around to the Gulf side and land on their beach." He grinned. "This has been too short a cruise."

"I'll bail," I offered, when a tin can came floating between my ankles.

I had thought the strait was rough, but the Gulf waves lifted us high and dropped us alarmingly on swell after swell. Duane rowed expertly, aiming the bow between the rollers, far enough off the beach to avoid breakers. My bailing was good distraction for both mind and stomach.

Okasassa House reared above the trees; I could see my own corner windows. The windows were empty, and the beach vacant.

"Quite some mansion!" He whistled.

Too bad he couldn't whistle loud enough to bring someone out to show us the path from beach to house, I was thinking, when Duane said, "Suppose we make our run for shore right here? You game?"

I nodded, as willing to die this way as any other. What else could we do—go bobbing around the island until the leaking got hopelessly ahead of my bailing?

He twirled the bow toward shore, and I hung onto the sides as we surfed on the smooth, glassy back of a swell. Wrestling his oars like an Australian lifeboat rower, he shot the boat from the back of one wave to the one ahead of it. Then he rowed furiously, so the next wave broke under us, and we rode it toward shore. When we spun in the foamy pull-back, he stepped over the side into knee-deep water, laughing, his ruddy face triumphant, his necktie not even damp.

"Made it!"

No more than my shoes got wet. "Were you a sailor?"

"No, just the son of a sailor. I've never been in the military, one reason I can't fathom why Keegan went and volunteered."

We were too busy beaching the boat to discuss Keegan's murky autumn motives.

"Y'really need a surfboard to do it right," he said, inverting the rowboat on the sand to empty it. He stashed both oars underneath.

"What'll we do? Leave it here? What about the tide?"

"It's beyond the high-tide line. See the shells? I'll shoot the waves in reverse, when I leave. Great fun."

We were standing on the beach in our wet shoes, facing our next problem—the path.

"Sorry they're so inhospitable," I said, "but they don't like the local people dropping in on—"

The first fascinating little spume of sand rose by my foot. Then I heard a pop, then a second, and a third. The sand rose like little dry geysers near us.

"Duck!" Duane grabbed my wrist and jerked me with him, into the sheltering trees. My feet hardly touched ground; I flew behind him like a banner, as he managed to carry both my purse and suitcase. He produced them once we were squatting under the mangroves, wide-eyed and listening. Not breathing.

"That's a mite too inhospitable," he remarked, adding, "Someone's shooting at us from the house."

"From the house?"

"I saw the flash in a third-floor window. It's a high-powered rifle."

"How dare they do this to me?" I snapped, driven beyond impatience.

"Might not know it's you. You said they valued their privacy."

"MIGHT not know me," huh? Even Duane left open the possibility of intentional assault. The shots did not continue.

"Let us hope, Dear Heart, that when we reach the house our gunman will have changed his mind," said Duane. "We can't go back to the boat and be targets again."

Keeping to the swampier places for cover, we found the path after clambering through branches and muck. After scrambling into a tree to observe, Duane reported seeing no one in any of the windows.

"You stay out of sight," he said. "I'll go wave a white flag at them. Then I'll come back for you."

"But they don't know you. They won't be expecting YOU." I hung onto him. "Let me go first. I'll be recognized. No one will shoot ME, point-blank!"

"Not a chance!" He held me and looked intently into my eyes. "But that's about the spunkiest, kindest offer a girl's ever made me. No. I'll trust to my honest face. I'm white, and wearin' a shirt n' tie. That'll help." He pushed me into the shadows. "You stay right there, Sweetheart!"

Duane strode out into the clearing behind the house, hands spread wide in a posture of innocence. Sick with apprehension, I moved sideways under the palmettos to keep him in view.

I lost sight of Duane behind some flower bushes, and when I sprinted to another rustling palmetto for shelter, he was gone. No shot rang out, but he was gone. For two, maybe three minutes, I crouched in dread, until my knees ached. As I decided to move into the open, I heard Ken's voice.

"Leslie! Where are you?"

I scrambled faster through the dry fronds. Searching for Duane, I found Ken in my path. Suddenly he was holding me tight, exclaiming, "Oh, Baby! You could've been shot!

My god, what a horrible mistake!"

I stood rigid, wondering who had pulled the trigger if he had not.

Duane was unruffled. "Now I'll have something to tell my kids, when I have some," he said. "Just like on TV, Daddy got shot at while escortin' a lovely damsel in distress back to her island."

That was one way to look at it, but it wasn't my way.

"Who shot at us?" I demanded.

"An over-eager watchman," said Ken, "who'll never do anything like that again, believe me."

"Who was it? Keegan?"

"I'll take the blame. I permit warning shots—"

"Why was I left behind in Gainesville?"

"Strike two!" He winced. "That fuzzy-brained old book-worm simply forgot you. Absent-mindedness. When he rolled into Okasassa without you, I could have slugged him—the way Keegan almost did! He hadn't given you a thought. He's a loner, as you well know. I got right on the phone to your motel, but by then you'd left. I was about to call the police or drive over there to find you, myself."

"Who shot at us?" I again demanded, seeing Duane's consternation at my sharp tone. He didn' know what else I had against my employer.

"I don't want to discuss it further, Leslie."

Ken's voice was still pleasant but firm. "It won't happen again. We've got valuables here, but no one would commit murder to protect them."

That angered me. The nearest bullet had struck the sand no more than a yard away. Ken now was guiding us into the house, his hand infuriatingly patting my back as if I were a small child.

"Livin' 'way out here, I can't blame you for makin' it a fortress," Duane said. "Havin' no police protection—"

"Thanks for understanding," said Ken warmly.

"It was just a trifle startlin'," Duane confided.

"I have something that'll really startle Leslie," Ken said. We were now in the living room, and his hand was again on my back. "A wonderful surprise for her."

I stopped dead in my tracks. "What?" I choked.

"What do you want more than anything else? What would help you most with Keegan? Guess."

"Duane can help me with Keegan." The last thing I wanted to do was play his guessing game. I scowled. "Duane was Keegan's lab teacher at the University, and he—"

"He's already introduced himself," Ken said, and spread his arms wide. "Leslie, listen to me. Can you guess what I've done?"

I guessed several horrible things he'd done. I maintained a stony silence.

"I telephoned your mother yesterday after you left and told her how much we need your sister. I arranged for her to come down here, all expenses paid."

"My mother? My mother is coming here?"

"Oh, no. Not your mother. Your sister. Little Cindy."

"Not my sister!" I shrilled. "What on EARTH—?!

"Day after tomorrow, Cindy arrives here." He grinned broadly.

"Isn't that just marvelous?"

"She'd just been sayin' how Cindy would enjoy Florida," Duane chimed in unhelpfully, his face beaming.

What could I reply to these two men whose faces shone in anticipation of my pleasure and gratitude? I wanted to run upstairs and cry, but I couldn't run away, and I'd have to swallow my tears. Cindy, down here? Bouncing merrily into this house for a fun-filled Florida vacation, unaware?

"That's really great of you, Ken," Duane continued. "I'm sure Cindy can do a lot for Keegan, from all the wonderful things I've heard about her. Leslie said Cindy didn't mind at all being deaf."

"Cindy doesn't know what it's like to hear. Keegan does," I stormed. "She has no sense of loss. What can they possibly have in common? Besides, she won't be able to understand Keegan. She can't speechread well, especially strangers."

"She'll be good company for you, though, Leslie." Ken maintained that sickeningly kind voice. "It gets gloomy around here, and a ray of sunshine . . ."

Seeing Duane's bewilderment at the way I was reacting to Ken, I wiped the pout off my face. "Thank you," I muttered, avoiding Ken's eyes. "It's a shock, though. I wish you'd consulted me first. "

"But we discussed it at least three times. I thought it was mainly finances that worried you, so I decided to pay her way; money couldn't be better spent. I told you I plunge ahead on things. . . ."

"May I go upstairs and change?" I needed to get away from them.

"Keegan's likely to show up for supper," Ken said. "He showed up for breakfast this morning, surprisingly, and asked me if you'd left."

"He did?" That stopped my flight.

"He even deigned to read the answer I wrote him."

Duane didn't catch the significance of this; he was still innocently smiling.

Ken picked up the "S.H.H." bag I'd forgotten and came upstairs with me, uninvited. As soon as we were out of Duane's hearing, he murmured, "You don't lose any time making new friends, do you, Leslie?"

"He's Keegan's teacher!"

"And he's a nice guy, but that's moving pretty fast, bringing him home with you." He chuckled rather mirthlessly. "I had the impression you were a rather starchy and decorous Midwesterner. Not a late-night gal."

"It was you who called?" I asked, trying to retrieve the overnight case from fingers that didn't let go of the handle. He opened my bedroom door and put the bag over on a chair, remaining in the room.

"Yeah, it was I. I was worried about your not coming back, so I checked. You were out at midnight and also at one-thirty this morning. You two really got friendly fast, Doll!"

"Your insinuations are uncalled for." I drew myself up. "And though it's none of your business, your assumption is ridiculously in error."

"Don't misunderstand me." Ken grinned. "I'm not scolding or insulting you. I admire women with spirit. I'm just surprised. Since you're no prude, I no longer have to watch every word and thought when I'm around you."

Though I'd been told that to excuse yourself is to accuse yourself, words rushed to my lips. "I was NOT with Duane all night. I met him in his drugstore yesterday, and he took me to lunch. The next time I saw him was today when he agreed to bring me home. After your buddy deserted me."

Ken put up his hands in mock self-defense. "Okay! Okay, Doll, I believe you!"

"Did you also call my motel yesterday afternoon?" I demanded.

"No, I didn't. Did someone call you then, too?"

"Yes. He tried twice. He hung up the minute I picked up the receiver."

"Well, then, I suppose you had two parties watching over you," he said, but he'd quit smiling.

I had arrived at the same conclusion, which didn't make

me smile, either. The trouble was, the motel manager implied that it was the same man all four times, a southerner.

"Hurry up and change. I'll keep your friend company." He winked as he backed out the door.

I groaned. When Duane returned to Gainesville, I'd be left here alone to deal with Ken. Until Cindy came. . .

I bathed, taking my time, and put on a demure pink dress with a ruffled neckline. I wondered if I could prevail upon Duane to spend the night. Walking over to the windows, I tried to see the boat we'd arrived in. Yes, there it was, a dark capsule on the distant beach.

For maybe twenty seconds I watched uncomprehendingly while a vertical speck left the treeline and moved to the boat, merged with it, and entered the water, heading out to sea. The boat—Duane's transportation home—someone was stealing it, right in broad daylight.

I marched angrily downstairs, clickety-click, and confronted Ken as both men sprang to their feet.

"If you won't tell us who tried to kill us, how about saying who is right now stealing our boat?" My tongue was adder-sharp in my mouth.

Ken didn't stop smiling, and now there was a chuckle in his throat. "Rufus Dean is taking it back to the mainland, Leslie. Duane can't row to town, after dark. I'll take him back in the SIGFORD, if he won't lay over with us for the night."

Ken looked from Duane to me, a teasing glint in his eyes.

"I have an early morning obligation in Gainesville," said Duane, "so I'd better head back tonight after supper. Would you believe the choir at St. Stephen's? But thanks, Ken, for the invitation. Another time."

Now Ken's glance cocked over at me seemed to ask, "Got yourself a choirboy, eh?"

I was awash with relief. So Rufus Dean, Margaret's husband, was the lookout who shot at trespassers? Never having met Rufus, I'd half forgotten about him. How could he recognize trespassers he'd never seen before?

My nose told me Margaret was preparing something with onions in it. My mouth started watering as I hadn't expected it ever to do again, in this house full of poisons. Someone else had also been lured in by the succulent scent. A door swung open from the kitchen, and there stood Keegan, jolted to see all of us standing in the livingroom.

Ken promptly made a little salute and headed up the stairs. I was moved with gratitude for that. Duane spread his arms in welcome.

"Remember me, Keegan?" (Good words to speech-read.) "From Bio. 101?"

Again I had the rare pleasure of seeing Keegan's face lose its stubborn stoniness. It blazed with joy.

"Gunlock . . . Mr. Gunlock! Duane! How'd you get here?"

I moved unobtrusively nearer Duane's broad back. Their handclasp flowed into a couple of playful punches on the arm. Just like some college reunion.

Duane said, "She came to Gainesville," pointing at me, and I spelled the city, knowing the "V" and "LL" would at least be readable on my fingers.

"And I met her." The sign for "meet" was two vertical index fingers meeting with a little bump.

Positioned as we were, my hands and Duane's mouth were almost superimposed. Muscles worked in Keegan's lean jaw, and I saw him for the first time really struggle to understand words.

"I drove her to Okasassa," Duane said, while I "drove" by gripping a steering wheel. I spelled the town, the round "O" emphasized, thumb against fingers.

It was faster than writing notes, even at this halting pace.

"How did you get across the water?" Keegan asked, and Duane did his own signing. He rowed, and said the word, and walked his fingers up the beach. He knew enough to leave out the rifle episode, although sighting a rifle makes a clear and easy sign.

"What do you do, Duane?" Keegan asked. "Teach at the U of F?"

"I'm a pharmacist."

"You're a what?"

"Pharmacist" would normally be spelled out; I tried signing it with "chemistry" (hands alternately pouring vials) plus "drug" (thumb grinding powder into left palm).

"Scientist? Doctor?"

I thrust my face forward and enunciated "phar-ma-cist," spelling it near my mouth. Keegan read it. Long words were the easiest.

"A pharmacist, huh? Great."

The logical next question was what Keegan was doing with HIS life, but Duane dared not ask that. Keegan stirred uneasily, and I saw on Duane's countenance the anguish I expected.

"Let's eat," I signed. "I want to eat." Claw-hands, palm-up, dragged "want" toward me; then I fed my mouth.

Keegan nodded, avoiding my eyes. In deference to Duane, he was polite.

Margaret rumbled through the door with a rolling cart loaded with casseroles and salad dishes. Rauenbauer? Here was Ken fetching him down the stairs. Margaret scowled at Duane, then scurried off for another place- setting. "He coulda tole me there'd be five. . . ."

The hot food was delicious distraction from emotional turmoil. Rauenbauer looked at me scornfully, as if I'd gone off and forgotten HIM. I didn't expect an apology, though I wondered if his alleged lapse had been simple absent-mindedness or fear that a scarlet woman might besmirch his chaste Buick.

Keegan wasn't interested in anyone but Duane, but he couldn't try to talk with Duane and eat at the same time. Duane chatted with Ken, who was as jittery as if he sat beside not a nephew but a short-fused dynamite stick.

Suddenly I realized how Cindy would change things around here. Enough silent language to make everyone dizzy would spin off our hands. You can fork food with one hand and fingerspell with the other. Let Keegan see that!

When Keegan passed me the biscuits, I thanked him in words and with my palm brushing outward from my chin. Red flared into his cheeks as if I'd struck him.

"I reached your mother at the number you gave me in case of emergency," Ken said. "She had me wire the plane-fare to Youngstown. Cindy will leave Ohio Monday morning. At Atlanta a pal of mine will fly her down to Cross City."

"Cindy's never been on a plane before. She's never even been outside Ohio. How can she manage that, all alone and deaf?" I fretted.

"Your mom didn't seem a bit worried. Maybe you shelter

Cindy too much," Ken said.

"Mother's honeymooning. She wasn't worried about MY coming here, either!"

Ken's lifted brow chided me for that outburst. He said, "Oh, and your mother said to tell you she was in paradise. I told her you were fine."

"Thanks," I muttered blackly. Fine meant not poisoned yet, huh?

Keegan ate fast and silently, eyes lowered, cut off totally from all conversation.

"Cindy will wear a blue outfit, so I told the Barbers to look for a tiny blonde in blue who doesn't talk."

I noticed Rauenbauer paying close attention to this, his little eyes darting from Ken to me and back; he chewed so carelessly that his beard got tomato-stained.

"Who'll meet her?" I asked.

"Al and Sue Barber. They're photographers who've given me a lift to these backwoods several times. They own a four-seater. Cindy ought to get a kick out of the little plane."

"Kenneth, you aren't bringing a deaf child here, are you? With all these precious books?"

Ken reacted before I could. "Cindy Fallon is fourteen years old. She's no child!"

"If she's a deaf-mute, it's the same thing."

"Look, Geoff, decisions about who comes here are mine, not yours."

"It's not your house, though, Kenneth," Rauenbauer purred. "It'll soon be Keegan's house. Has HE invited her? Does he even know she's coming?"

"If you want to try telling him, fine. We can use all the help we can get to keep Keegan informed, Geoff. Try it! Meanwhile, let's cut the chat. Duane? Ready for dessert?"

Rauenbauer leaned across Keegan toward me and whispered loudly, "I'd think you'd care more for your sister than to bring her to this house!"

What a person to have as an ally! I made no response. We finished dessert in record time, every one of us now uncomfortable. To my disappointment, after dinner, Keegan slid away like a wraith, but Duane had plenty to confide to my ears alone.

"The poor guy!" he began. "I never realized! He's stuck here with no way to communicate, with nothing to do! What can he do, read all the time? No way to finish his education, to have a profession, accomplish what he wanted and deserved to. His life's goin' to be completely wasted!"

"It doesn't have to be. I need—"

"A man needs something to aim for, some goal," Duane rushed on. "If he were—say, paralyzed, he could at least share his suffering with someone, talk about it, but he's totally cut off. Lord a'mighty! Bein' blind wouldn't be worse!"

I could only agree with him. We walked outside, shuffling through the sand by the lagoon.

"I was worried about your gettin' the wrong pills," he blurted, "and now here's Keegan goin' through hell! Do you think your sister will make any difference? Does she sign real well?"

"It's her first language; English is her second. We can communicate from further away than you can yell, across a football field or through sealed glass windows."

"It's sure interesting. I'd like to learn how to sign."

"In less than an hour, Duane, I could teach you finger-spelling. If Keegan knew its value, he could learn to sign in no time. But he has other things on his mind."

"His uncle seems a nice guy, don't you think?"

"He appears to be." (Gloriously ambiguous.)

"Leslie, I'm sorry to be rude, to eat and run, but I really do have to get back to the city. I want to see you again, though. Soon."

"I'll go ask Ken about the boat."

Hoping that Ken would somehow prevent Duane's departure, I headed for the house. Keegan needed Duane, and I dreaded the thought of spending another night in a house with five people I did not trust or had not met.

"I want your phone number," I called back to Duane, "in case I ever need you."

"Get me a scrap of paper, then." He was vainly rifling through his pockets.

In the house I tore a slip off Margaret's grocery pad, carried off someone's pen, and asked Ken if the SIGFORD was available.

"Yep," he said, "in a few minutes. I have to go to the mainland anyhow, to bring Rufus home."

Going out again, I stopped short on the porch.

Keegan, his back to me and facing Duane, was trying to read words off Duane's lips. Drooping shoulders, tensed arms, and tilted head all told me he was failing. When Duane saw me, he waved me over.

"Boy, do I never need a pen and paper, now!"

I handed him what he asked for. He scribbled a note and tore off half the sheet for Keegan. When he wrote his address and phone number for me on the other half, the paper was divided and distributed. He had no more.

"My phone's unlisted," he said. Then he forgot himself and said, "Look, Keegan, Leslie's here to help you. Let her teach—" He reached out to stop the retreat of the uncomprehending deaf man.

A bit too loudly, Keegan called, "I'll drive up sometime and see you, Duane. So long."

"He can still DRIVE?" Duane asked in astonishment.

Keegan understood him and stiffened.

I jumped right in. "People always ask that! The deaf have been proven safer drivers than hearing people."

I signed as I spoke, and hoped Keegan realized that I was defending him. He warily watched us.

"Sorry, Buddy!" Duane stuck out a hand in apology and farewell as Ken came galloping down the steps to join us.

"Ready to go?" Ken led Duane to the boat, calling over his shoulder, "Now you've got Keegan out of hiding, use this chance, Leslie. Talk to him."

Sure, but what could I say? Discuss Mary Ann? Never. Tell him Duane identified as dangerous the capsules that Keegan might have sent me?

He was turning away, escaping. I ran a few steps through shoe-grabbing sand to catch at his arm.

"Keegan! Wait!"

"I can't understand speech—yours or anybody's. Or the stupid hand-waving, either. Leave me the hell alone!"

On the back of the slip of paper with Duane's phone number, I wrote the first words that came to mind.

"You still can dance!"

I forced the note on him. He read it and sent me a black look.

"You're a fool to say that, and you won't make a fool out of me. Why don't you get off this island?"

Like my first note, this one he shredded and buried in the sand, murmuring, "Isn't one man—Ken—enough for you?"

Flabbergasted, I watched him stride away, realizing I'd lost Duane's phone number, and for nothing. What an asinine thing to have written on a valuable scrap of paper. Keegan knew he was deaf to music, forever, so how could he possibly—? But he'd loved dancing, and so did I.

I walked slowly upstairs, grieving. We'd come a long way. Keegan had been a gentleman in front of Duane, till my display of pantomime-signs and my stupid mention of dancing humiliated him.

Up in my bedroom, I was changing from my dress into jeans when I noticed a bra lying on the floor. I opened the overnight case. Its contents were well stirred. Nothing seemed to be missing. I ran to my purse where I'd tossed it on the bed. From that, things indeed were missing—both Sigrid's letter and the portrait of Mary Ann and Keegan. All the money was still there, but. . . I spun around, seeing my room anew. Bureau drawers were slightly open, the bed-spread was disarranged, clothes pushed to one end of the closet bar. My room had been searched. By whom?

And when? While I was in Gainesville? No. When I came back, my room was okay. It was during dinner, or while I was talking with Duane outside. Someone had ample time to come up here, search and steal.

Furious, I shoved the chair under my doorknob. I plunked myself down in the window, hugging myself in a fury of indignation. I'd stay here till someone got a lock for my door! Someone? Everyone here was suspect.

That letter Sigrid wrote—whoever had it might assume I was in contact with the missing woman. Had Mary Ann ever showed it to Keegan? Did it come to Mary Ann enclosed in a letter to him? Undated, without a name at the beginning, it could just as well have been written to ME, urging ME to marry Keegan.

And who would want the photograph? Not Ken, who could ask for it back and didn't. To whom could I complain about this theft. . .who was not the thief?

Grimly, I sat behind my barricade while outside the sun touched the horizon. It flung an orange carpet from cloudless infinity to the surf-line, a carpet bumpy with wavelets. Lovely scene, a lovely place—full of deception, violence, and now murder. I'd braced my door shut, but I couldn't do that when I was out of the room. Anyone could slip in—not that I had anything left worth stealing.

My resolution to stay put was sorely tested around nine p.m. Ken sent Margaret up to fetch me, and when I opened the door to her, faint music came wafting up from the living room. I brought my purse along with me and accompanied her downstairs.

"Yo' li'l sister is comin' here?"

I had known exactly what her tone would be. "It's not MY idea, Margaret. He acted on his own. I was amazed."

"You want a lil' chile to see the ghost?"

"What can I do?" I grabbed her arm, habituated to the deaf world's necessarily uninhibited touching. "Whatever can I do?"

"You can rise up and leave this house. Go away."

"That's what you and Keegan want, isn't it? And if I don't leave, you'll hurt me and scare me till I do, right?"

"This here's a house full of death . . . and deaths ain't done with. All the hurtin' and scarin' ain't done with!"

"Is that a prediction or a threat?" I cried. "Did you—or Keegan—send me those capsules?"

She didn't answer.

"Did you ransack my room this evening?"

Her eyes widened. "Ran-sack?"

"You brought me pills the first morning, in a little envelope. Now my room's been . . ."

"I din' know what was in that envelope with yo' name on it."

"And you said Ken went away for a shot, but he didn't leave the house!"

Refusing to halt, she had dragged me along with her down the last flight of stairs. Now Ken was in earshot.

"What's the matter, Leslie?"

Margaret took advantage of his interruption to flee into the back of the house, rocking along rapidly with the gait of a frightened hen.

"Cheer up, little glum face," Ken smiled. "We're going to decorate a pretty bedroom for Cindy, before she arrives here. Is it Rauenbauer who's got you depressed? Aside from his leaving you there and the horrible mistake with the rifle, is there anything else?"

Anything else! Imagine!

"Was the motel nice? I mean . . . look, I've offended you, teasing about Duane. He seems a nice guy. And that was an awful welcome for him, too, after he so kindly brought you home."

I walked over to the stereo, miserable and wanting to tell him why.

"Oh, may I have that motel's matchbook back, Leslie? Do you still have it? My friends often need an address to lay over in Gainesville."

I dug into my purse and found it to return to him. At least that wasn't stolen.

"The fat man I met when I arrived here, that Baker Johnson—who was he?" I asked, to avoid blurting out what I most wanted to hit him with.

"Oh, didn't I make that clear? He's Brad's attorney. Baker handled my brother's legal affairs for a long time. Now he's handling the estate. We're all sitting here month after month while he sees it through probate."

"The attorney's in Gainesville?"

"No. He's a Tallahassee lawyer. Very busy man. I think he puts this estate-settling on a back burner."

He was leading me to the coziest corner of the living room, onto ankle-deep tan rugs. I had to sit down on—or rather in—a couch, low and contoured to my rump. Ken sat close beside me.

"Now tell me how much you accomplished with Keegan this afternoon. Got him talking to you and Duane twice, didn't you?"

"Talking TO us. Right. He's embarassed by sign language—the variety I showed him, anyway. We couldn't talk to Keegan, more than a few phrases. He still tears up my notes or doesn't read them. He's worse now than when I told him about the ghost. I've lost ground."

"Sad. but I have high hopes for Cindy."

I didn't want to sit there with Ken, listening to Mantovani records. But I did approve of his audio system. Both stereo speakers stood on the hardwood floor; the amplifier was studded with knobs. Using that, I could show Keegan he could dance to music.

"Sorry it's been so rough on you," Ken went on soothingly. "Meeting Keegan in the worst possible way, then that knife-episode! Remember, he was in a nasty war; he had screaming nightmares for months, and he still has daymares, I think. Then the apparition, and today. . . Poor little gal!" He edged closer.

"I want Cindy to room with me."

"Oh, no. We have so many empty rooms— Leslie, you even think I'm a threat to you, don't you?"

I couldn't deny that. I said, "This very evening, Ken, someone got into my room and searched everything. Stole things." I was circulating so much adrenalin by now that I added, "Was he, by any chance, you?"

"ME? Search your room? Steal?"

"You know I wasn't with Duane all night. Now you know exactly where I was, right?"

He sighed, reaching in his pocket. What he pulled out was the motel matchbook. He read slowly, "'Four Palms Motel, 368 Live Oak.' That's where you were, and again I apologize for teasing you about Duane."

"Thank you," I said icily.

"Which still leaves you a very pretty girl who might like a little warmth and comfort after all this harrowing strain. I'd like to hold you, Leslie."

I gave him an astonished look.

"Okay, okay, I can read your mind. I throw you at Keegan, then I make a pass at you, myself. Look, Keegan certainly doesn't appreciate you. Duane's a choirboy. But I admire you, man to woman. I like you. And I need you."

The matchbook fell onto the couch in the swiftly closing space between us, and I saw my handwriting on the inside. There, in full view, was Mary Ann Monahan's phone number and address.

His arms went around me.

Steadily he drew me to him. So stunned that I'd left evidence of my trip to Starke, I did not duck Ken's kiss. His mouth captured mine, held it, and he fed on lips parted in astonishment.

"So sweet and young," he murmured. "I could teach you so much, give you such pleasure . . ."

Yep. I'd never been kissed like that before, never by such an experienced man. He didn't wait for cooperation to kiss me more fiercely, arching my back and sliding his arms further around me. Considering my fear of him, I shouldn't have melted, even for a moment. "Seduction!" I thought. Hunger for a man's arms, innate longing to be caressed and conquered must not leave me open to this man—of all men!

Keegan at first sight had grabbed me even more fiercely than Ken did. Keegan's own uncle, now—! Ken's graying sideburns lay before my eyes, evidence of his years of success at charming, then seducing women far more sophisticated than I.

"You've got . . . plenty of models!" I gasped.

"Where? On my walls? Pictures? You're kidding me! Where, in this God-forsaken wilderness, can I find a sweet girl—a lovely, intelligent woman to share joy and—"

"You im—import them!" I cried, struggling at about half strength.

"You're single. I'm single. I've never gotten anyone in any kind of trouble. I know my way around."

His arm under my bosom made cleavage flash right up to my collarbone, attracting his starving stare.

"You think I'm too old for you, Leslie, but many things improve with practice. I could give Keegan a run for his money . . ."

"But NOT with the same girl!" I flared. Keegan's name broke the spell. Keegan? Ken had everything; Keegan, nothing.

He sat back, and my hand slid under my hip, feeling for the fatal matchbook. I got it, but he took it from me. He read my writing, and his eyes were no longer beseechingly amorous. They narrowed.

"Leslie, what's this? Starke? Mary Ann?"

I sprang up. "Not that you don't know already! You emptied my purse this evening!"

He retained a grip on my left wrist.

"You didn't go up to Starke! Why? Why?"

I forced myself to despise him, though his hands had left trails of heat winding around my body, my quivering, ambivalent body.

"This isn't going to be a conversation for other ears to hear," he said, rising and forcing me toward the door. "We're going for a little boat ride."

"I don't want to!" I wailed, hugging the purse he shoved into my arms, but we were already through the door and headed across the porch. My strength didn't even slow his strides.

"I won't hurt you. We just have too many listening ears in this house."

One pair of ears too few. Screaming wouldn't bring Keegan. Mr. Rauenbauer? No help there. Margaret would see this as just a lovers' quarrel.

We headed for the dock as if I were not digging my heels into the sand at every step. Ken half-shoved, half-carried me along.

For the third time I was lifted down into the SIGFORD, but this time I was crammed unceremoniously into the cabin under the forward deck. I heard the door snap shut and the engine start. Keegan couldn't hear a boat engine, either.

I pressed my nose against the porthole, as the SIGFORD crossed the lagoon. Lights from the tall windows shone down on us. When we rustled into the mangrove trees, the scene went black.

We'd traveled what seemed only a boat-length when the motor cut off, and we rocked between trunks and limbs. I could feel them rubbing the boat like huge fingers. Leaves rustled close overhead.

The click of the door-latch sent me squirming into the farthest end of a bunk, huddling in the bow, as blind as Keegan was deaf.

"Calm down," Ken's voice said, and he struck a match. A kerosene wall-lamp flickered to life, illuminating dark paneling, a sink, a table, and the two wide bunks. He stood against the door, his fingers laced together in front of his chest. Dense shadows under his brows and cheekbones turned his handsome face into a movie ghoul's.

"I tried to keep you clear of this, but again I underestimated your curiosity. You know what curiosity did to the cat, Leslie."

"I had to find out the truth. Somehow."

"You went all the way up to Starke to find Mary Ann Monahan," he marveled. "That's where you were all night. You spent the night up there. I can imagine what she filled your ears with!"

I didn't reply. All I could think of was, "Name, rank, and serial number," the latter which I didn't even have.

"What happened? You have to tell me everything now," he said.

"I will NOT," I cried, but if he decided to hurt me, words might come tumbling out.

"Leslie, you can't guess how serious the situation is. You can't interfere. Lives are involved. Sanity—"

"You wouldn't tell me how your brother died."

"The cops said suicide. I don't give a damn what Mary Ann said."

"You know what they suspect. Margaret, too, and Keegan. Not just Mary Ann. They think someone killed Keegan's father. Poisoned him."

"He deserved it!"

His words shocked me horribly. I realized then how much I wanted Ken to be innocent. Please let him be an unwise, bungling uncle and an overly passionate boss, but nothing worse.

He continued, "But I didn't do it, didn't poison Brad. It was a setup. You stay out of it. Enough people are already busy prying, believe me!"

He was silent for a moment. I dug into my purse for the little pharmacy vial. I spilled out of it onto the table the pair of black and green capsules. Going on the attack, I said, "There! Explain those!"

"What are they?"

"Capsules that Margaret said you sent me. Capsules that Duane says would've poisoned me."

"How'd you say you got them?"

"A couple of mornings ago, right after Keegan stabbed you, these came with my lunch. They were in an envelope, wrapped up in a note signed 'Ken.' "

"Brother! I've never seen capsules like these. And I never caught Margaret telling a lie. Keegan? You think HE sent them? The idiot kid doesn't want you here . . ."

"They're powerful sedatives. Who takes drugs for severe nervousness?"

"I don't know. Keegan refused to take what the VA hospital prescribed for his nerves. Look, this is proof of the danger you're in. Why, WHY didn't you confide in me?"

Suddenly he leaned forward, bracing his palms on the cabin walls beside my shoulders. He boxed me in. I shrank away from him as far as I could.

"Now, the person who searched your room this evening stole something, you said. Stole what? Tell me."

"I'd give him rope and see if he'd hang himself. "He stole your photo of Keegan and Mary Ann from my purse. And a letter Mary Ann gave me from . . . from Sigrid Howell."

"From Sigrid?" he cried. "My god! Dated when?"

"No date."

"A recent letter? Does Mary Ann know where Sigrid is? Do they write to each other?"

"You act as if Sigrid's alive," I said. "Mary Ann thinks she may be dead."

He backed away, straightened up. "If I hadn't felt so much like . . kissing you, I'd slap your mouth for that, Leslie. I didn't kill Sigrid, and I didn't kill Brad. My own brother! What Mary Ann does not know is that Brad wrote a suicide note before he poisoned himself. He wrote a whole suicide-correspondence, in fact!"

"Does Keegan know that?"

He shook his head.

"Why in heaven's name don't you tell him? If it was suicide, why let him think it was murder?"

"Because it's . . . it's an unusual suicide note. It would only hurt him worse. Sigrid read it, and I did, but no one else. Brad wasn't a sane man. You'd have to be able to read between the lines."

"Yeah, I'll bet!" I said.

Ken shot a hand over to the cupboard and produced a bottle. He poured a drink, asked with raised brows if I wanted any, and accepted my emphatic negative before he continued.

113

"Look, Brad's fingerprints were on the cyanide can; cyanide was left in his glass; he wanted to frame me for murder. Isn't that enough for you? He knew he was dying, slowly suffocating. He thought he had lung-cancer."

I couldn't argue. I watched him bolt down the whiskey.

"The letter, Leslie. What did it say?"

"Very little. Sigrid was praising Mary Ann— What's—?"

I'd suddenly heard the slurp-and-dribble of oars. Ken heard it too. He froze, then whirled for the door of the cabin; I followed him out of the light into blackness, the door swinging shut behind us. We were moored in the mangroves, tucked nose-first into a cave of tree branches. I could see moonlight glinting here and there on water. I strained my ears toward the sound of watery movement, and felt Ken tighten on my shoulder his cautionary grip.

The silhouette was recognizable first to Ken.

"It's Keegan, prowling. Spying, as usual."

It was folly to consider calling out to Keegan; he couldn't hear a voice a few yards away as he paddled the skiff toward the tunnel-like channel.

The SIGFORD blocked the channel, just in the shadows.

When Keegan saw the boat and saw us, with a paroxysm of motion he reacted. I heard the rasp of a paddle falling on wood; then Keegan's silhouette arced, and the water boiled white.

"Not coming to chat, but to spy," Ken said drily. "It's nothing new. But he'll break his fool neck one of these nights."

Ken leaned over the rail and caught hold of the bobbing skiff. "I'll haul his boat back for him."

After he tied it to the SIGFORD's stern, he started up the engine and started in on me again.

"Cindy arrives Monday. Things will improve then. That is, if you can control yourself, stay out of mischief."

I scarcely heard him. All I could think of was Keegan, in that murky water.

Docking the boat, Ken led me toward the house. I paused to sweep one last look over the moonsheen of the still lagoon. Keegan must be swimming out there, watching us, eyes just above the surface like a crocodile's. Ken, on the pretext of helpfulness, had deprived him of the skiff.

Ken was unpredictable and too persuasive. Before we

parted company that night—very promptly—he dragged out of me the fact that Sigrid's letter was handwritten, signed, and lacking a salutation. Yes, it did sound, conceivably, as if it might have been written to me—that is, if I were Keegan's fiancee.

"Dammit, Leslie," Ken said at the front door, "I wanted to take you out in the boat for a very different purpose. Not to shout at each other, but to touch each other. To give each other ecstasy. Liquor and pills can't compare, as tranquilizers."

"YOU need a tranquilizer?" I muttered.

"Leslie, don't consider me a Casanova. Since I was out of my teens, I've never made love to a woman I'd be ashamed to marry."

"Why didn't you ever marry, then?"

His eyes measured me and concluded I did not rate an explanation.

I slept very late Sunday morning, glad to find myself alive when I awoke, safe in my tumbled bed. After pulling the chair (plus a table) away from in front of my door, I peeked out.

In the hall not three yards away was a cot with a pillow and blanket. Someone had slept there last night. I didn't know how to feel; it depended on who the watchman was.

Breakfast had been kept hot for me. Ken sat by me while I ate, nursing his coffee cup. He explained the cot before I asked.

"Rufus Dean slept there, and he'll sleep there till we figure out what's happening around here," he said.

I asked to meet Rufus Dean, and Ken was surprised that I hadn't yet run into him.

Margaret's husband was tall, narrow shouldered, and gray haired, his dark face accordion-lined. His smile was so apologetic that I didn't mention the rifle-shots. I liked his face and his bass voice so much that having him sleep uncomfortably in my hall grieved me. I insisted that the precaution be discontinued. The Deans had their own problems. I'd handle mine.

Ken reluctantly agreed to dismantle the cot, but he wouldn't agree to let Cindy share my room. Adding a bed would make my room too crowded. He should have seen the size of our apartment back home.

I thought about Rufus Dean, who'd insisted he'd been comfortable last night. He didn't exhibit the same scorn for Ken that Margaret displayed. Was Rufus a better dissembler, or just more polite than his wife? For one thing, he was an excellent shot.

"Leslie," said Ken, "last night I looked up something I remembered about the eighteenth-century Spanish painter, Goya. He went deaf suddenly at forty-five. After that he painted monsters and demons with soundless, screaming

116

mouths. Horrors and atrocities—no more sweet pastorals. What a testament to the agony of deafness."

We were silent for a moment. Then he said, "What deafened Cindy?"

"Mother probably had German measles—rubella—during pregnancy, but she doesn't even remember being ill."

"Maybe it's better that Mary Ann did run off," Ken remarked. "She'd be shocked at the messes Keegan gets into."

"Like what?"

"Like flooding the bathroom when he forgets the tub's filling; he can't hear water, running. Like plowing into Margaret when she's behind him with a stack of dishes in her hands. He always liked to cook, and helped out when his mom fixed Brad's elaborate special diets. Now he's deaf, he lets things boil over and burns food in the frying pan. He can't hear them. So Margaret discourages him from cooking anymore."

"How sad." Ken had successfully loosened my tongue. "I have stories, too. Deaf people have maddening problems with cars—not hearing the motor stall, not knowing when the radio is left on, or whether the door is shut tight, or when the car needs repairs. One deaf man was shot when a policeman stopped him, and he reached for his pad and pencil. The cop thought he was reaching for a pistol.

"You haven't seen much, since Keegan is stuck safely on this island. Just mistakes with gas-station attendants, waitresses, and clerks can be humiliating."

Ken groaned. A depressing topic, but better than the topics of last night. He kept his hands to himself. He dropped his face into his hands, in fact, and groaned aloud.

"The poor kid! I remember Keegan blew up at Rufus a few weeks ago. First time I ever heard him say a harsh word to Rufus, and just because the man was tapping his fingers on the table."

"Vibrations—even little ones—can be maddening to deaf people."

"And I thought all that would happen was that we'd hang a hearing aid on him. I was more worried about his busted legs than about his ears." He sighed and rubbed his face. "You ever noticed suicide seems to run in families? Look

117

at Ernest Hemingway and his father, and I've heard of others. I'm afraid . . ."

"So am I." But, I wondered, WAS Brad Howell's death a suicide?

After I finished eating, we climbed the stairs to work on Cindy's boudoir. Ken approached the project like a man starved for diversion. In the deeply carpeted bedroom across from mine, the high bed was stripped of linens. I had to pick out her colors from an assortment of bath and bedroom accessories in a walk-in closet big enough to serve a palace. I stuck to shades of blue, Cindy's favorite color. Her curtains would have blue daisies, and her bedspread was woven of blue and gold. Add thick, pale blue towels.

"What else would a girl of fourteen like?" Ken's eyes shone.

When I admitted Cindy still seemed to be in the horsy stage preceding the boy-mad stage, he produced a huge blowup of horses and colts frisking in a meadow against a blue sky. We hung it on her wall. All the blues reminded me of something, though—Brad Howell's face, after he gulped cyanide. I struggled to blank it out of my mind.

Ken seemed to be cured of his depression over Keegan's condition. He was happily busy, and it's hard to distrust a cheerful personality, even keeping in mind that prototypical Shakespearean uncle who "smiled and smiled" but was a villain.

"Why are you doing all this for my sister?"

He paused in the task of installing a cafe-curtain rod in her window. "Because she's your sister. She's also special, isn't she? To me, she's not handicapped; she's got talents I don't have, that YOU don't even have."

"Will you learn sign language, too, If Keegan does? Signs and fingerspelling?"

Here was a test. So few deaf kids Cindy's age had parents who could sign. Often a brother or sister could, but hearing parents the age of ours tended to say, "My child can read my lips just fine."

Even Mom said that. She was wrong. But she wasn't as maddening as the parents who refused to study any sign book, but would turn right around and enroll in French class, if they got to go abroad.

"Just you watch me," Ken said. "When he learns signs, I'll sign to him."

Descending to the living room after we finished the interior decorating, I almost ran into Keegan. His back to me, he was, however, unaware of my presence. He stood staring at the fireplace, where—to my horror—was displayed in full view the stolen telephoto shot of him with Mary Ann. It was propped up on the mantelpiece.

Keegan's grunt was angrily visceral. He must've just noticed the photo. He convulsively jerked it off the mantel and bent to study it closely. I felt convinced that he'd never seen it before. Like Mary Ann, Keegan never suspected that a camera had captured their loving gaze.

Keegan hissed out a curse, tore the photo in two, balled the pieces in his fists, and flung them into the cold hearth. Who'd dared to stick that up on the mantel for him to find? It sure hadn't been there after breakfast.

Breath whistled through Keegan's nostrils as he spun toward me. As quickly, I sank backwards into one of the libraries, almost treading on Geoffrey Rauenbauer, who knelt by a teetering stack of books.

"Watch it!" he snapped, glowering. Then, "Have you told Mr. Howell what mischief you were into in Gainesville?"

The question stunned me.

"You have no right to ask that. It's my personal business. Why'd you leave me behind in Gainesville?"

"Considering what you're up to, young woman, I hardly think you'd be chiding ME."

When I whirled to depart, he shocked me again.

"Where is Sigrid Howell?" he asked.

Keegan might still be right outside the room! But then I remembered he couldn't overhear us.

"I need to know," Rauenbauer continued, "because it's very much to her advantage if we can contact her directly, without going through her brother-in-law. Her son stands to lose a lot of money if Kenneth Howell knows what I've found in this house."

"What are you talking about?"

"Can you find out for me if she's alive? It would mean so much that I'd pay well for the information. Tell me some way to reach Mrs. Howell."

119

"Why don't you write Keegan a note asking that?"

"You're aware of what he does with notes," he said with growing agitation. "Young woman, surely you see what's happening!"

"Can't Ken help you?"

"Ken?" he snapped. "Our friend Kenneth Howell will soon find himself in prison!"

A new note in this symphony of revenge and threats. Earlier Rauenbauer had threatened Keegan with prison; now he was indicting Ken? Plenty of people distrusted Ken, but why Rauenbauer? I sought some way of testing him.

"Have you by any chance recently seen a letter and a photograph?" I asked. "I misplaced them. I may have dropped them somewhere in the house. The letter's on yellow stationery, and the photo is of Keegan and a girl—"

"There was a picture of Keegan and some girl up on the mantelpiece. That may be it."

I pretended to go look, just to get away from him. I was happy to abandon Rauenbauer to his work.

The rest of that day was uneventful, except for the surprise that Ken and Rufus brought back from the mainland along with the week's groceries. It was a cage containing a blue parakeet.

Ken took it upstairs to hang in Cindy's room. I'd no idea how he'd come up with the bird—plus half-consumed boxes of seeds, gravel, and cuttlebone—in Okasassa. We never had pets in Toledo, except for stray cats we girls lured into the apartment, and my short-term pup. Ken said the talking bird was Cindy's, as long as she stayed here.

"Does it talk?" I asked, echoing the first question everyone asked me about Cindy: "Does she talk?"

"Yep," Ken said. "Sweetie has quite a vocabulary."

I didn't tell Ken about the photo on the mantelpiece. Another accusation might mean I'd be dragged on another boat-ride. I'd wait till the letter turned up, too, I told myself cynically.

On Monday I was beside myself with anticipation. Going to meet Cindy would mean briefly getting off the island, seeing some harmless people—the helpful pilot and his wife.

But at ten, when Ken untied the SIGFORD, Ken forbad me

to leave Okasassa House.

"It sounds cruel, I know, but I don't want you running off from me, or spilling all our woes to the Barbers at the airport," he said. "The other time was enough of a scare—your not being in the motel at one in the morning and then not showing up with Rauenbauer. Just calm down, Leslie. In a few hours I'll be back with your sister, safe and sound."

"She'll expect me to meet her. She'll be scared!" I cried.

"Stop babying her!"

"She's only fourteen!"

"Leslie, Cindy can survive without big sister, from Cross City to Okasassa."

Very true, unless Cindy's host was really a murderer.

He left me standing infuriated on the dock, tempted to swim after the boat. I didn't want to be left behind in that house. Worse things happened• to me in Ken's absence than in his presence.

His last words reached me across the widening gulf between dock and boat.

"Notice that I'm ordering you to stay there. I didn't abandon you or drug you. I don't do things like that, and I hope I never will!"

Considerate of him. But he'd forcibly kidnapped me on Saturday night, when our desires were reversed—when he wanted me on the boat, and I prefered the house.

I took a roundabout route back to the house, wandering across the sand, then kicking a path through knee-high yellowed grasses. I came out nearer the back door than the front, so I went up the steps to the kitchen door, climbing past nodding pink and white periwinkles ringing the garbage cans.

Inside, I heard Keegan's baritone voice.

"I know how far the boat went. Into the mangroves. He moored it there, but not for long. They saw me and came back across to the house."

Margaret was bent over the formica counter, laboriously writing on a pad. When she heard me enter, she immediately straightened, hid the paper in her fist, and poked Keegan.

I'd never felt less welcome. Margaret wouldn't meet my eyes, but Keegan boldly looked me up and down, his wide mouth like a scar tight across his face.

"I'm sorry," I said, "I didn't mean to barge in."

Margaret snorted, and Keegan glared, his dark brows drawn down.

"Margaret, does Keegan know my sister is coming?"

"Ask him yo'self," she said.

"How can I?" I said, turning to Keegan, wincing at his winsome tanned face, his lithe, strong body and pale hair. I hated to think that Keegan, unlike Ken, regretted kissing me.

"My little sister is coming," I said, enunciating clearly. He tossed his head as if a fly were buzzing near his face.

I said it again, hand on chest ("my"), and indicated her height with my hand. The "female-same" sign meaning "sister" wouldn't communicate. Instead, I outlined a girl's shape between my hands. "Coming" was gesturing toward me, but an airplane was clearer. My little-finger-plus-thumb wings flew my right hand to land on my left.

"My SISTER," I said.

"Your what?"

"My deaf sister." But "deaf" was the wrong sign to use. He remembered that from the night less than a week ago when I'd lied to him about my hearing.

"You're not giving me that DEAF crap, again! You're not deaf!"

I took two steps toward him. "Keegan, please!"

"Why all this hand-waving stupidity? I'm no blasted deaf-mute! His voice came close to breaking. "I just . . . can't . . . hear!"

"Okay!" I snatched up the pad and wrote, "My 14-year-old deaf sister is coming today. Please be nice to her."

He actually read it. "Is SHE deaf? Not another lousy faker?"

I nodded, flushing hot. "She is."

"Why expose her to this madhouse? What's he gonna use HER for? Babies of fourteen don't turn me on, believe me!"

His words lashed me right out of the kitchen. This time I was the one furiously to walk out on him.

Why was Cindy coming here? Merely to liberate you, Keegan! To furnish you the skills to get off this damn island and go back to college. We could help you more or less to use the telephone!

"She might give you what I can't give you, Keegan . . . a fighting chance!"

I waited until I was sure the kitchen was empty. Then I returned, filched three cookies from the selection cooling on a rack, and looked around the sunny room so spotlessly clean. No wonder Keegan made this his headquarters and ate with Margaret and Rufus instead of the three of us—sour Rauenbauer, Ken the poisoner, and me, the fake-deaf, fake Mary Ann.

I glanced into the kitchen waste can. On top of coffee grounds and orange peel lay two wads of paper. If everyone else around here could spy, sneak, and steal, so could I. I whisked the paper wads right out of the trash and up to my room.

I winced. Unwadded, Margaret's notes to Keegan did seem to justify Rauenbauer's criticism of her English grammar. Her grammar was very original, and she couldn't spell. Both she and Cindy were bright people, but their schools had obviously failed them.

Translated, the notes read, "I can't hear them say anything about your mother." Then, "He said no more shooting at people." Then came the note I must have interrupted: "They were arguing, and he kissed her a long time, and . . ."

Keegan had a diligent spy, but what a way to get almost all one's information!

Noon. I couldn't see the lagoon from up here, so I trotted downstairs and planted myself in the front porch hammock—like a fish in a net, waiting. Everyone was waiting for something else to happen, around here.

Noon came, then twelve-thirty. I felt as if I'd lived here not a week, but a month. Margaret arrived on the porch and gruffly announced lunch. My stomach growled an affirmative, so I trailed her indoors—after nearly falling on my face getting untangled from the hammock. Was Ken feeding Cindy lunch enroute?

Would Cindy search through the menu, pointing out new

words? Menus and recipes . . . she needed them put in simpler language, but she was becoming a gourmet cook. "I can't hear, but I sure can taste!" she'd sign.

For lunch I had the doubtful privilege of dining with Rauenbauer, alone at the round table in the bay window. Envying Keegan his meals in the kitchen, I hungrily spooned up cream of celery soup, my eyes cast down.

"Have you reconsidered?" he asked.

"Reconsidered what?"

"Helping us find Sigrid Howell."

I sighed. "She's Norwegian. Maybe she returned to Norway."

"I think she's much closer than Norway," he murmured, "but where?"

How much did this man know about the circumstances of Brad Howell's death, I wondered. Refusing to furnish him information, I merely said, "I don't know. I don't consider it any of my business." (What a whopper!)

"You know what happens if harm befalls that deaf boy? Ken Howell gets everything."

"It seems to me that Ken is concerned for Keegan. He's tolerated things few men would. You said so yourself when Keegan stuck a knife in Ken."

"Oh, yes! That's how it appears. But you don't know what Ken's doing behind our backs. Bradford Howell's lawyer came down from Tallahassee Friday to confide in me. Baker Johnson can't stomach these machinations any longer. Ken got his brother out of the way and then the wife. Now all that stands between him and a fortune (the books alone are worth over fifty thousand dollars) is a helpless deaf boy. Baker's coming here soon with proof."

"Of what? Proof of what?"

"Proof from Bradford Howell, his client. Baker has some um, documents that he's agonized over since Fall. Evidence that will prevent the estate's being inherited by Bradford Howell's murderer!"

I gaped. Rauenbauer put his hand on my arm and whispered, "Baker IS a backwoods southern lawyer, slow and fat, and he may not impress people, but he's a man with a conscience. Do YOU have any conscience at all?"

That stung. "I didn't think you liked Keegan one bit."

"I haven't a trace of affection for him; you're right.

No excuse for the way he acts. But I have even less respect for his slick, deceptive uncle, who can gull anyone into cooperating . . . especially women!"

He watched me take each bite, which was hard on my appetite. I decided again to test his reactions.

"Did you come into my room and take something from my purse Saturday evening?"

He did not speak for a moment. His eyes got round and darkened. Then he said, "No, I certainly didn't! But I can tell you exactly who did."

And of course, at that suspenseful moment, I heard the motorboat coming in.

Racing to the porch with my mouth still full, down the path, out onto the dock, I was in time to see the white bow poke through the wall of mangroves. As if he knew how I'd feel—hopping around on the dock, straining to see— Ken pivoted the boat sharply to give me a side view of the SIGFORD, complete with small, waving passenger in blue.

Cindy, veteran of two airplane flights and a ride to the island in very questionable company, was smiling and gesturing as if to show me what a change she'd make at Okasassa House. The waiting was over. I hoped the shocks and terror were over, too. At least help had arrived, signing "beautiful big big house!" from halfway across the lagoon.

She rushed into my arms, not waiting for Ken to hand her out of the boat, not with her agility! Her fingers gave me the tale of her travels faster than her soundless, moving lips could keep pace. She signed and spelled:

"I flew . . . airplane . . . big one . . . many people . . . breakfast . . . eggs . . . milk . . . bacon . . . on plane . . . Atlanta . . . tall man say you Cindy Fallon? Pilot . . . his wife . . . small plane . . . fly like this . . . wild . . . scary . . . beautiful . . . all down there . . . trees . . . rivers . . . Florida . . . wife hold me. . . . I not throw up . . . a new man . . . Ken Howell . . . friend and wife. Ken drive me . . . eat lunch . . . nut candy . . . (She had a box of pralines). Boat ride here . . . SIGFORD . . . Okasassa House . . . I love you!"

That was the English gloss of Cindy's American Sign Language.

I'd last seen Cindy at Easter vacation. She'd grown to at least five feet tall, making her skirt a bit too brief. She was even prettier than in April. She'd found some way to smooth her blonde hair down. Farewell to the gossamer halo of yesteryear. She hadn't developed a figure yet, though. Perhaps she owed to Mom's rubella this long delay in maturing. She wasn't wearing glasses, though she'd been threatened with them. She had no more than average eyesight, but used her eyes well. Deaf people do that. Never for them the dull-eyed look of hearing people, accustomed to sounds, who close visual shutters to cracks.

"She's a marvel! She's one helluva smart kid," Ken cried, putting her suitcase on the dock. "What she can get across . . . and understand, too!"

"It's a necessity," I said, still hugging her. "And she's had life-long practice."

"The signing— It's beautiful. Her fingers fly like little butterflies. There's a rhythm to it, too, as if she hears silent music."

"From now on," I told Ken, "I'll sign and speak, so she'll get the same input we do. Keep that in mind. Other kids can overhear; Cindy will 'oversee.'"

"Suits me. I'm looking forward to watching you two."

Simultaneous method, total communication, they called it. I said and signed to Cindy how much I'd missed her and how super she looked.

"I swim? Water warm! Water deep! Fish here? We dive down?"

"Now be fair, Leslie," said Ken. "I can't read hands, so tell me what she says. Translate."

"Name trees? Those trees, there?"

I spoke and spelled the names I'd so recently learned: "Mangrove, palmetto, hibiscus, oleander." Cindy spelled them back to me, frowning intently, self-disciplined to remember names. Always she was demanding names, names, names. For six years she'd lived with no names, no questions, and no answers. Now she was a word-monger. Knowing names, you can talk about things that you can't point to.

Touch things, stroke and weigh them, sniff, taste what one politely can. Her hands were as active as her eyes and brows and lips, always learning, learning, and hunting for people she could pump.

Ken watched us closely—listening to us, nodding, and smiling. Keegan was still the only uninformed, unreachable person on the island, for all his education and his talent at inventing insults.

"I took Cindy to lunch," Ken explained as I whipped his words into visible form. "She had me struggling to explain 'hush puppies' on the menu, so I pretended to hush a loud dog"—he made a shadow-puppet of a dog's mouth barking— "by throwing it food."

"Wonderful! That's exactly what you should have done!"

"The word 'grits' on the breakfast menu sure caused a lot of frowning and rubbing fingers together. I had to order some just to show her they weren't sand."

"Grits . . . creamed what? Corn?" Cindy spelled.

"Yes, 'cream of what?'" I laughed. "Looks like cream of wheat, doesn't it? Not corn, like on cobs."

"Al and Sue really got a kick out of her," Ken said.

His slang had to be restated; otherwise, she'd think he said that she kicked Al and Sue. I signed that the couple "enjoyed" her, then carefully signed the exact words Ken used. Giggling, she responded, "I got . . . a . . . kick . .out. . . of them, too!" She'd sure remember that one, and grasp it when she read it, too. The crazier the figure of speech, the more she loved it.

Cindy was full of love. Her frequent spurts of temper cooled quickly. Her attention-span was short, however, since she'd never attended church-services or patiently endured adult conversations before she got signs at six.

Her love was abruptly and physically expressed. She gave Ken a hug, which startled him and made me shudder. (Watch out whom you're hugging, Sis!)

"Thank you!" she mouthed carefully up at Ken, so he'd understand.

"Why, thank YOU!" he answered, and she lip-read that.

"She never speaks aloud?" he asked, and was treated to Cindy's impersonation of a hearing person's reaction to a deaf voice. First came shock, then revulsion and retreat. After her "hearie" had drawn back, grimacing, Cindy showed Ken why. She switched roles. In the metallic monotone of a robot, she ground out her two best words: "Cindy Fallon."

It was all Ken could do to keep his face steady, behind

a frozen smile. When he recovered, he murmured, "She's a gift from God, isn't she?"

He got a melting smile in return, and then she was off, running to smell all the flowers and try out the hammock.

The rest of that day was breathtakingly exciting for us both. Keegan did not appear, but Margaret did, and her black face underwent scrutiny. Cindy had never lived in a mansion with a housekeeper, and I held my breath until she gave Margaret a ferociously merry squeeze. Margaret had passed inspection.

Cindy passed Margaret's inspection, too. Margaret hugged the tiny, skinny form, and patted her back, not trying to say a word to Cindy.

Now came Cindy's silent question: "Deaf?"

"No. Hearing."

All Cindy knew about the island she learned from my first-day, Pollyanna letter. I'd leave it at that, for now. She was plenty perceptive. We often made games out of her uncanny perceptiveness. Watching someone telephoning, for instance, she'd guess how the conversation was going just from body English, and she was accurate.

Unfortunately, perceptiveness could work against Cindy. People who thought her a freak or mentally defective couldn't hide behind bland faces. She read eyes and posture. As a result, she gravitated to deaf people and the few hearing folks who understood. I had a judgment handed me before I asked for it.

"Mr. Howell likes me," she signed, "He's better than George. Not afraid of me."

Ken and I took her up to her room.

"Beautiful! Blue! Everything blue for me!" She danced across the rug, flew from window to window. "So high up! I can see Gulf of Mexico! No boats out there. It's bigger than Lake Erie?" Then she spotted the blue parakeet.

"Parrot? Little parrot? For me?"

"Parakeet," I spelled, and she spelled it several times, feeling a new word on her fingers and imitating my lip-movements. She coaxed the bird over to her along its perch.

"Tell her we can shut the windows and let it fly free. Tell her it's hers on long-term loan," said Ken.

"Fly around? Sit on my hand?" she marveled, in signs

clear enough for Ken; her right hand represented the bird.

"Yes."

"Can it talk? Tell me if it talks," she signed and I said. "Is it talking? Or chewing?"

"That hurts!" Ken whispered. "You now get to be the interpreter for a BIRD!"

That's exactly what I was. I listened closely to the quiet avian muttering. Having ears, the parakeet did better at producing human words than most deaf people can. I translated.

"Pretty birdie," it said, then, "Kiss pretty Sweetie." It cocked an eye at Cindy and confided to me, "Birds can't talk!"

Cindy danced in astonishment, immediately seeing the comic irony of that. I explained, "Remember, Cindy, it has no idea what its words mean."

A consoling thought for a child who'd never speak half so clearly herself.

When Ken left us alone, she changed into shirt and shorts. As she tucked and buttoned, she kept one hand free to spell, "Where's Keegan?"

Like Ken, I tried to explain and excuse his absence.

"He's the only deaf here?"

"Yes. He knew the hearing world, though, for twenty-one years. He's new to the deaf world. He has to learn so much."

She pondered, then asked, "Are you in the hearing world completely? Or are you half and half? If he learns, will he and I be together and apart from you, or will he still be more like you than like me?"

That question made my head spin. So much for the pronouncements of many "experts" that deaf children—and adults—"cannot handle abstract ideas."

"He'll be partly like you and partly like me. He can read and write and talk well, like me. But he can't speechread, yet, nearly as well as you can, and he is just as deaf as you are. A hearing aid doesn't help him."

"Will hearing people be afraid of HIM?"

"Not when he talks, but when they see he doesn't understand them, they'll get nervous. Right now, he wants to be alone; you must be patient with him."

She sent me a scathing book—how could I imagine

otherwise? Then dimples.

Cindy found the library where Rauenbauer was working, and shrank away from the thousands of books full of idioms she was trying to memorize. When I introduced Cindy, the scholar arose with dread in his face. He blurted something wonderfully stupid: "She doesn't LOOK deaf."

I managed a straight face. Cindy speechread him and giggled up at me. It was almost as awful as the notorious question, "Is Cindy learning Braille?"

"He's a freak!" she signed, as I towed her away to inspect the rest of the house.

"Where's the TV?" she wanted to know, as addicted as I was. She preferred comedies with enough action to make them halfway understandable. I explained that Keegan's father had loathed the "boob tube," and Ken had not yet bought one. She spotted the stereo, and ran her hand over a speaker to find out if it was playing.

At that moment, Ken materialized.

"Ah, I'll bet Cindy loves music!"

When he realized what he'd said, he gulped, strangling on his words. The ironic thing was that he won his bet. Cindy did love music and danced all the time. To music. And so could Keegan.

"Let's show you my darkroom, Cindy," he offered.

I would enjoy translating his explanation of the magic that turned light-rays into pictures printed on paper.

In his studio, Cindy instantly noticed the nudes. She grinned up at them, her eyes sparkling with devilment.

"Your girl friends?"

Dutifully verbalizing her signs, I blushed more than Ken did. She looked both of us up and down, my spindly little pixie in the midst of that display of mature bare limbs.

"Leslie's too young for you, isn't she? You're old."

"Aw, come on!" he cried.

She laughed at his aggrieved expression.

"Who takes off clothes for pictures?"

I let Ken field that one.

"It's a job. Some women are professional models."

Cindy closely studied the nudes, then spun back to me. "You have a job here. You're pretty. You bulge. Will you take off YOUR clothes for pictures?"

I didn't need to translate that; her signs were a vivid pantomime of a stripper.

"I haven't asked her, Cindy. Should I?"

I blushed scarlet, to Cindy's delight. But Ken didn't get off easy, either.

"Ken will be like a daddy to us, won't he?"

I'd despaired of trying to graft tactfulness onto Cindy. Tact melted into thin air when described. "Be kind," was all I could say. "Be kind to people," but many people were not kind to her, so she had few examples to follow.

We ate supper, the four of us. Rauenbauer rushed to finish and hurry away from all the "hand-waving," as Keegan would've called it.

Margaret brought Rufus to meet Cindy, and my sister noticed how cold the woman was to Ken. I grew weary of Cindy's restless, "Where is Keegan? I want Keegan!"

Ken went out to look for Keegan. No luck. The deaf boy I'd promised her could not be found.

"Boy"? Wait a minute! Did I think of Keegan, a man of twenty-one, as a boy, just because he was deaf? Ken called him a "kid," which was okay. Was I no better than parents who got shocked that I dared refer to their "poor little deaf child" as a "deaf kid"?

"Keegan has no sign language, remember," I cautioned. "Not one word."

"Well, I have!" was her succinct reply.

Around seven p.m., Cindy started to droop, and I urged her to head up to bed. It was eight-thirty, however, before I won out over her insatiable curiosity. I had to promise to retire when she did, so that if she missed anything I'd miss it too!

I tucked her in—a golden-tressed princess in the high, antique bed—nuzzling and tickling her until she squealed.

"What do you think of Ken, Cindy?"

"He loves you," she twinkled, "very much. He looks at you when you don't notice." She imitated a leer. "Maybe you'll marry him. He's not too old, really."

"Does he seem to you like an honest man?"

"He's tense. In this house he's so tense I can feel prickles. But before the boat, on land, he was happy and calm."

I pondered that. "Well, tomorrow see how you read Keegan."

I wasn't making or taking bets on what tomorrow would bring. Just get her through the night, in her room across the hall from mine—another room with no lock on its door.

14

The next morning, after I fetched Cindy from a safe and sane night's sleep, we found Ken sitting at the breakfast table and Rauenbauer already rising, wiping his mouth. I knew he didn't want another meal with fingers flitting over the plates like twenty butterflies.

On the other hand (so to speak), Ken watched our communications with fascination, resting his chin in his palm. He treated Cindy with awe, seeing her, apparently, as a miraculous airy creature who honored him by alighting here. She watched attentively while I translated her signs into sounds.

Keegan still hadn't appeared, and after our eggs and bacon were gone, Cindy popped up and headed for the kitchen with her dishes, as I had a week ago—the morning of the knifing. But she wasn't fleeing Ken. She was simply a neat housekeeper. Her slender blonde-in-blue figure disappeared through the swinging door, and I followed, carrying my own plate and cup. Keegan, however, was not eating in the kitchen.

He had isolated himself still further. Outside the screen door I saw him, sitting on the back steps, a dish of melon resting on one knee and a mug of coffee beside him in the sunshine.

Cindy saw him too, and signed, "He's deaf? All lonely?"

I nodded, suddenly chilled with anxiety.

Margaret, elbowing through suds with our dishes, muttered, "How can she be such a happy child? She can't hear or speak one word!"

In the space of that distracting comment, Cindy was past me, out the back door, and standing two steps below Keegan, gazing straight into his startled face. I could see them both through the rusty screens that concealed me.

Keegan spooned himself another bite of melon. Not surprisingly, he completely shut her out.

I also wasn't surprised at Cindy's move, knowing deaf

134

people's aggressive, tactile approach.

She took hold of Keegan's wrist and stopped his spoon in mid-air. Smiling engagingly into his face, brows lifted, she lipped a much-practiced word: "What?" and pointed at the melon. No fingerspelling or signing for this deaf one.

Keegan sighed. "Papaya."

He didn't communicate.

Cindy whipped out of her shorts pocket her trusty 2x4 pad and stub of pencil. She shoved them at him. He didn't respond, so she turned up the wattage of her smile.

He wrote a word and shoved the pad back to her.

She read it, frowned, then tilted her head to watch her own hand spell it: "p-a-p-a-y-a." Then "p-a-p-a?" She looked puzzled. I knew her hand would drift to her temple, thinking in signs: open hand with thumb tapping her right temple was the sign for "father." She mouthed "father" questioningly at Keegan, then "papa." "Papa-ya?"

"Not connected with 'papa,' " Keegan said curtly. "It's a plant grows down here. Spanish word." Frustrated at her uncomprehending patience (how well had "deaf" Leslie lipread in the moonlight for him!), he said, "Oh, hell!" and I feared she'd lost him with her problem in semantics.

He was digging his spoon into the melon, but not to dismiss her. He offered her a bite. Never lacking courage, she daintily poised finger and thumb over the bright orange lump on his spoon.

"Hey, I'm not worried about germs!" (a scoutmaster's voice). "Here!" He cupped her chin in his left hand and spooned the morsel carefully into her mouth.

Cindy wrinkled her nose, savoring it with deep concentration. Ever-ready fingers twitched into "peach" and "cantaloupe," while her brows outlined her puzzled contemplation. Keegan didn't understand.

Patiently, she wrote it down, "Peach + cantaloupe = papaya."

I could read it over Keegan's shoulder.

"That's right! That's pretty good!" He squinted up in surprise. He wrote, "Spanish word, a fruit, not 'father,'" and gave the pad back to her.

There was a moment's suspense while Keegan finished his melon and set the dish aside. Cindy didn't budge, her legs braced apart, pad back in her pocket, fingers twitching. She could sense him slipping away even before he moved.

"Your name?" she mouthed and spelled to him. Then she signed it.

He shook his head, starting to rise.

She pounced at him again, seizing the same wrist, this time to lift it vertical from the elbow. She forced his fingers into a "K" (probably the hardest letter in the alphabet, poor guy), thumb propping the forefinger above the second finger, others bent. He didn't resist her struggling hands, as she bit her lips and set each joint in place. He couldn't slap a pretty little brash child, one no bigger than a twelve-year-old.

"K!" she mouthed. "E!" She fought his hand into that letter, four fingernails digging into the top of the thumb. The commonest letter in English always hurt! She nodded his "E" hand to show the letter doubling. Then to the difficult "G"—best called a tipped-over open bird's bill. "A" was easy—a girl's fist, thumb vertical. Then "N" with two fingers hanging over the closed thumb.

She spelled the word for him and, in grim determination, made him imitate her. "K-E-E-G-A-N" spelled faster and faster. I prayed he had agile fingers, but any biologist who dissected beasties under a microscope—

About the time I was expecting him to spring up and leave, he pointed sternly and said, "Who are you?"

She knew those words. Grinning dazzlingly, she spelled her name. He surely recognized the curved hand of "C," the little-finger "I," the typewriter lower-case "D." The "Y" was little finger and thumb up, hard for stiff hands.

"Cindy?" he asked. "Cindy?"

She jumped for glee when he said it and then tried to spell it after her. By some fast arithmetic I found he had one third of the alphabet already. My little sister was hypnotizing him.

She had him saying, "Go on, your last name?"

"F-A-L-L-O-N," she spelled, with the "OK"-sign of "F," the two-fingered "L" and the ball of "O," and he had almost half the alphabet.

She pointed at him and spelled "Howell." "H" and "W"

were added. She outlined my figure, batting her eyelids significantly, and spelled my name: "Leslie." She made the sign for Negro, then spelled "Margaret." Keegan had the fist of "S," the three-legged "M," the crossed fingers of "R," and thumb-under-index-finger "T."

Three-fourths of the alphabet, already!

Keegan hunched toward her, one knee drawn up to his chest, one hand near his face to compare his finger-positions with hers.

"My gracious, look at that!" Margaret gasped, making me remember there were three of us watching from the kitchen. Ken was shaking his head, his brown face shining.

Keegan pulled at his chin and drew a mustache on his lip. Instantly Cindy put "Rauenbauer" in the air.

"How can she spell that long name . . . it's his name, isn't it?" Ken said. "I keep forgetting how he spells it, the sour ole kraut."

"She saw me spell it twice. A deaf kid is embarrassed to spell errors in sight of everyone."

I spoke at normal volume; Ken and Margaret kept whispering, though Keegan and Cindy wouldn't hear anything softer than a dynamite-blast.

"Write! Write!" she mimed. "Anything" (shrugging).

He wrote a line I didn't see, and Cindy grinned as she read it and signed it, word for word.

"Now is the time for all good men to come to the aid of their party."

She'd recognize that from typing class. She signed it over and over, diminishing the amplitude of her motions until her hand movements seemed little more than beating time to music.

Signs were faster than speech; fingerspelling, slower. Keegan nodded solemnly at Cindy.

Pointing to the melon, she spelled "papaya," again.

"What's the sign for it?" asked Keegan, forming with his hands a tentative, papaya-shaped globe.

"Yes!" She grinned widely. "Invent signs or spell new words and names."

He pointed to the coffee mug.

She signed "cup," setting a "C" on her left palm, then looked to see what it held. "Coffee" was right fist grinding on left. ("Tea" was a dandled teabag.)

Keegan was impatient. "Okay. Man. What is 'man'?" He slowly spelled "M-A-N."

Cindy, sterner than I, shook her head no. He still had five letters of the alphabet to learn. She taught them to him.

Would he retain all twenty-six letters? She ran through the alphabet four times, faster and faster, and Keegan watched, then followed suit, the tendons taut in the side of his neck. I held my breath until "Z"—the bitter end—which sure was sweet.

He remembered. He wasn't an agile-handed honor student with a "photographic memory" for nothing. "S" and "A" got reversed, of course, and "F" and "D." But I'd never seen anyone learn that fast before. I hoped he remembered that I had manual language and ears as well.

Keegan was pointing to things and asking for signs, now. The house, that tree, the shoes he wore. Cindy's hands eagerly flew into a roof-peak, a finger-limbed swaying tree, a pair of fist-shoes.

He slid off the steps and marched Cindy out into the yard, gripping her wrist as she had gripped his.

I asked Ken over my shoulder, "Do you think he'll stick with it?"

"When that kid takes on a project, he sticks with it to completion. Always has, since his Tinker-Toy days."

Now Keegan was hesitantly spelling words to Cindy. "Fish," and her hand swam away from her. "Home," and she touched near mouth and ear for "eating-sleeping-place." "Learn" was pulling knowledge out of the left palm up to the brain. Keegan began building sentences.

"I learn my name . . . my house here . . . fish come home . . ." Sign and spell, sign and spell, and ask for more vocabulary.

Keegan was no longer beating his head against the metaphorical "glass dome" which encloses profoundly deaf people. He'd found a crack in the glass and was breaking out.

Cindy suddenly ran for the back steps, sprang up them two at a time, and burst the door open in our faces.

"Did you see?" She wheezed with excitement. "See? He learns! He's smart!"

She grabbed Ken's hand and mine and hauled us down the

back steps. Keegan rose. The glare Keegan flashed at Ken was obvious, but Cindy was too busy to tolerate nonsense.

"Talk to Ken," she signed to me. "Make him talk, too. Say anything."

Facing Ken, self-conscious, I spoke and signed patter about today's beautiful weather. Too fast for Keegan to grasp, yet, but he saw one sign per word, big and clear, instead of tiny, ambiguous lip-movements, each of which could represent several different sounds.

"That's all it takes? There's a way to sign EVERY-thing?" Keegan asked. "It's not ugly, when you do it now—"

I nodded, not trusting my voice even if he couldn't hear it.

"Unbelievable. Really. I didn't realize. I'd never watched deaf-mutes closely—"

Putting his words into signs for Cindy, I didn't stop in time. She read my lips, shuddered, and then marched up to Keegan. She slapped his face. Not hard, but the blow shocked him.

"What'd I DO? What made you—?"

I mouthed "deaf-mute," shaking my head, making a face. I don't think he understood "deaf-mute" is as insulting as "nigger."

Deaf people aren't mute. They can laugh, cry, and yell as loud as anyone. At least Keegan didn't say "deaf and dumb," which would have netted him a fist in the gut!

Cindy was quickly over her pique. Clapping her hands, she exploded into new action, our little trainer, shoving the three of us around like big circus animals.

Her right hand flew to her face in a Y, little finger at lips, thumb at ear, for "telephone." She winked at me.

She forced Keegan's hand into that shape of a telephone receiver. "Talk, talk!" she signed to him. I already had my "receiver" ready, but Cindy had me hunch my shoulder to hold the receiver in place and free both hands.

The third receiver on the line was Ken's.

Keegan caught on immediately.

Ken talked on the phone. I listened and signed. Keegan could read my signs and use his voice to talk back to Ken.

I was interpreting via telephone for Keegan. Cindy bounced up and down with glee at the new gift she'd given her eager student.

I wasn't the least bit jealous. I was proud of Cindy.

It was disorganized, but textbook-teaching couldn't have been faster. Keegan sponged up signs, and few, if any, appeared to drain back out. He got numbers, colors, months of the year, and even the finger-snapping, thigh-slapping sign for "dog." Cindy loved animals.

By dinner-time he still retained the alphabet, and many signs I knew he'd seen only once, like "house" and "dead." We hadn't paused for lunch, hadn't even thought of food.

Margaret came to get us for dinner, down to the dock where Keegan was spelling species of fish, and Cindy was slipping him prepositions like "to," "for," and "with." Cindy had remained in control throughout. When Keegan spoke aloud to me, Cindy sternly pointed to his hands; no silent talk,* just because I could hear.

"You kids ever goin' to eat?" Margaret asked.

I might have asked her to bring food outside, let us have a picnic, but I didn't want to inconvenience her.

If only I'd been less considerate of Margaret, I thought later, but how could I have foreseen? I'd tried to forget all the troubles on this island.

At the dinner table, Keegan had eyes for nothing but our hands. Cindy, by pointing, gave him signs for everything on the table, non-stop. Rauenbauer had deigned to join the dinner party, even though this morning's two signers had now become three.

I ate hurriedly without attempting to translate the hearing men's remarks. I could sense Keegan's desire to be free of Rauenbauer and Ken and back to full-time learning. Forking and spelling simultaneously is tough.

The meringue pie disappeared rapidly. Cindy licked her fingers to show Keegan "taste" was middle finger to tongue. He laughed.

But he had nothing else that day to laugh about.

Just as Keegan rose from the table, Rauenbauer caught at his shirt-sleeve. Then he tried to communicate something.

"Tell him I must show him what I found," he said.

Uneasy, I spelled, "He found something."

Rauenbauer stuck a piece of yellow paper toward Keegan. Just as it changed hands I recognized the stationery and handwriting. My stomach plummeted like a broken elevator.

Keegan read the letter, right down to the signature, "Sigrid."

Not monitoring the volume of his voice, Keegan shouted in the old man's face. "Where'd you find this? Where, damn it? Where?"

Rauenbauer slowly lifted his right hand and pointed his finger at Ken.

Keegan spun furiously toward Ken.

"YOU had this letter? Where's my mother? What have you done with her?"

Now Keegan grabbed MY arm. "What about YOU? You know what happened to Mom? Is she alive? Talk, Baby! Spell!"

I had nothing to say or sign. Ken was as speechless as I. Rauenbauer was backing away. Cindy stood paralyzed by Keegan's rage.

"Is she alive?" Keegan hissed at Ken. "If you wanna stay alive, Uncle, you better tell me!"

"I . . . I don't have her!" Ken said. Keegan needed no translation.

"Is she shut up in this house, and I can't hear her?"

Involuntarily, I looked upward, thinking of all the empty rooms in this old house. . . .

Keegan saw my gaze lift and was maddened. "Where IS she, you louse?"

Ken did not try to communicate with his nephew. His lips stiff as a ventriloquist's, he hissed, "Both you girls get out of here. Run!"

I grabbed Cindy's hand, and dragged her toward the stairs. Up on the third floor, safely behind my barricaded door, I saw her frantic question.

"What? What?" Cindy demanded. "Explain!"

Using "K" at her temple for "Keegan," she signed, "Keegan went crazy!"

My hands gave her a simplified version of Keegan's tormented life. I left out the ghost, my trip to Starke, and my capsules. I wouldn't have told a hearing sister any more. She understood Keegan's frenzy better than anyone else. She'd often felt victimized, too.

"I saw he hated Ken," she said. "'Sigrid'—strange new name, like the boat?"

"Oh, Cindy," I concluded, "It's a tragedy. Everyone

hates Ken. He must've done something horrible to deserve it!"

Cindy shook her head. "Forget Ken. I must teach Keegan. He's coming free. Free from prison," she signed, wrists breaking bonds, bars torn aside. "He scared me. Was he yelling?"

"Yes. He scared me too."

I was listening in vain for sounds from down below. There had been bumping and a cry, but now all was silent.

For us both.

15

Half an hour later, Cindy's back went rigid, and I soon heard what she had felt. I ran to the door.

Keegan stood there, his elfin face aged into a gnome's.

"May I come in? I won't harm you."

If I hadn't let him in, Cindy would have; she rushed to pull him into the room, signing faster than he'd be able to read.

I hated to translate all his cruel words, but he wanted us both to know what was going on—everything that had happened. He stammered at first, his shoulders sagging.

"I . . .I almost killed him."

Keegan watched my hands flick the words over to Cindy. She gasped, not needing to ask whom he meant.

"I had Ken by the throat. Rauenbauer picked up a knife from the dinner table. I took it away from him before he could stick me. With it, I almost. . . cut Ken's throat. I could have. I wanted to."

"But you didn't?" I whispered, and he understood me.

"I've always wished him dead. He was saying 'Mary Ann!' Did he mean the letter was to Mary Ann, long ago? I thought—"

"It was an old, old letter." I made him understand that. Then I asked for reassurance. "Is Ken alive, Keegan?"

"He came back and came back for years," Keegan mumbled, "He tore our family apart. These last months I've wanted to tear him to pieces. But today, holding that knife at his throat. . ."

He paused.

"Now I know I can leave here and let him do what he pleases. It doesn't matter any more. I can live. I can find some job. I can learn where my mother is, alive or dead. I can get along. . . if I just have an interpreter."

Cindy and I didn't say anything. Our four eyes were

143

already spilling tears.

"Can't I work," he asked, "even if I can't hear? I want some career. At least a job. Could I ever go back to school? To some school?"

Cindy answered him with slow fingerspelling. She was snuffling back tears. "Deaf can work. Good work. Many jobs. You go to college. You can talk. You can read."

He glanced at me for assurance, and I nodded.

"Learn. Study hard," Cindy spelled. She went over to the window to blow her nose. When she came back, she had a sign language book under her arm.

Keegan took it from her as solemnly as if it were the Holy Bible.

"We teach you," she signed.

At this pont, my own hands lay at rest. My mind was on that letter of Sigrid's. Rauenbauer said Ken had it. Had Ken rifled my room, or the thief's room? Should one even believe Rauenbauer?

"How do deaf people go to college?" Keegan asked.

"Copy notes. Read lots," I spelled. "There's a college for the deaf, too."

It took ages to spell the words for which he knew no sign, but I spelled close by my mouth. Lip movements helped him.

"How would I get up in the morning for classes?" he asked. "I've used no alarm clock since . . .I got hurt. Seven months. No school, no job, just sitting around rotting. How does Cindy manage?"

Cindy pantomimed. Going to the lamp by my bed, she flipped the light on and off, on and off, and pretended to be awakened. We saw understanding brighten Keegan's face.

"Light flashing instead of bell ringing?" he said. "Would that work for a doorbell, too?"

"Yes! And for telephone, and baby crying," she went on. "Deaf see light when machine hears baby."

"Deaf people have babies that can cry?"

Shockingly ignorant! We gaped at Keegan. Cindy sent me a mischievous look, grabbed Keegan's hand and pressed it against her throat. She let out a roof-raising yell. He couldn't hear her, but he could feel her larynx vibrate and see me recoil. I wished I had time to explain to him that clear speech requires tiny accuracies of tongue, lips, teeth, glottis, and larynx. A shout is merely forced air. When would he grasp facts like that?

"You move your lips. Are you talking?" he asked Cindy, slowly spelling the words.

"I say words without sounds," she spelled and lipped, while I intently listened at the door. Would anyone come upstairs to investigate Cindy's ruckus?

No one came.

"I sure have a lot to learn," Keegan said, and sighed.

"We will teach you."

Right then, Cindy saw me flinch—Leslie the human sound-sensor—my eyes flashing a visible alarm. I wasn't hearing footsteps in the hall. I heard the boat's engine.

We ran into Keegan's room overlooking the lagoon. The SIGFORD was just entering the tunnel through the mangroves, but we were too late to see who was in it. The dock and shore were both empty. No one said anything.

I assessed Keegan's room by the light of day. Books, hundreds of them, lined the walls—boys' adventure stories to textbooks in physiology and calculus. There were maps, bottled crabs and insects, snake skins, and a microscope on a shelf, very dusty. A radio was even dustier.

Keegan's voice brought my head around.

"I want Rauenbauer out of here, too. Rauenbauer and my uncle, both. I can handle my own affairs, now."

I contemplated his handsome, winsome face. Twice he had almost killed Ken with a knife. Ken dead and Keegan in prison for murder made a picture too hideous to imagine. Who had left in the SIGFORD? I hoped it was Ken. At least Ken. Maybe Rauenbauer, too?

Cindy was running a finger down the spines of his books, frowning at the titles. "Big words! Smart man!"

"He can graduate. He can still be a techer, maybe teach deaf kids. Lots of deafened adults do that," I reminded her. "Even if he can never be a doctor—"

"Why can't he be a doctor?" she demanded. "I'd love to have a deaf doctor; deaf like me!"

No one seemed eager to go downstairs. Finally Keegan braced his shoulders, chin up, and we made for the lower regions of the house. He led the way.

No one was visible on the first floor, and I shook my head when Keegan asked if I heard anything. We headed for

145

the Deans' apartment, and Keegan knocked.

"Who is it?" asked Rufus' voice suspiciously.

"Us three," said I.

Their sitting room was cozy, decorated in red and black with bright rugs and windows full of potted plants.

"My Howell done went away," Margaret announced instantly. "Mr. R went too."

"When will they come back?" I asked.

She shrugged. "I dunno. We got us plenty of food and fuel, though."

Rufus added, "Don' you younguns worry. We'll watch after you. I got me a good rifle—"

He stopped short.

No message of any kind had been left for us. Not a peep.

"We better stay here?" I said doubtfully. "For a while?"

"Yes, stay!" Cindy insisted. "I have to teach Keegan."

"We can't get off the island very well without the SIGFORD," Keegan said, guessing the drift of the conversation. "Of course, I can easily swim the strait—"

I pictured the manta ray, sharks, and alligators.

We didn't even have a phone, out here, to summon a boat to come fetch us.

Margaret surprised me. She reached for both my hands and held them sandwiched between hers. This proved to be not a gesture of reconciliation, but her way of preventing me from signing to the others.

"Miss Fallon, I tole you I was scared of another killin'? Well, we just about had us a killin' today. Keegan got that knife, and he was kneelin' atop his uncle, and we daren't do nothin'. This boy I raised up since he was your sister's age—I'm not about to see him goin' to no 'lectric chair. Now you and your sister make Keegan smart enough to get off this island. Don't meddle. Just forget all that's past, and you teach him good."

"Did you learn anything about Keegan's mother? Before the men left?" I asked.

Rufus made his judgment in a whisper. "To my mind, poor Mrs. Howell done herself to death. She din' have no other choice."

Cindy and Keegan were justifiably irritated at being

left out. I immediately gave them the gist of these confidences. As we strolled outside, my head started whirling. Suppose Keegan really HAD cut Ken's throat? Would Margaret and Rufus turn Keegan in? Not a chance! They'd pretend Ken left; they'd get rid of the body. They'd do that for Keegan, whom they loved.

Then was Keegan lying? Had Keegan killed him, and was Ken now lying in the cellar—if this house had a cellar—or in some shallow grave, or at the bottom of the lagoon?

I found it difficult to look at Keegan. Suppose Sigrid really had killed herself? The loyal Deans might have prevented scandal by burying her on the island. Or Ken might have.

Because my morbid thoughts were invisible to them, Keegan celebrated the men's departure by asking for more signs, Cindy happily agreeing. She gave him the cluster of feminine signs by the cheek: "woman," "girl," "mother," and the masculines at the temple: "man," "boy," and "father." Keegan seemed almost too attentive. While he absorbed the pretty fluidity of visual words, I dwelt on the horrors of today.

Nonetheless, as dusk fell, the absence of Ken and Rauenbauer did lighten the atmosphere. Keegan began treating me as warmly as he did Cindy. At bedtime, Margaret gave even me a smile as she and Rufus called us into the kitchen to share cocoa and chocolate chip cookies.

We made up a sort of family—a multi-language family of southerners and northerners, deaf and hearing, young and old, black and white. Keegan's frustration and the rage it spawned seemed to be a thing of the past. I prayed for that, at least. He was even beginning to do some accurate, unconscious speechreading, meanwhile amusing me by saying, "I sure better learn signs. I'll never be able to lipread a single word!"

Two afternoons later, I heard sounds that brought me out of my room. Who on earth—?

The sounds came through Cindy's door. I invaded without warning, finding her sitting in the window, her yellow head bent over a ten-string guitar half as large as she. It was expensive and had seen heavy use, from the looks of it.

She pressed her temple against the wood near the tuning pegs, and plucked the strings as if it were a harp.

"Cindy?" I stamped on the floor, making her jump. "Where on earth did you get that?"

"It's Keegan's."

"Did he say you could—?"

"He gave it to me, after I found it."

"Found it where?"

"In his room. Hidden way back in his closet."

When were you in his room?" I did not keep my face blank enough; Cindy decided to be evasive.

"Oh, sometimes. We talk. He used to play the guitar."

She smiled, feeling none of the anguish those words gave me. She'd never heard guitar music. Keegan had.

She acted out the scene while balancing the instrument on her knees: her own surprise to discover a guitar, pulling it out, playing with it, looking up at him, Keegan's waving it away from him with tight lips. She gave me the whole poignant picture.

No wonder Beryl's guitar had worried Ken. He'd mentioned the dancing, but I did not know that Keegan also had been a guitarist.

I asked Cindy to keep the thing out of sight, and she said she would, not understanding why, frowning in perplexity. It was fun to feel the different vibrations of the different strings and to sit there cuddling this instrument that singers were always holding on TV or by the roadside, their mouths open and feet tapping. . .

From where she sat she could see herself in the bureau mirror. She rearranged her legs and hair, placed her fingers on the frets and the strings, and did a beautiful imitation of a folksinger.

Except for the folksinging.

In the sunshine, fourteen hours a day, we taught, and Keegan learned. Margaret furnished gallons of lemonade, stacks of cookies big as pancakes, cornbread, gingerbread, and clean towels for wet bodies.

Cindy was head-teacher, but Keegan himself did a lot of biology teaching. She kept pumping him for the names of everything from hermit- and fiddler-crabs to kinds of sea-weed and the sandpaper discs of sand dollars.

She thrilled me, one day, by "hearing" water for the very first time. She'd always asked me what water sounded like, but a washing machine was the best I could offer—a machine at the laundromat to embrace, her face close above the sloshing suds. Today, at a very high tide, tall breakers thudded on sand like boulders striking. Each roller crashed right at her toe-tips.

"I hear it! I hear it!" her hands screamed in delight. "I can hear water! Hear waves!"

I hugged her nearly in two, almost as delirious as she.

As for Keegan, he remembered sounds so acutely that he couldn't believe he wasn't hearing the surf that shook the sand beneath our feet.

Teaching him was like trying to stay on our feet in front of a man-sized vacuum cleaner. His need to learn sucked knowledge out of our brains. He wanted every skill of ours to be his, immediately! Now! No, yesterday! Total immersion in signs.

"Watch my lips," I reminded him. Keegan dropped his gaze—remembering, perhaps, our first meeting, in the moonlight in my bedroom. He'd kissed the lips he now was trying to read.

"Is this sign right? Is this 'animal,' or 'bear'? How is 'salt' different from 'train' and 'name'? They're made with the same four fingers!"

"Teach me, teach me . . ." until Cindy and I were exhausted, and I understood why Duane Gunlock hadn't forgotten Keegan Howell from Bio. 101. He wore both of us out, and once I padded down the hall at two a.m. just to find out if he really did study our sign books all night. Yes, I saw a yellow slash under his door and could faintly hear the flap of pages turning.

We swam twice a day, and Cindy's small, wet hand would appear just above the surface, spelling to Keegan. He was intrigued that miners and ironworkers needed signs during their noisy work, and deep-sea divers invented signs as well. Keegan tried to sign to me under water before sliding past me, smooth and golden, so very good to look at, so very tempting to touch.

My cutaway white bathing suit usually drew a whistle. At least I did wear a swimsuit. I didn't skinny-dip to remind him of Beryl, as my face had once reminded him of Mary Ann Monahan—now Mary Ann Parker.

Underwater, out of Cindy's view, Keegan swam close behind me, nuzzling my neck. "Affectionate," Ken had called him, and it was sure true, wonderfully true. I let air bubble out of my lungs, as we looked at each other through water-flattened eyeballs. The only time he'd kissed me was by mistake. Now he wanted to kiss ME, Leslie Fallon, but he held himself back.

Up in the sunshine, gripping an inner tube, he gasped, "I think you've forgiven me for the way I once treated you?"

I blew him a kiss (hearing people use more signs than they realize) and dived again. On that ascent I got very promptly and properly kissed. It felt wonderful.

He was splendid in the water, our former college athelete. Not tall enough for football at five-ten, his brown body was beautifully muscled, and his strokes hardly disturbed the surface. When his hair was wet, I could see dark Ken in him. Brad had married a Norwegian girl, and they'd had a son whose hair sun-bleached in the summer. I'd never seen a picture of Sigrid, but I imagined a Viking with hip-length yellow braids under a fur cap. A fur cap in Florida? No, I imagined her in Norway, just as the Deans and Mary Ann imagined her in her grave.

"What you thinking of, pretty little Leslie?" asked Keegan, in a tone so much like Ken's that I shivered.

"Of your . . . family," I admitted, and Keegan's

reaching hands never completed their circuit of my waist. His eyes darkened.

"We three make a family now. The five of us, here."

Asia, his war was another forbidden topic, not because he cut me off, but because pain broke out on his face like sweat. I didn't ask how many people he'd killed over there, or how many of his buddies lost their lives before and after he had lost his hearing.

I watched Cindy carefully. She was proud of him, wrapped up in him, but if she thought of him romantically, she didn't show it. Her age and immaturity seemed to limit her to idol-worship. She and I were close; each of us, in a crunch, deferred to the other.

I even enjoyed their teasing me, laughing when something fell or when a door slammed, making me jump. They signed behind my back, and Keegan already used his eyes more efficiently than I, noticing things I didn't and reading my feelings when I tried to cover them. Good. Good! I grieved for what they lacked; let them take full advantage of what they had.

"After twenty years of hearing, you'd think I could speechread better than Cindy, but I can't."

To reassure him, I showed him the identical appearance on the lips of "red" and "green," and of "baby" and "paper." The deaf made jokes about it: Hearing person to deaf child, "Never cross the street on a green light," and the child does the opposite. Or, "Where did you put the baby?" "In the incinerator." "Where's the paper?" "In the playpen."

Keegan was incensed to learn that some teachers used to tie or bag deaf kids' hands. To "make them talk," people denied them even natural gestures everyone uses.

"I don't want to go through life guessing what's said, never being sure!" Keegan growled.

When Cindy told him that many deaf kids think they'll never live to grow up, he cried, "What're you talking about? That's crazy!"

"Deaf kids who've never met any adults like them would assume that, or they'd expect soon to start hearing."

"Why don't they meet deaf adults?" he innocently asked.

"Who does? Hearie parents and teachers don't mix with deaf people. Deafness is invisible. And formidable."

There was a break in our idyll on the third day after the men's departure.

"This might prove interesting," Keegan said after lunch when we were headed through the living room to study on the shady porch. Keegan reached into a shelf below the window where Ken often sat. He dragged out an elaborate camera with a long snout of a lens.

A telephoto lens, no doubt.

"The film's still in the camera," Keegan said. "Just for kicks, I think I'll develop it."

He had no trouble arousing our curiosity. We raced each other up to Ken's studio.

"While I do the negatives, you can gape at these," he said, jerking out a drawerful of photos. "He used to try to impress me by flashing these around."

More candid shots, but these were of famous people. The Duchess of Windsor was patting the head of a basset hound that resembled the Duke. Lyndon Johnson was licking an ice cream cone. Football stars ogled a cheerleader. Hundreds of them—anecdotes on film. I wondered why Ken didn't publish his collected photos. He'd make a fortune!

"Okay. It's about time!"

Keegan summoned us into the darkroom to stand over metal trays in the red glow, sniffing the vinegary chemicals. I was eager for Cindy to see pictures emerge magically upon blank paper. I looked away quickly when I saw above us on a shelf a can standing near the red light bulb. The label read: "Potassium Cyanide."

In their chemical bath, ghostly images began to rise into view. Cindy oohed and ahhed as Keegan sloshed them around. With forceps, he transferred the photos to the fixative.

I stood staring down— At myself. Dozens of me. On every white square was Leslie Fallon! He had telephoto close-ups of me, building my sand castle.

Why? Why did Ken take them? I experienced the same indignation Keegan and Mary Ann had felt, earlier. Cindy, however, was enthralled, clapping her hands and pointing.

"You've got a sand-box, Leslie! A beautiful castle!"

While I'd played kid in the sand on my second day here, my image was being sucked into a camera. I had to admit they were the most beautiful pictures I'd ever had taken, but. . . !

Kneeling, my profile white against the curtain of my dark hair, my fingers gracefully flitted over shimmering sand, towers of crystals. Leslie the water-nymph, and in other shots, a serious sculptress, no sandbox juvenile.

My face wore a range of expressions: shy amusement, satisfaction, wistfulness. In two shots I'd raised my head to look for Keegan—sad, searching eyes, my hands still alight on my fragile architecture.

After this series came five more in brighter light, morning sun. I shook my head in disbelief. Ken had been ready with his camera when I pulled that axe out of my castle. There was my forlorn, slumping pose as I stared down, then my incredulous examination of the sand-caked blade. The last shot was of me as I retreated, glancing back over my shoulder at the flattened castle.

It made a parable; indeed it did. Beauty created, and beauty destroyed. But it also made something else very clear. Keegan didn't hesitate to say it.

"See? He slung an axe into your sand castle, just to stage his pictures. That may be minor, but he's done things you wouldn't believe. All my life he's meddled in our family affairs."

I stared at the photos. In this "minor" case, was the set of exquisite talking pictures worth the trick played on me? I shared neither Keegan's rage nor Cindy's unalloyed delight. I didn't know what to feel.

Cindy furnished me plenty to feel when Keegan left us putting away photos we'd spread around the studio.

"Too bad he hates Ken, since he looks and often acts exactly LIKE Ken," she observed, before she went running after her idol.

"What?" The explosion in my head sent me reeling into the nearest chair. Keegan so much like Ken? The Ken who stayed here and looked after Keegan, dangerous as that was. "Think what all you know," I told myself. Brad and Ken had fought over Sigrid, and Brad married her. Sigrid ran away after the suicide/murder. How often I'd shivered because Keegan spoke or looked like Ken . . . his uncle. Or WAS Ken his uncle?

I couldn't say it, could scarcely think it. His uncle? Or his—? I tried to put the notion out of my head, along with the horrible fear that diving into their lagoon might someday bring me face to face with Ken . . . green and dead and sunken there.

Cindy was bothered by no suspicions or suppositions. She took swimming lessons from Keegan, stuffed herself from a bottomless freezer, played with Keegan's microscope, and examined Australian pines that were Australian but not pines and helmet-shaped horseshoe-crab mothers leading their babies through sandy shallows.

Keegan discovered that he could still teach biology—to deaf kids, at least.

The next morning he took us climbing along the track he'd cut in the mangroves, deep into the green gloom of leafy caverns all mucky and organic, smelling like a greenhouse.

An upthrust of sand in the trees furnished him space for a lean-to made of boards. He had jugs of water and food sufficient for several days' stay, and even a rifle wrapped in plastic. Where we sat on a pad of blankets, eating tuna on rye-crisp and sipping instant orange drink, sunlight shafted through branches and quivered on our sunburned legs. It was warm and contained, among the pale arms of the mangroves, and felt very, very safe.

In exchange for Keegan's sharing his hideaway with us, Cindy turned on the stereo that night. From her excited face, I guessed what was coming.

She presented Keegan with a dozen record albums and asked which he preferred. He drew back, the old hard look solidifying his winsome face.

"I can't hear music! You know that! I'll never hear music again!" he said bluntly, without self-pity.

"Neither can I!"

She pulled his hands down, tapping a record album sharply. "Choose!" her fingers ordered.

Refusing to cooperate, he let his eyes fall too long on the Bacharach and Simon and Garfunkel albums. Cindy put those two on, and snapped one sign to him: "Watch!"

When her hand on the speaker told her music was filling the room, she spun dials. Treble down, bass up all the way. The pulse of low-frequency sound pounded almost uncomfortably under the soles of my feet. The polished wooden floor, flexible with age, interfered with my heartbeat: thump, athumpa, athumpa, thump, thump.

Cindy made good use of it. She danced.

Trained with metronome and vibrating floor-boards, she bent and swung, supple, her bare feet adhering like suckers to the dance floor. As cartilaginous as Keegan's shark skeleton, boneless, she interpreted "Bridge Over Troubled Waters," arching, flowing, sailing with the silver boat.

Keegan stared, open-mouthed, unblinking, reading the amplified signs and pantomime flowing from every limb. Cindy had memorized these lyrics from sheet music.

"Haven't you seen drama and dance on television by the National Theater of the Deaf?" I asked him.

"I scarcely knew deaf people existed!"

"Do you feel the beat?"

He nodded. "And . . . I think I can see the words!"

I brought him the record jacket and pointed out the songs as Cindy danced them, her face shiny with perspiration, flitting, leaping, gliding through that record and the next. Raindrops fell on her, she never fell in love again, and we were knee-deep in little green apples.

She flipped the records, hauled Keegan out on the floor, and challenged and brow-beat him into dancing with her, not losing the beat, remembering it in his head, receiving it through his feet.

He seemed to dance in a dream, stunned by the fantastic discovery of silent music. He was still a good dancer, as graceful in the air as under water.

Halfway through the record, he bent, kissed Cindy on the forehead, went to the stereo, and picked up the record jacket. Once he made sure what song he was feeling, he grabbed for me.

"Don't you try to lead," he cautioned.

I didn't. We danced a two-step, walking on the music.

"A good excuse to get closer to you," Keegan murmured, his arms tightening. I closed my eyes, not resisting Ken's nephew. Our hearts bumped together.

"How did you two know I danced?"

Lips on my cheek, Keegan could whisper to me, but I could not reply. That was fortunate, considering his question. He didn't yet know I'd met Mary Ann.

He went on, "You're lovely. Not because you resemble

anyone else, or because you can help me. You're lovely as you. Leslie, I have to warn you, if you don't want a deaf man—and I'm deaf for life; you know—making love to you, you better speak up."

I swallowed, my knees weak, moving with him, wanting him to whisper in my ear forever, making blood beat in my skull, filling me with warm contentment.

"You still listening to me, little ear?"

In answer, all I could do was move one hand from his shoulder onto his neck for a moment, and then into his sun-bleached, salt-stiffened hair. --

Cindy disappeared. Tactfulness? Or resentment that he talked to me alone? I didn't care which. How could I ever have responded to Ken, after I met this young man, this beautiful, heartbreaking man my age, deaf and tender, brilliant and courageous. . . ! Ken was old enough to be my father. Or Keegan's.

When the music stopped, I urged Keegan out onto the porch to cool off; my desires were out-distancing my mental processes. I ached for him and couldn't take my eyes off him. I longed for his baritone voice, already sliding into a drawl, blurring—but I liked being called "Lezlie," and "Sandy" was okay for my sister. At least those were easier to speechread than "Ken" or "Keegan," those so-similar names. Say "Keegan" rapidly, and you'd have "Ken." I couldn't control my imagination. Appalling!

Mary Ann had asked me if I'd ever consider marrying a deaf man. Far, far too early to entertain any thought of that, but. . . I'd met two men who were deafened in their teens. Both were strong, confident, successful men with wives who could hear. The marriages worked. Wives and kids could all sign. The families shared both deaf and hearing society.

"Where do you think Ken went?" Cindy frequently asked. "Why would he stay away so long?"

Every day I grew more curious, too, but Keegan coldly replied, "I don't know. I don't know, and I don't care."

Keegan could make signs for "I" and "don't" and "know," or use the ASL reverse-"know"—his hand flung off his forehead, but the answer was still the same, "I don't know." I began to keep my eyes open for the "freshly-turned earth" of murder mysteries. I stared into the lagoon; I tried to pry open locked doors.

Cindy drew from Keegan a little more information.

"Keegan said he was like me," Cindy boasted. "I fooled you for two whole years, and he fooled the doctors for two weeks that he wasn't deaf. They thought it was medicines or—" she reached for the word—"shock?"

"Yes, shock."

"He got blown 'way up in the air," she mimed, "and broke his legs coming down, and nobody found him for eight hours. He thought he was screaming loud."

So Keegan told her things he didn't tell me: Cindy had a talent for worming facts out of people. I didn't think to ask what she'd told Keegan in exchange. I was too busy marveling at his mastery of her ASL syntax. Already he concentrated on Cindy's sense over her syntax.

There was so much that I wasn't supposed to know, and that Cindy didn't know. Should I tell them everything? Surely Keegan didn't tell her things that neither of them told me.

"Keegan," I ventured, when Cindy was off cooking supper for the five of us, busy in the kitchen, "you say Ken murdered your father, destroyed your mother, and hurt Mary Ann."

"Did he convince you he didn't?"

"No. But he said your father poisoned himself, right in front of everyone, and your mother disappeared. He claims there was a suicide note. . ."

Keegan was silent so long that it frightened me. Finally he said, "If nothing else happens, if we can be peaceful and happy, I want to forget all that. Let me forget, please!"

What could I do but kiss lips for once unresponsive, and postpone my other questions?

On our idyll's sixth day. I found Margaret melting a large candle and struggling to cast from it many tiny candles. It was not my birthday, or Cindy's.

"Keegan's gonna be twenty-two." Margaret said. "He figgers ain't nobody remembers, but ain't no way I kin forget his birthday. I done bake him a cake with the last two eggs we got."

"A birthday party? A rebirthday party; oh, good!"

Cindy, warned in advance, had cooked fudge for her

present to him, and Margaret had made him a shirt. I felt totally left out, with no gift to give, and the meal was already being served. The cake was a surprise for dessert. One thing I knew he wanted, but I didn't know if we could afford that, yet. Me.

Keegan was startled by the chocolate cake bearing twenty-two flickering, crooked, mud-colored candles. "Happy Birthday to You" was sung by three voices and four hands. We gorged on sweets, the only sour note coming after the party, when Keegan and I were rubbing up frosting from the edges of the cake plate.

I'm lucky to have had twenty-one years and five months of hearing," he said. "Cindy had none."

I froze, fingers immobile at my lips.

"Y'know, this will sound maudlin, but it takes a person twenty years to realize life's a fatal condition. Everyone dies, even us. I'm luckier than Cindy, but this is the only life I'll ever have, and all the rest of it—maybe fifty or sixty years—is going to be silent!"

I backed away from him and turned aside, hiding my tears. Keegan followed and caught up with me on the staircase. We sat on the cool wooden steps holding onto one another. I couldn't offer to be his ears for his lifetime—only because my hands were around his neck, his arms were around me, and he was kissing me with the intensity of a man who has discovered he has just three months to live.

That day, Keegan's birthday, was not over before our peaceful idyll ended. Margaret came to me just before bedtime and confessed what they had been hiding.

The "blue gose." That's what her stricken face indicated. I was right. Ken wasn't back, but the "gose" was.

Twice since the men left, she said, the blue face had appeared. On two hot, quiet nights when the three of us upstairs slept hard after swimming and signing, the Deans had seen the ghost.

"Why didn't you TELL us?" I exclaimed.

"An' scare yo' sister, poor lil child?"

Margaret, who'd shown such merriment at the birthday party, now was grim. "I can't hide it no longer, Miss Leslie, and Keegan don' halfway understand my writin'. You

158

'splain it to him."

Rufus added his worries, more about his wife's mental
health than about their safety. The ghost never did
anything, just grinned, but Margaret had fainted last
night.

"Who's doing it? And how?" I cried.

"Ain' nobody doin' nothin'," Margaret objected. "It be
the same face, Mr. Bradford Howell's dead, poisoned face.
Mr. Bradford's still in this house. His bones be buried in
New York State, but his spirit done never left here. It's
seekin' revenge."

I wasn't believing any such explanation, but I reported
to Keegan every word she said. We left Cindy in ignorance,
for now. Keegan offered to sleep on the Deans' couch from
then on, frantic to see the phenomenon. We both swore it
was man-made, but by what man?

That same night, the Deans saw the thing again. Hearing
the ruckus, I hurried downstairs without waking Cindy, and
found the Deans' bedroom lamplit and unhaunted. Margaret
was shaking with a chill, Rufus and Keegan leaning over
her.

"She needs a doctor," Keegan said. "We've got to get
her to a physician."

"Her heart ain' good," Rufus admitted. "Maybe a little
rest is called for. Maybe up at our daughter's in Georgia.
But we can't leave you younguns alone. Supposin' I take
her on up there and come right back? You reckon you kids
be all right for a day or two?"

Of course we would. Cindy was a fine cook, I had ears,
and Keegan would inherit Rufus' rifle. Kneeling by
Margaret's bed, by a Margaret swathed to the chin in
blankets on an eighty-degree night, Keegan managed to
persuade the Deans to leave.

"We need a boat, of course," he said. "I'll swim over
to Okasassa and see if I can find the SIGFORD. I should
have done that a week ago. If she's not there, I'll rent a
rowboat, same as Duane did. You row Margaret back to the
mainland, Rufus, and stay as long as you need to. She
deserves some peaceful rest."

The next morning we persuaded Rufus to accept half our
mutual hoard of cash. I helped Margaret pack, and Keegan
started swimming. We told Cindy only that Margaret had

taken ill and needed a doctor. Cindy's deafness made secrets almost too easy to keep from her.

To my relief, Keegan came back alive, not in the SIGFORD, but in the leaky rowboat. We had some trouble urging Margaret into the little craft. Since it was not built for three people, we couldn't get it back. Once they left, we'd be stuck again without a boat.

Out on the dock in the ten o'clock sunshine, Keegan wound the line from the boat around his hand while Margaret got settled in the stern, her suitcase across her knees like a life-preserver, her feet up on a block of wood to keep them dry. We waved them away.

Keegan began muttering the jingle, "And then they were three."

"Don't you two leave," he joked. "We started with seven people here, then five, now three. Three's fine."

No mention of "two's company, three's a crowd." We needed every one of us. Now mine were the only ears on the island. Two girls and one man. . . and my baby sister must be protected.

Lazying on the porch that noon, Keegan said, "In Okasassa, I tried to talk to several people I once knew; I think what they said was Rauenbauer had claimed his Buick and drove away, but no one saw either Ken or the SIGFORD."

"NO one?" The old terror rose in my throat again. "You did communicate okay?"

"Only when the answer came as a nod or shaken head. I didn't catch more than a few words . . . not with the accent in this county! And no one came up with anything to write on, those who COULD write!"

"You need. . ." but and I couldn't say it.

"I need my own pad and pencil, like Cindy's. I know it. When I'm not swimming someplace, I'll carry a pad. My ego can stand it now."

"Did you tell anyone we . . . we have problems out here?"

"No. Our problems we have to solve ourselves, you and me. One of these nights, someone's going to bite off more than he can chew, and get it shoved down his blasted throat!"

Cindy slept with me in my big bed that night, because I said I was nervous with the Deans gone.

I was busy thinking. What was going on? Someone wanted us off the island, or perhaps wanted everyone gone except Keegan and Cindy and me. Why? To launch an invasion and take over the place? Again, why? What was of value? Well, the books. Rauenbauer said the old books he was appraising would bring a lot of money. He had to appraise them for probate. I gave some thought to wills and estates and probate . . . Inheritance . . . and inheritance taxes.

Keegan had no money, he said. The Army disability pay was a pittance. But once he got the house and the island, he'd have inheritance taxes to pay. An uncle of mine was once caught in that bind. I remembered hearing that he had to sell a house he inherited just to pay the state and federal inheritance taxes.

Keegan might lose everything—lose both house and island if the taxes were enormous. How fast would he have to find a buyer, and did anyone want a haunted house on an inaccessible lagoon? It sure wasn't tourist territory. The books he could part with, though. Sell them to pay the inheritance taxes, and he'd keep his home.

So much for sleeping, that night. I turned over and brooded on another topic. I began thinking about the ghost. My bet was that whatever it was would keep to pattern and appear in the Deans' room downstairs, where Keegan had stationed himself as watchman. Maybe tonight he would finally see the blue face, before something drove it away.

I was wrong. The ghost visited us.

When the memorable blue glow crept under my eyelids, I awoke, but Cindy didn't. The blue light proved less effective in awakening her than her alarm-clock flasher; her head was almost buried in the feather pillow, and she daintily snored.

The grinning face I squinted up at was the same, no less horrible the second time around.

I put a hand over Cindy's eyes, pulled the sheet off her, and slid out of bed with her nested in my lap as if we were spoons. I couldn't explain, and her giggle reassured me that she took this as some game. I got our feet on the floor and pushed her to and through the door, keeping her eyes shielded.

In our similar, flowery Mother Hubbard gowns we ran downstairs to the Deans' bedroom. We burst in on Keegan, finding him awake and half clad. Instantly he read the fright on my face—by flashlight. We shushed Cindy. No sound and no lights on. Cindy's confusion as she dragged on me, spelling into my palm, "What? What?" was short-lived. Suddenly the Deans' bedroom glowed blue, and there, against their ceiling, lengthening and widening, the hideous face vibrated like protoplasm

Keegan and Cindy didn't stand frozen beside me. They ran to the window, Keegan jerking Cindy behind him so neither would be seen. I reached the window while the narrow blue beam was still splaying the face-pattern on the ceiling. It originated from a spot of light, which resembled a distant automobile with one blue headlamp.

"I'll kill him! It's Ken!" Keegan choked in a whisper. He readied the rifle on the windowsill and thrust the unlit flashlight at me.

"Shine that on the source."

"No," I whimpered. "No, Keegan, Ken's your—" But he couldn't hear me. I had to flip the flashlight back on and intersect the blue beam.

In the pale yellow glow was a man's figure, crouching.

He leaped to his feet. Keegan's rifle cracked, and glass tinkled. Keegan fired again. He emptied the rifle, but the last shots went awry. I'd shoved the barrel up, trying to ruin his aim.

"What d'ya hear?" he demanded.

A crashing in the trees told me someone was retreating fast, but I had no time to spell to Keegan.

He bolted. Keegan dropped the empty rifle and hurdled the windowsill. With the flashlight, he ran into the trees. Cindy and I headed for the back door.

Just as Cindy switched on the kitchen light and made her assessment: "A bad, bad movie!", Keegan returned.

"I hope you're happy you let him escape," Keegan snapped. Stamping into the kitchen, he threw down on the counter a slide-projector, its long snout of lenses shattered. He pulled out a slide of a blue face. Above the serial number of the machine was scratched the name "Ken Howell."

"KEN did that?" asked Cindy.

"I . . . don't know," I signed.

"You DO know!" Keegan snarled. "Look, it has his blasted name on it! He's a photographer! This slide looks like some painting of a face . . . and he saw my father die. Blue in the face! From drinking potassium cyanide. From his darkroom. Who else saw Dad die? Who else would do this? Set up a battery-operated projector—" He punched at the machine. "You fell for Ken, so you protect him."

He refused to look at my answer; he ran upstairs with Cindy and I at his heels. From my room we could see a spot of light faint on the beach. Keegan leaned on the window frame and cursed.

"Comes in a small boat, probably towed by the SIGFORD. When it's calm, with little surf. Calm and hot when everyone's blinds are open on this side of the house. No wonder Ken put you in this room."

"Why would he . . . ?"

"Look at the results. He's scared the Deans away. He could've scared you off even before that, but you hung on.

"That's crazy, Keegan! Ken wants me here. He didn't even want me going to Gainesville—"

I stopped myself, but he wasn't watching my hands, anyway.

163

"Now there's only three of us left and two of us deaf," he hissed. "You wanna leave?"

I shook my head emphatically.

"I won't leave. If I give up the house, it'll be my own decision. No one's going to run me off this island."

I could argue no further. Everything contradicted my assumptions. Ken wanted Keegan weaned from the island. I was supposed to accomplish that. Why the scare-tactic of the ghost, night after night, both while Ken was here and after he vanished?

Before we went back to bed, I tried to cool Keegan's anger.

"It might not have been Ken out there. And even if it was Ken, or his man, you cannot shoot and kill a person, Keegan! That's murder, or at least manslaughter. I had to stop you."

"You think I'm still mentally in Southeast Asia, don't you?" he said. "Maybe I am. Maybe I'm off my rocker. Only because Cindy shouldn't witness a murder—"

I got my good-night kiss, a brief one.

"What we need is a big, fierce dog to roam the place," I said.

"Yeah," He conceded, "now that Dad's. . . My dad was allergic to animals."

Life had to go on, and everything was normal, again— For thirty-six hours, anyway.

We resumed sign language studies. Now Keegan complained that in the dark, sign language was useless. I quickly showed him how to read fingerspelling in his palm. Cindy and I often communicated that way under the covers, after lights out at night.

"Hey," said Keegan, "You could reach me this way even if I went blind!"

"Don't think such a thing!" I cried. Helen Keller might be the patron saint of deaf people, but how they dreaded blindness! Some very heavily insured their eyes.

I was glad Keegan could face such ideas, though. He'd enjoyed Cindy's story of the boy and girl at her school who both wore dual hearing aids. They couldn't take the aids off to neck because without them wouldn't hear anyone approaching, but left on, the four cords got tangled. Cindy's acute sense of the comic buttressed her sanity.

164

Signing day and night, never writing, we had our student as proficient in eight days as I'd been after eight months of study. His motivation, however, was more than thirty times greater than mine.

On the third night after we shot the slide projector dead, we were all back in our three separate rooms on the top floor. I still withheld the gift of myself that I longed to give Keegan, and withheld information about Mary Ann's marriage. Rufus hadn't returned. That night I failed in my role as listener for the others; I failed tragically.

In the middle of that hot night, voices downstairs made me sit up in bed, astonished. A radio was on? For whom? My watch said one o'clock. I sprang out of bed, left my room, and heard nothing through Cindy's closed door. In a thin little shift pulled over my nakedness, I descended to the second floor, past Keegan's open door and empty room.

I saw light, white light, on the lower flight of stairs, making a silohuette of Keegan. He stood on the stairs, rifle in his hands, his head turned aide. Three brilliant beams were shining full in his face.

My feet on the landing must have been visible to those in the living room, because two of the beams swung up and blinded me.

"A broad!" a man's voice cried. "The deaf kid, or the sister?"

"That ain't no little kid!" another one said, and whistled.

Keegan turned his head further, saw me, and snapped, "Get back upstairs! Get her and go hide. Now! Run!"

I couldn't move.

"They aren't armed," Keegan yelled. "I can hold them here. Run, before they—"

"Who are they? Who are you?" I called down.

Rough voices laughed. The lights moved enough for me to make out six bare feet on the floor. Three men, young, by their voices. Faces were invisible behind the glaring flashlights.

Keegan dared not turn to face me. He already needed more than two hands to hold the rifle and shield his eyes, and he stood only ten steps above them.

"Get the hell out of here!" he shouted. "Get out, or

you'll be shot! I'm warning you!"

The men muttered among themselves. They'd expected to awaken and confront me, not meet an armed deaf man.

I retreated a few steps, but I couldn't run hide and leave Keegan there, aiming at targets he couldn't hear or even halfway see.

Keegan's brave insults continued. "Shove off, you dirty louses! Scram!"

One offered to throw something at Keegan. My hearing this did Keegan no good at al.

The beams jiggled wildly, and something came sailing through the air. He ducked it. A heavy book. A second book struck the rifle aside, and a bullet slammed into the wall. Then the men stormed the high ground, and fell upon Keegan. He lost his rifle.

"Like takin' candy from a baby!" one chortled.

"Sure talks big fer a blind kid!"

"Deaf! He's deaf," corrected another, laughing.

I descended, furiously screaming, "Leave him alone! Don't hurt him!" Then I retreated, fearing for Cindy's safety, now I saw them—big men with nylon stockings over their faces . . . fish-flat pale faces, their features deformed. They wore work pants and sweat-soaked tee shirts.

"Don't hurt him!" I cried. "He's handicapped!"

"This yer babe?" one taunted Keegan, grasping his chin to yank his head around. "Gun big as yew are!" "This yer playmate?" "She done woke him up!" And they snickered.

Keegan, boxed against the bannister, continued to curse them. One man, with an open hand, coolly slapped Keegan across the face. Not much harder than Cindy had slapped him for "deaf-mute," but how utterly humiliating. They were playing cats and mouse, watching his reactions.

As for me, I didn't retreat fast enough. One man lunged, projecting his body up the stairs. He managed to seize my ankle. Without doing Keegan one bit of good, staying too near for too long, I was hauled down the steps, bump, bump, bump, on my rear, fighting to keep my skimpy garment over me.

"Boy, ain't she a ripe little peach?" asked my captor. "No wonder Ken Howell wants her!"

Keegan couldn't hear that, but he saw where one man

nonchalantly cupped his free hand.

"He'll just halfa sit here, tied up, and watch us take his ole books," one said.

"And her, too," another added.

That suggestion must have relaxed a few muscles, because Keegan suddenly was free and springing at us. A karate-chop across the larynx threw my tormenter backwards, choking. A death-blow, if ever I'd felt the breeze from one!

". . . play rough fer a deafie!" was all I heard before the man with the rifle swung it like a bat, swatting Keegan across the back of the head. Keegan sailed face-first down the steps to crash at the bottom. Their flashlights found him lying crumpled on his side.

"You've killed him! Murderers! Murderers!" I shrieked. No one was holding me. I slid down the stairs and crouched over Keegan, feeling warm wetness in his hair.

"You've killed him!"

It was real hysteria, first-time, screaming hysterics. Agony. My insides were being dragged up out of my throat in screams. I couldn't stop screaming, because I loved him.

"Get out! Get us a doctor! Send him a doctor! He's dying!"

Keegan hadn't stirred.

The men surrounded me, arguing, the injured one still bent double, gasping and clutching his throat. Their words got tangled in my screams.

"You've broken his neck! Killers!"

They didn't touch me again or bother Keegan; muttering "police" and "murder rap" and "no guns, he said," they crowded toward the open front door.

"Don't hang this on US!" "Ken Howell sent us!" were the last words I heard.

Dragging with them their damaged colleague, they left. They took the light with them. I was no longer screaming, just keening over Keegan in the dark, my fingers blindly examining his head and vertebrae—the crucial chain of bones from skull to hips.

I felt around for a lamp, listening to a boat's engine reving in the lagoon. No moonlight to see out. Inside, in lamplight, I discovered blood on the back of Keegan's skull where skin split against the bone. Move him? Did I dare? Could I budge a man considerably heavier than I?

In the kitchen I got a wet cloth. To revive him, I bathed his face with it, and laid it over the back of his neck. He moaned. He moved one arm, and I knew the spinal cord was intact in his neck. Carefully, I rolled him onto his stomach and spoke comfort into his ear—forgetting, always forgetting, that he could not hear me. He did feel my hands on his naked back.

"Leslie?" he mumbled, "where are they? Are you. . . ?"

Resting the heel of my hand on the floor by his face, I spelled, "Gone."

He sighed. I moved my hand down over his jeans to his ankle and squeezed. He moved his foot. Thank you, God.

"I'm okay," he panted. When he tried to pull up to hands and knees, I pressed him down. I spelled more words to him; this time, "Back hurt?"

"I hurt all over, but no bones seem to be. . .broken."

This time he did pull himself up off the floor. He had his own terrors.

"What'd they do to YOU? How long was I out?"

"Nothing! Nothing!" my hands said, flung out from my chin.

Keegan's eyes were as frantic as my screams had been. His searching hands explored my body. He glared an unspeakable question at me till my lopsided smile made his scowl lessen.

"True? They let you alone? And Cindy, too? That's too good to be—" He pulled me against him.

I loosened his grip enough so I could sign to him.

"They thought you might be dead. I was shrieking. One of them said, 'no murder rap.' They ran. I heard a boat. They were burglars, Keegan, not killers or. . . rapists."

He snorted. "They could've done anything to us. They took my rifle, I bet, the rifle I should've used on them. But you said quit assaulting people!"

"Three was too many, even if you had a gun."

"A deaf guy against three hearing guys. Go ahead and say it!"

We went out onto the porch, Keegan weaving a little and holding the back of his head. We walked barefoot on gritty footprints, gazing at the black lagoon.

"I heard their boat leave, but I didn't see what it looked like."

"Sound like the SIGFORD?"

"I dunno."

Our feeble flashlight beam traced their progress from the dock to the house. They'd jimmied the front door. Keegan had surprised them before they'd unshelved more than a dozen books—very old, thick books with gilded edges.

One thing I still withheld from Keegan—their mention of Ken's name.

Cindy was thumping downstairs at last, rubbing her eyes. The sight of blood in Keegan's hair sent her running back upstairs again.

"Let's tell Cindy that you fell and hit your head, Keegan. Shall we?"

"Nope. No more discrimination against anyone deaf. Our Cindy's in this up to her eyebrows, too." He glared at me. "Please tell me everything that happened," he prodded. "every single word they said."

"Well, they did. . .they did use Ken's name twice, Keegan. . ." Keegan managed to swallow his retort; Cindy was back.

"I sleep too hard!" Cindy complained, marching up to him with a bottle and a wad of cotton in her hands. "I didn't help!"

Keegan bent his head to let Cindy frown into his hair and dab his wound with alcohol-soaked cotton until he grunted and pulled away.

"Losing the rifle was bad," he said. "We can't stay here completely unarmed."

"You have another rifle," I said. "Out in your lean-to."

"That old thing's not been fired in a year. It's a 22, just good to threaten with. But all I did was threaten, didn't I?" he added bitterly. "If you hadn't scared them off . . ."

"You think you have a concussion?"

"Probably, but it won't slow me down much."

"Were they robbers?" Cindy asked.

"They wanted my books. Ken's stealing them. Ken scared off the Deans, leaving just us, then sent in his men. He risked their dealing with Leslie. He figured I'd stay asleep, but the whole damn house rocked under their tread!"

Cindy got a kick out of staying up the rest of the night. We put out the lights so we wouldn't be sitting ducks, and I made cocoa by the refrigerator light and the stove's blue propane flames. Keegan armed himself with a knife and a fireplace poker, but we didn't expect anyone to come back that night. Maybe Ken himself would come next time, to make sure the job was done right.

"Did you ever have burglars before?" I asked. "Since Rufus took pot-shots at trespassers, I figured—"

"Trespassers, yes. Rufus assumes the books are worth a fortune, and the locals are all bent on cleaning us out."

"The books are worth over fifty thousand dollars," I said.

"Where'd you hear that?"

"From Rauenbaucher."

"I had no idea! Worth fifty grand! No wonder . . !"

Keegan's pointed remark about discrimination toward deaf people persuaded me at last to tell him everything. When every detail of my trip to Starke was out in the open, he sat wide-eyed.

"Keegan? Are you upset Mary Ann got married? And so very promptly?"

"No. I'm glad she's happy and cared for. I don't wish her ill, even though she left me with no farewell. Hell, I might not be able to accept a deaf wife. What amazes me is that you'd go all the way up there, secretly, take all that on you. I've never even been to Starke. And back then, you must've been furious at me!"

I answered him with a kiss, and then tried gently to explain Ken's destruction of Mary Ann's "Dear John" letter.

I said, "Anyone would hate to let a message like that get through to you, Keegan. No one should open another person's mail, but he was concerned about—"

"Quit making excuses for Ken! He does NOT mean well!" Suddenly he added, "Leaving a lover because you can't cope with his deafness is saner than its opposite."

I did not grasp what he meant. Not then.

"Ken feared you'd be crushed. . . ."

170

"Quit defending him!" He glared. "Suppose—" and the next words were said without signs, for my ears only. "—suppose his burglars had gotten hold of Cindy?"

We took turns napping after the sun came up. Our sweet paradise had become a fort, unarmed and undermanned. Where was Rufus, gone three days now? Keegan could ferry us to the mainland, one at a time in the rowboat, but what then? We had no car, no money, and no phone numbers. Besides, what could we expect either Duane or the Deans to do for us?

Cindy remained calmer than we, because she missed meeting our uninvited guests. She compared us to the family in THE DIARY OF ANNE FRANK, Jews hiding from Nazis. I'd helped her get through Anne's book last Christmas vacation. Of course we had only criminals, not a whole military machine after us.

"But we're like Anne and her sister, and we've got a handsome young man. . . and we can't leave the island, and Leslie loves Keegan. . ."

How could I hide it from those piercing eyes?

"And Keegan . . ."

She didn't finish. Love? Already? I knew Keegan was at least frantic for my safety, so worried now, in fact, that the lessons stopped for the whole day, and he sat brooding like a blond leprechaun on a toadstool, his chin on his fist.

I awoke from a nap to find Keegan and Cindy sitting on the rug below me, silently and emphatically signing. I did not eavesdrop—eye-drop?—though I was tempted. They ceased the moment they saw me stretch and yawn. Keegan's glum face, a sense that his healing self-image had been wounded anew by those thugs, made me vocal.

"It wasn't your ears at fault," I said. "You couldn't see them well enough. I couldn't, either. They could've thrown a book at anyone to disarm him."

He didn't want to discuss it. He waved away my signs.

"You sacrificed yourself to keep me from being hurt. You nearly killed one of them, and they were huge men, big lugs hired to carry off—"

He withdrew his gaze from me, chopping off all communication like a hearing person's sticking fingers in his ears. Cindy shook her head at me irritably.

171

I rapped on the floor to retrieve Keegan's attention.

"I admire you for holding a gun on them! You were wise, and you were brave!"

Cindy rose to her knees. "Shut up!" she signed. "You talk too much!"

I was appalled. What did she know that I didn't? Angry but chastened, I put my nose in a magazine; if Keegan and Cindy wanted to cut me out of the conversation, okay. Swell!

By twilight, I began to shiver as if I were coming down with the flu, but it wasn't that. We'd reached no decision on what to do. And I expected more visitors.

We had visitors.

I heard an engine. An engine, here, could only mean a boat was nosing into our lagoon. I signed the alarm. "A boat! A boat!"

It was not the SIGFORD, but a military-looking cruiser larger than the SIGFORD, painted two shades of blue-gray. Its name was the MANTA.

It headed right for our dock, and bumped it raspingly.

"Fool didn't cut his engine in time," Keegan snorted.

Three men climbed out onto the dock, and two of them waved at us. One was short and wide; the second thick and tall, the sunset making silver coins of his spectacles. Rauenbauer. The third was a young man with black hair, who tied up the boat.

"Miss Fallon!" Baker Johnson, though he was puffing the hardest, was the first to greet us. "Can you interpret for Keegan? Splendid! Wonderful what you've accomplished. Look at her hands fly! Geoff, introduce us; she probably doesn't remember me at all. Is this the little sister?"

Geoffrey Rauenbauer mumbled introductions and let us know that Pete Brokaw, the young man, owned the big boat.

"What do you want?" Keegan asked.

"Leslie, tell him we have good news for him at last." Johnson smiled. "Leslie can guess what it is!"

"Please talk directly to Cindy and Keegan. I'll interpret. Don't talk just to me." Their revelations were delayed to teach them some manners.

Baker Johnson turned to speak toward Cindy, letting me give her the words. "I heard how pretty you are, my dear. And such a good teacher, too, at your age!"

Rauenbauer didn't do so well; from him we got the idiotic line, "Did you teach Keegan Braille?"

Johnson seemed a lot smarter than Rauenbauer, and I regreted my bigotry against very fat men. Pete examined me so boldly with his nice-looking blue eyes that he reminded me of Ken.

"Ken Howell hasn't come back, yet, has he?" Rauenbauer asked.

173

me of Ken.

"Ken Howell hasn't come back, yet, has he?" Rauenbauer asked.

"YOU tell US where he is," said Keegan.

No reply. They wanted iced tea. Cindy, playing hostess, offered to make it. She scurried off to the kitchen. The sun was below the horizon, but it was still warm, and the men's faces were reddened from sun and stinging salt air. I heard ice cubes crashing into the sink.

"Wellll!" Johnson sank into a deep chair—deeper with him in it. His exhalation reminded me of a deflating basketball. "Well, we have good news tonight, as the man said. Welcome news for Keegan."

"What news?" Keegan leaned forward, perched on a chair-arm, up higher than the other men.

"Your mother. I finally hired us a detective, and he traced her," said the attorney.

Keegan sprang to his feet. "Where? How is she?"

"Just a minute now, son." Johnson waved him back. "It's a long story. Let's take first things first. She's here in Florida. She's been ill."

Behind Johnson's shoulder I was stationed, to flick words across to Keegan. I was bug-eyed.

"She's had a small stroke—sit down, Keegan—and I haven't had the heart, yet, to tell her you're deaf."

Keegan's mouth twitched. The cross he bore was not only heavy but unmentionable. He subsided onto the arm of the chair again. His lips tasted the bitter word. "A. . . stroke, you said?"

Johnson resumed his drawl. "You can go see her, son, but not immediately. It's got to be broken to her gradual. She thinks you're just now back from Asia, and that you're still angry at her."

"Oh, Lord! How is she now? Is she paralyzed?"

"She's okay. She's pretty young, and it was a nervous stroke. A little one. Spasmotic hypertension."

My hands stumbled on those big words. "Just a little weakness is left. You know what she's gone through since last Fall. Her only problem now, besides wanting to see you, is her brother-in-law."

"He's everyone's problem!" sneered Keegan.

"I thought if we started with you just writing her a

letter . . ."

Keegan headed for the writing desk.

"Wait, wait, son. There's plenty of time. We'd like to spend the night here. Is that all right with you folks? Mr. Rauenbauer had to leave here in a hurry. Under duress. He needs time to pack his things, and it'll be dark by then. We had the devil of a time finding the way into the lagoon, with him guiding us, and that was in daylight."

Keegan shrugged. "Sure, we can accommodate an army. But talk about my mother. Where is she?"

"I hate to alienate a boy from his own uncle," Johnson irrelevantly continued. "I've heard about yours and Ken's confrontations. I'm a family-man myself, and I like to see respect for the older generation, but—"

"What's he done now?" Keegan pressed.

"Well," Johnson looked helplessly at Rauenbauer, "Ken Howell has your mother so harried and frightened—"

"Did he know where she was and keep it from me? All that time?"

"Afraid so, son. She said he was on her trail. He knew she ran off to Norway (what a place to spend a winter!), then returned to the States. he knew the hospital she'd been in after she'd had her stroke."

"That . . . that LOUSE!"

"I hate to see anyone so angry, but can't say as I blame you."

It was hard to be a good interpreter—to keep my reactions to myself with no raised eyebrows, no embroidery. Just the men's words, stressed with their emphasis, not mine.

"I brought you a letter from her. You shouldn't just take my word for it." Johnson hunted through his pockets. "We visited her where she's recovering from tests and surgery for an aneurism in an artery. We said that you were on the island, that you had been wounded slightly and sent home. She wrote you this letter."

He extended a folded paper to Keegan, and even before opening it, Keegan let me know I could come read over his shoulder.

Immediately I recognized Sigrid's pretty script, erect and peaked.

Dear Keegan,

It is a shock to hear you are back in this country and
injured. Ken lied about you. He's harried me about the
country until I've become ill. I can't come home until I'm
released after this surgery, but you come to me, Dear.
Brad's lawyer, Baker Johnson, will bring you. He and his
friend have been trying to save the estate for you. Please
trust them. They're protecting you.

I'm sorry to be so weak that I've worried myself sick,
but I'm afraid Ken was involved in your father's death, as
you suspected. He said if I did not marry him, he'd hurt
you and steal the books.

Please come as soon as you can. Bring your new girl and
her sister.

I love you.
Mom

It was dated three days ago.

"I want to see her. Right now! Tomorrow." Keegan's
fingers unconsciously stroked the paper, smoothing it and
resmoothing it on his jean-clad knee.

"Write to her. Let Leslie and Cindy take her your
letter. After they break the news to her, tell her how
well you're doing, you can go see her."

"Let us, Keegan," I interjected, thinking of what Ken
put Mary Ann through. "Let us see her first. She's ill!"

"Okay," he sighed. "But if I'm to be patient, at least
I want to know exactly where she is."

"Let's keep that vague a little longer, son," the
lawyer cautioned. "If you don't know, you won't jump the
gun. I don't want to put an additional burden of self-
control on such young shoulders."

Keegan was distracted for only an instant when Cindy
offered him and then me glasses of iced tea from her tray.
She cocked a brow interrogatively at me, seeing our grave
faces.

"My fingers buzzed out, "Sigrid's found. She's in
Florida."

Cindy let the tray sag, then caught it, unable to reply
with both hands occupied. She served Rauenbauer last,
having never adopted standard etiquette. She followed her
personal protocol, and fed people in order from the most

to the least favored.

Keegan said, "I'll go with them, at least stay nearby. Let Cindy and Leslie see her first, then maybe I can talk to her doctor, get clearance from him." He looked miserably embarrassed.

Johnson whirled the ice cubes in his glass. "Maybe that's satisfactory. If you stayed the night in . . . in that city and met her the following day—day after tomorrow—it might not hurt."

"Let's go!" Keegan cried.

"Not until tomorrow morning," Rauenbauer objected. "I am not a well man, and I've been badly mistreated. Ken Howell struck me. I need a night's rest, and I must pack—"

Keegan nodded impatiently, as I studied our three guests. One egotistical, sick old man; one ugly, fat, middle-aged man; one silent, leering young man. I must not judge so much by appearances, I told myself firmly. Could I have been so patient with Keegan if he'd turned out to be an acne-studded, wimpy kid instead of a handsome athlete? Still, I gave thanks for Cindy's blonde beauty; it would be a big plus all her life.

We offered each of our visitors a bedroom on the second floor. While Pete fetched their bags from the MANTA, Cindy and I headed upstairs to prepare rooms.

Keegan surprised me on the stairs. He spoke in silent signs, right in front of the two older men.

"I saw Rauenbauer pop a pill with his tea. Get those capsules you showed me. I want to try something."

Keegan helped make up two extra beds. Then we went to Rauenbauer's old room. Before the men came upstairs, before the ascending tromp of footsteps reached us, Keegan dropped one of my big capsules on Rauenbauer's cluttered bureau. He handed me back the vial with the other green and black capsule, and loitered in Rauenbauer's doorway.

I fussed around, waiting for Keegan, ignoring the silent young man who had captained the boat and now tagged after me.

They'd had supper, Johnson said, and wanted to turn in early. Good night. We three rushed up to the third floor to compare notes.

"Guess what?" Keegan whispered. "He lighted on your

capsule right away. I glimpsed him when he picked it up. He took out a vial and popped it in. It was HIS medicine."

"Really?"

"Yeah. He didn't see me watching. Must be pretty expensive stuff he doesn't want to lose, if he risked betraying himself."

"That means Ken didn't do it, then. Ken didn't try to sedate me to death." Relief was visible on my face.

"It means Ken filched the capsules from that old goat to give to you, Leslie. Use your head! If you don't want to suspect Ken, who did you think gave you the pills? ME?"

I nodded. "Sure. You wanted me out of here, Keegan, and it was Margaret who brought them to me—Margaret, your only close buddy."

Keegan was already on edge, frustrated. I should have kept quiet.

"Leslie!" he slapped his jean-clad thighs in furious exasperation. "I'm just deaf, not criminal!"

"And I was a tutor, not a kept woman!"

He put his hands into his hair, shaking his bent head.

"Okay, okay. Let's not scream at each other. I'm sorry. You had a right to suspect me—at first. I treated you rotten. But now. . . I'm getting paranoid—probably a common affliction of deaf people, huh?"

I put my hand in his. He kissed me lightly, and we stood with our foreheads touching, our hands clasped tightly, anger melting out of us.

Tomorrow would answer . . . would have to answer so many questions.

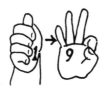

By dawn, Cindy and I were as nervous as Keegan. My hand
was shaking when Baker Johnson, all smiles, put into it a
business card.

"Robin's Nest Convalescent Home," it said, in—of all
places!—Gainesville, Florida!

We were all set to go. Cindy's parakeet got enough food
and water to last it three days, and by seven a.m., all of
our suitcases were on board the MANTA.

Pete, the helmsman, kept gazing soulfully at me, but
ignoring Keegan. He was so leery of Keegan that he
rendered himself mute. Johnson had a sudden suggestion to
make, concerning Pete Brokaw.

"Let's have Pete leave us off at Okasassa and then go
right back to the island," Johnson said. "He can guard the
place. You mentioned you had prowlers recently. That place
shouldn't stand empty. As Bradford's attorney, I do advise
that you keep someone there at all times."

I didn't remember mentioning our masked invaders, but
Keegan agreed. Yes, let Pete play guard; but, Keegan
asked, did Pete have a gun?

"I don't believe in firearms," Johnson said. "Weapons
usage sure makes attorneys rich, but they scare me—I was
accidentally shot in the leg as a child. Besides, it's
manslaughter to bring in the corpse of a mere trespasser.
Their posting Rufus Dean as a sharpshooter was dangerous
lunacy."

We disembarked at the Okasassa dock, and got into the
Buick. We continued inland with Rauenbauer unfortunately
but necessarily at the wheel. At Cross City, Baker Johnson
mentioned pressing business—including Howell business—
waiting for him up in Tallahassee.

We cheerfully offered to take the bus the rest of the
way to Gainesville. Let Rauenbauer chauffeur Johnson to
Tallahassee. Rauenbauer said he needed to go up there to
file the completed appraisal of the books. On a bus, we'd

179

reach our destination in no time at all.

In Okasassa, Keegan had picked up the mail. Not a word from Rufus or Margaret Dean. In Cross City he took us with him to his bank to cash a pile of disability checks.

When the pretty bank teller smilingly asked Keegan for his driver's license, he caught that phrase on her lips. He fished out his wallet and showed her his license.

"It's expired, Sir. May I see some other identification, please?" She was still batting her eyelashes enough to make me feel jealous.

He squinted at her scarcely moving lips. "What?

Was it preferable to sign to him in front of all these watching people, or to tip off the bank teller?

"He's deaf," I murmured, and saw her face go blank. Then she actually backed away from Keegan.

"I can interpret," I said.

Hearing that, of course she moved nearer to me and talked only to me, watching Keegan with pitying anxiety.

"Needs other identification," I told Keegan.

Social Security card, military identification card, credit cards, abruptly, he thrust them at the woman. Scowling.

"In what denominations does he want—?" She seemed really scared of him now.

"Twenties!"

She dealt him his twenties with the jerky motions of a keeper feeding a tiger through cage bars.

Thus began Keegan's initiation into what people call The Hearing World.

I began my little homily right outside the bank. "She didn't understand deafness, Keegan; she was afraid to embarrass you . . ." Cindy stilled my hands.

"He KNOWS that, Dumbie!"

Stung, I tagged along behind them, on our way to the bus station. Suddenly, Cindy punched Keegan, held out her hand for a contribution, and when he caught on, she took the coins and dashed into a five-and-dime store. Keegan followed her. She came back with him in an instant, flourishing candy bars for each of us.

"Speed!" she spelled. "Smile and point. Fool them. Never talk, or THEY'll talk."

On the bus everyone stared at our busy hands. I was

speaking without voice, but Keegan talked audibly for my benefit. Since his was the only voice that people heard, they assumed that he could hear. I planned it that way, hoping to ease his embarassment, but my plan failed.

A man leaned across the aisle and whispered to Keegan, "Are them pretty young girls both DEAF?"

That wasn't speech-readable, so I had to give our game away. Keegan was learning too fast how it feels to be judged "handicapped," "unfortunate," or worse. He cringed. At the next stop he bought himself a paperback book and buried himself in it until Gainesville.

Cindy made sure he kept his word to let us meet Sigrid first. She led Keegan into a restaurant, her fierce signs preventing any rebellion. "You wait here. You promised!"

When we saw him wavering, Cindy made the ultimate sacrifice. She groaned, "I'll stay with you!"

I left them sitting tensely side by side in a booth. I went by myself, solo, to find Sigrid in the Robin's Nest Convalescent Home. It wasn't far away, that small, yellow stucco building not far from the University. I walked up the red brick path, entered the lobby, and asked for Mrs. Sigrid Howell.

I wasn't gone long. All the way back to the restaurant to find my sister and Sigrid's son, my stomach quivered in response to my dread.

Keegan spotted me immediately, and sprang to his feet.

"How is she? Did you see her? When do I see her?" He came right out of the booth to interrogate me in the crowded aisle. I had to push him back into the booth to let a waitress past. His voice rose, became too loud from nervousness. "TELL ME, LEZLIE!"

"She left there," I signed. Diners all stared at us, alerted by Keegan's excited voice. "They said she was there till two days ago, and then she had to go down to St. Petersburg to another specialist."

"Where in St. Pete? Let's go!"

"Wait a minute! She had tests here at the hospital, then surgery," I told him, watching him ease back into the booth again. Cindy was jiggling up and down on the squeaky plastic seat, eagerly watching our hands.

"Johnson told the truth?" Keegan demanded.

"I think so. She got an angiogram, a brain-scan—"

I carefully spelled the words. What else could I think of to delay my news? More data. "They've got her blood-pressure down, and she's not paralyzed at all."

"Great! Go on!"

Two kids nearby were aping our signs, while the blasted parents grinned at us over their french fries. Though I knew enough to ignore them, Keegan did not. Seeing them, he hissed, "Damned nosy idiots!"

Then he needled me again. "How did Mom get all the way down to St. Pete? By ambulance?"

"She's stronger than that. Strong enough to go in a car, Keegan," I stalled.

"Who took her?" Cindy burst in, assessing my face better than Keegan did.

"The description fit . . . The nurse said he had the same last name as. . . as your mother." That was all he needed. I waited apprehensively for the violence to come.

"Damn!" Keegan struck the table so hard that dishes jumped, and every head in the restaurant came around.

"He's got hold of her! He got there first!"

"Another bus ride?" Cindy asked, ready for any new adventure.

"I'll find her. I'll KILL that louse," Keegan growled. "Johnson told the truth, then. Her handwriting wasn't quite right, so I'd felt a little suspicious, but my uncle's kidnapped her, now. What's this about some doctor in St. Pete?"

"I did get the name of the doctor there. We'll find him; then we'll surely find her, Keegan."

I forced down my half of the superburger Cindy had ordered for us both, while Keegan bolted a coke. His rage at Ken overflowed onto the nosy diners; he glowered at them, stared at people till they looked away. He was deaf to their whispers about "deaf-and-dumb deaf-mutes." The offending children made faces at him.

Outside the cafe, Keegan's next move surprised me.

"Where's Duane Gunlock's drugstore?"

It wasn't far, right on the edge of campus, but we didn't find Duane. Another pharmacist said it was Duane's day off, and he'd be gone on a trip for two additional days.

How disappointing! Duane ought to see the new Keegan, and Keegan needed some distraction to give him time to cool off.

We persuaded Duane's colleague to furnish us Duane's unlisted phone number. In the booth from which I had once phoned Mary Ann's house in Starke, I dialed. Keegan crowded into the booth with me, pulling the mouthpiece up to his chin.

Duane—bless him!—answered on the third ring. Keegan read my face and said, "Duane? This is Keegan Howell. I'm in your drugstore. Any chance of seeing you? Enlisting some help?"

I listened to a long silence, standing there with the receiver stuck against my ear and both hands ready.

"You got your hearing back! Keegan, that's great!"

I anticipated exactly what Duane would say, and my signs followed just one second behind his words.

"You're usin' a PHONE, Keegan! You can HEAR, again!"

"Not THAT much improvement, Duane, but a lot. I'm on the trail of my missing mother. . ."

Duane ordered us to stay put, and hung up with an ear-bursting crash.

Keegan bounced out of that phone booth as bright-eyed as an Olympic medalist. For an instant, I saw him forget Ken, and maybe Sigrid, too. He'd used a telephone, again!

Cindy squeezed him, laughing with delight.

Duane took less than five minutes to get there. Without comment, he stuffed all of us into his Volkswagen and took us straight to his apartment. He thrust a cold beer at Keegan. I grabbed ginger ales for Cindy and me.

Only then did Duane make his announcement.

"Another ten minutes, and you'd have missed me; I was just headin' over to Okasassa to fetch you. . .to go an' see Ken Howell."

When he saw the "KH" sign for Ken, Keegan spilled beer down his collar. Duane tossed him a dish towel without pausing in his explanation.

"Ken was visitin' your Mom at the hospital, and figgered he'd drop in to see me. Said he'd found her only a few days ago, usin' information pried out of that guy Rauenbauer.

"Ken wants your mom to meet Leslie and Cindy," Duane

said. "He took her to St. Pete to another doctor; today I was to head for Okasassa to fetch them and take them to meet him. Fancy all of you showing up here and saving me the trip!"

"Where is my mother?" growled Keegan.

"I'm not sure, but I'm supposed to bring Leslie and Cindy over to the coast, to Cedar Key. The boat'll be anchored off Cedar Key."

"What boat? The SIGFORD?" Keegan demanded.

"No, a yacht, he said. A friend's yacht."

Keegan looked like a watchdog with its hackles rising. "You're helping that louse who's kidnapped my mother? He's hunted her down and threatened her!"

Duane blanched. "Never heard a hint of that," he said. "I never met your mother, but Ken and she— Well, he said she sure liked him. It was . . . mutual."

"I have a letter from her." Keegan's voice was icy. "It's dated four days ago. She says she needs help to escape Ken Howell."

Duane's face changed rapidly from white to red. "Beats me, Keegan. All I know is Ken wants the girls to tell her about your hearing. I mean, your not hearing. She's been in Norway all winter. I didn't hear that you lost your dad last Fall."

"No, Ken wouldn't mention THAT," Keegan said. "He's stealing from me what I'll inherit from Dad. We had to leave a guard on the island. Not to mention that he, himself, murdered my dad!"

Duane shook his head, his honest long face miserable. "God help me, Keegan, the only thing that sounded fishy to me was Ken's saying he couldn't come pick up the girls. Said they might not trust him."

"How astute!" Keegan muttered.

"Do you and Cindy want to go to Cedar Key with me?" Duane asked. "If murder's involved. . . Lordie, what's goin' ON around here?"

Keegan dropped his head into his hands. "I think I'm going insane!"

Handsomely dressed up to meet his mother in gray slacks and the new maroon shirt, if only Keegan felt half as good as he looked!

"I want to go!" Accompanied by sparkling eyes, this

came from Cindy.

I did too. With big Duane as our escort, we'd be protected. Maybe the three of us could free Sigrid—if she needed freeing.

Keegan was busy reading my thoughts, glaring over his beer can at me from his corner of the couch.

Duane kept trying to explain what Ken told him.

"Your uncle's got this buddy with a big yacht, okay? Well, after so much doctorin', said Ken, your mom oughta get some sea air, have a nice cruise. Right? His friend offered use of his yacht. Cedar Key's just an hour or so drive from here. . ."

"Oh, hell!" Keegan stood up. "So my dear uncle is no poisoner, no thief, no kidnapper. He's everybody's hero. I'm going back to the island. You do what you want!"

"Aw, Keegan, don't feel like that!" Duane cried. Then I saw him get an idea.

"Hey, if you won't come with us, Keegan, why don'tcha ride my motorcycle back to Okasassa? It'd sure be more fun than the bus. We can all meet at the island, once the rest of us get there by boat. Then, afterwards, I can ride my motorcycle back here from Okasassa. Clear as mud?"

Moved by this offer, Keegan managed a crooked, fleeting smile. We promised him we'd reach the island just as soon as possible, bringing his mother safely home.

Keegan looked thoroughly worn out and tired of us by the time Duane hammered him fraternally on the back, handing him a shiny blue helmet and a brown leather jacket for the motorcycle-ride to Okasassa.

"Just slam the apartment door behind you," were the last words I made visible to Keegan. Keegan made a wry little salute in farewell, as Duane swept me out the door, his palm warm on my back.

Cindy and I piled into Duane's car. As we drove out of the parking lot, I thought I recognized someone. Was he someone from the restaurant? Or—?

The man sat in a car parked across the street. Just a typical sunburned, skinny, fortyish Floridian, I told myself. I added, "I'm getting more paranoid than Keegan," when the notion hit that he somewhat resembled the beggar who accosted me ten days ago outside my Gainesville motel.

Duane's praise began immediately.

"You've sure done marvels, Leslie. He's like the old Keegan I remember, if he weren't so unhappy about this confusion over his uncle. Hardly notice his eyes flickin' over to you for the signs. How'd he manage to talk on the phone? Bet he thought he'd never use a phone again!"

"Cindy broke through to him. I was just her ears. Keegan's an incredibly fast learner, just as you said. Very few could accomplish what he's done."

Duane's little VW accelerated past ranch-style homes with sprinklers raining on their lawns, past parks and a golf course.

"That memory of Keegan's, wow!" said Duane. "Can he go on in biology, at least do research? Surely with a sign language interpreter. . ."

Cindy stuck her head between us from the back seat and signed "Leslie" (pointing at me) "loves" (wrists crossed passionately on her heart) "Keegan" (pointing back toward Gainesville). Her lips formed the three words accurately.

Then the reverse motions: "Keegan loves Leslie!" her eyes sultry with sentiment.

Even keeping one eye on the road, Duane understood.

"Is that true? Are you already in LOVE with him?"

"I like him very much. Yes, I think I love him!"

"You'd get serious about a DEAF guy?"

"Of course! Look what I can do for him, and he's just marvelous—as you, yourself, told me."

(I failed to translate this conversation for Cindy, who stuck her tongue out at me, pouting.)

"I think you're foolish," Duane said, "but, then, I'm prejudiced. I volunteered to help Ken out mainly for a chance to see you again." He didn't look at me.

"Why don't you question Keegan's loving ME?" I mused.

"But of course he'd love you! You're lovable, Leslie, and you're . . . you're NORMAL."

"Oh!" I gasped, as if struck.

"You'd never consider marriage, would you?" he said, staring ahead down the highway, his lips twitching. "You want just a . . . relationship."

"A late-deafened man will often marry a hearing woman."

"A woman who pities him?"

"A woman who loves him! Pity, indeed!"

"The lady doth protest too much," he said. "See how

186

angry you get? Think about it, Leslie. Would Keegan want you to mistake pity for love? Keegan's too much a man to marry you for your hands."

I sat there furious, with Cindy punching me for an explanation why. Five minutes to control my temper, then I said (and signed), "You don't know how comfortable I feel around deaf people. I wouldn't trade Cindy for any hearing sister in the world. I know Cindy's school friends, I belong to the deaf club, and I'm studying to be a teacher of the deaf."

"I see." He sounded grim. "I see, but I don't like it."

"Who would make him a better wife?"

"He's young, Leslie. I'm still single at twenty-six. Don't rush it."

"He's twenty-two," I persisted, "and he's been through hell—war, killings, tragedy. . ."

Having missed the beginning of this conversation, a puzzled Cindy asked, "Me, a wife for Keegan?"

Wincing, I translated that, and Duane said, "What a good idea!"

"No! Eight years difference in age, and insurmountable differences in talents and knowledge? Oh no!"

With those words I signed, "Keegan's much too old for you, Cindy."

Cindy giggled, startling Duane out of his assumption that she was mute.

He said, "You can handle these family problems of Keegan's? You got any notion what's goin' on between Sigrid and Ken Howell?"

"I'm totally perplexed. Did you keep back anything from Keegan? Anything at all?"

"I'll let you find out for yourself," he muttered.

The rest of that hurried trip was silent, though my hands kept pointing out sights to Cindy: veils of Spanish moss, public shuffleboard courts, "mermaid" spectaculars for tourists, and, further south, wild animal parks.

In an hour and a half we were at the Cedar Key waterfront, looking for a yacht named the SILVEN SEAS.

When we pulled up at the right dock, Duane let out a whoop. "A yacht, huh? Look at that luxury liner! Wowee!"

Ken's buddies owned planes; this pal must be even richer. The SILVEN SEAS dwarfed the SIGFORD, which bobbed beside her. Dozens of portholes opaque in the early afternoon sun . . . a railed forward deck . . . an upper deck under a canopy . . . The great white side rose above Cindy as she ran out on the dock, her face tilted up.

I held my breath as a man left the rail and came bounding down the gangway, arms open wide. It was Ken Howell, snazzy in white duck slacks and a black shirt, and of course a black and white yachting cap.

"Leslie! Cindy! Good work, Duane! You're here ages before I expected you. Gee, it's great to see you again, gals. I've got someone for you to meet!"

Ken's aplomb dazed me. Was this the man I'd feared was dead? The one Keegan kept trying to shoot or stab?

"At last you'll meet Sigrid." he went on.

Then Ken added—now grinning broadly—"Mrs. Howell, that is. Mrs. KENNETH Howell, this time!"

I stood paralyzed with the name half-spelled on my fingers. I stopped after "K-E-N—"

Cindy was stamping her foot for the rest of the words.

Ken had married her! Duane knew, but never told Keegan.

No wonder Ken wanted someone to smooth his way. All I could think was, "Keegan will kill Ken. Keegan will kill him!"

Belatedly, I signed, "He married her!" I kept remembering Sigrid's letter. Had Ken bribed her into cooperating? Drugged her? Controlled her by withholding word of her son? Their son?

Cindy wasn't very enthusiastic about Ken's hug, and here he was, coming for me, his arms spread in greeting.

I ducked his hug.

"No congratulations, Leslie?"

"I dunno what to think," I mumbled.

"You thought I was a hopeless old bachelor at forty-three? But this is what I've been waiting for, Leslie. For such a long, long time."

He motioned Duane and Cindy up the gangway to explore that floating mansion. My sister began touching things, gazing appreciatively at polished teak, shiny brass fittings, cranks and pulleys, rope and canvas. She'd cheerfully accept any luxury people forced upon her.

Ken put a hand on my shoulder, asking, "Can Keegan understand speech, now? He's okay? Is his morale better?"

I let Duane catalog Keegan's successes, but Ken's eyes stayed on me, a puzzled gaze.

"Good . . . good . . . great!" he said. Then, "Leslie, sorry I left without any word, but I practically had to wrestle Rauenbauer out of the house. I dragged him to Okasassa and made him phone Johnson about Sigrid."

"I see," I said, though I didn't.

On deck, we met a dark, wiry man in jeans and tee shirt whom I took to be a crew member until Ken introduced him as Jim Silven. He was a publisher. He and his wife, he said, "sailed north instead of south to help out a buddy."

"Cedar Key's not the direct route from St. Pete to Jamaica, is it, Jim?" Ken kidded him.

Looking at that yacht, I'd thought, "Mafia!" but I liked Jim and Mrs. Silven. She was clad like her husband in rumpled blue denim. They must walk the decks of their wealth instead of wearing it.

"Sigrid's taking her nap," Ken said. "She's not very strong, so I put her down for a before-supper snooze like a toddler."

His words made me dizzy. I'd imagined Sigrid chained hand and foot below decks.

"Look, Leslie, while she's napping, I need some time alone with you. Jim, how about giving Duane and Cindy the royal tour while I have a little chat with Leslie?"

My sister and friend were eager to sightsee. Ken got me alone in the stern of the vessel, where he vainly offered me my choice of refreshments.

"Wine? Coffee? Tea? A glass of water, then?"

I shook my head, refusing to admit I was thirsty.

"I want to thank you for all you've done, Leslie," he began. "Sticking to your work out there with only Keegan and the Deans." He sat leaning forward, mangling his yachting cap between his hands. "Trusting me to come back and pay you, when you had no idea where I'd gone— I couldn't write you and alert Keegan, until . . ." He grabbed my hand, squeezed it, and dropped it before I could pull away. "Leslie, what Keegan's been telling you, what everyone's been telling you about the Howell triangle is untrue."

I parted dry lips, ready to say, "Sigrid's own letter condemned you. SHE should know!" but he rushed on.

"Hear me out. I was dating Sigrid back when we were your age. She and I fell in love. I introduced her to my older brother. Worst mistake I ever made; a capital crime. I graduated from Cornell, got a newspaper job, and went overseas on a long photo assignment, one July.

"Brad was a year older than I, but he'd missed a couple of years of school, being sick all the time—asthma, it was, back then. He started trying to convince Sigrid that he needed her far more than I did. Big-hearted Sigrid—who loves babies, animals, and old folks—was easy prey. Brad badgered her to marry him and save him; he admitted his ills were psychosomatic; he led her to think she could cure him. He gave her a lot of garbage about how rough our father was on him—though I never remember Pop being cruel; he just didn't enjoy having a whiner for a son. Anyway, Brad even threatened suicide if she didn't marry him, which should have made her cautious. It didn't. It made her pity him even more.

"My louse of a brother told Sigrid that I'd phoned him from Europe to say I'd married a French girl. It was an outright, dirty lie, but Sigrid hadn't received any mail from me. Brad got Sigrid's mother to intercept my letters—weekly letters. Her mom didn't much like me.

"Without my letters, Sigrid believed Brad's lies. On the rebound she married him in September. When I heard about it a month later, phoning from Paris to find out why no letters from her had reached me yet, I rushed back, ready to throttle Brad. It was too late."

"Too late? She could have left him."

"She was already expecting a baby—Keegan."

One of my fears was exploded. Ken was in Europe when Keegan was conceived. "Are you telling the truth?" I managed to ask Ken.

"Sigrid will vouch for it. Now that Brad's dead, she needn't protect her liar of a husband. Or her son. Leslie, Sigrid is a person who keeps her vows, no matter how much she regrets them. She took care of Brad for twenty-two years . . . almost to the day!"

"But . . . but—" I protested, unable to break into his fluent flow of facts . . . if they were facts. Ken Howell dressed and spoke too well. It was like watching an actor give a reading.

"Brad hung on her like a second child. In fact, by about the age of eight, Keegan was more mature than his father. Sigrid wouldn't leave a hopelessly neurotic man, and she had no job-skills yet. There was no money. I contributed.

"As Keegan grew up, Brad doted on his son. He managed to be a fairly decent dad, I will admit. No kid ever had more paternal attention and encouragement. Sigrid was a super mother. You've seen the results by now, I hope—

Keegan's self-confidence and his generous affection.

"None of that, of course, got directed towards me. Brad cast me as a menacing villain. You can see why. Brad knew that Sigrid and I still loved each other, and he got her only by deceit. He had to turn Keegan totally against me, make him hate me."

"Why on earth didn't Sigrid tell Keegan the truth about you?"

"Think a minute. That would mean telling Keegan his own father was a filthy liar. She'd have to explain why. She'd ruin a father-son relationship—IF Keegan believed her. If he didn't, then he'd consider her a liar, or worse. At best, the only one to benefit would've been me. I asked her to keep quiet."

"Wow," I whispered.

"Here was Brad, wrapped up in Keegan, knowing his wife didn't love or respect him, though she was so loyal. I pity the poor bastard. His illnesses multiplied, one psychosomatic disease after the other: asthma, dermatitis, colitis. Then he developed emphysema, which he mistook for lung cancer. And he detested doctors!

"Sigrid raised Keegan to be kind hearted like her. He waited on Brad, took care of him, and blossomed with all that loving attention. All their love went to him, not to each other.

"I played fair, Leslie. I didn't see Sigrid for years at a time. I sent them money, which Brad never refused. Sigrid studied to qualify for a job I got her with a printing company. My photography took me all over the world—the way it kept me abroad from July to October of that terrible year when I lost her.

"In Norway, I found another lovely Norwegian girl and married her, but she wasn't Sigrid, and we got a good-natured divorce. I tried to forget Sigrid, but Brad kept losing jobs. I got him started in Florida. He bought my friend's rare-book business so he could work from his bed. Sigrid let him handle all their money, invest in foolish ventures and buy himself luxuries. I kept coming down and straightening out the finances, but Brad convinced Keegan I was behind all his failures."

"When Brad . . . died, she ran away instead of telling Keegan any of the truth?" I asked him.

"You forget. Keegan vanished without warning. We didn't even know he joined the Army. He left because Sigrid wouldn't turn me in to the cops as a murderer."

"Because she loved you."

"Because I'm not a murderer. Brad finally did what he often threatened to do. He killed himself, after brainwashing Keegan into thinking I could murder my own brother."

I was silent, trying to absorb all this, decide how much I believed.

"For two decades, Sigrid allowed herself only one safety-valve. She wrote to me. Sometimes she kept a post office box so I could reply."

"Ken, did you keep any old letters of hers?"

"I've never destroyed a single letter she wrote."

"Then why on earth didn't you show Keegan proof of your innocence?"

He sighed. "When could I? When, Leslie? Sigrid didn't want to hasten Brad's death by cutting Keegan off from him. Then Brad died, Keegan fled, and I didn't see him between last September and this March. He came back from the war deafened, injured, with his life shattered. His fiancee dumped him. When was I gonna say, 'Hey, Nephew, your father was a lying bastard who bled me white for funds and ruined your mother's life'?"

"I begin to see. . ."

"Brad should have been an actor. He got Margaret's sympathy. He courted the citizens of Okasassa by dressing like them and drinking their home brew. He didn't entirely fool Rufus, but by the time Keegan was ten, he was like a little time-bomb. You've seen him take a knife to me, once. That last day on the island—whew! I thought I'd had it. I almost got my throat cut for doing the kindest thing of my hardly saintly life—protecting Keegan's sanity."

"When Keegan finds out you've married his mother. . ."

"Yeah. I'm glad you didn't bring him with you. Everything he's assumed about me is wrong, Leslie. And when he learns the truth, what'll it do to him? He won't share a penny of the estate with Sigrid, if I'm her husband, but that's okay. I can get back to work and support a wife. But my wife needs more than me; more than money. She needs her son's love."

"You really love her, don't you?"

"She deserves love. Sigrid even blessed my brief marriage, but no one can compare with her. We think the same, react the same, love the same things. Not even you can compare, Leslie, though you're such a bright, lovely girl. I'll never feel sorry I desired you. Lonely as hell, thinking Sigrid might be dead, knowing my own detective couldn't find her all winter . . . I hope it's some proof of love that I married a woman my age who's ill and has six thousand bucks worth of medical bills to pay. To me she's still priceless, at any price."

He paused to slide a fingertip unobtrusively along each cheekbone.

"Why did Brad die last September? Why, then?" I asked, remembering Mary Ann's conclusions.

"He was convinced he had lung cancer but refused to get xrays. He was in pain. He knew Keegan would soon marry and move out. With Keegan gone, Sigrid might at last leave him. He figured out a way to keep Sigrid his even after death. If she married me, I'd be framed for his murder."

"But if the coroner ruled it suicide, what proof could anyone use?"

"Brad wrote out a statement saying that if he ever died violently, his death should never be judged accidental or a suicide. He said I was threatening to murder him, and marry Sigrid. He turned the townspeople against me in advance, said I was a pornographer. The sheriff would get me convicted easily, if I weren't lynched, first."

"Who has a copy of that statement?" I demanded.

"I do, and so does Brad's henchman, who threatened to send it to the sheriff, if I didn't leave the island. Now I'm off the island, but once this marriage becomes known— I've married Brad's widow, and Brad—by proxy—will try to get me hanged."

"At Okasassa—" I dropped my voice for fear of being overheard. "Keegan . . . Well, he hasn't softened toward you, and he has new suspicions. Awful things have happened—"

"I'm not too worried about Keegan, but I better find Brad's henchman and expose the scheme before the local people are brought into it. The same man who helped Brad lose money, selling books at a big rake-off, is not above framing me, now his client is dead."

I didn't understand business dealings. What I was visualizing at that moment was Sigrid. She'd suffered a loveless marriage and a stroke, and she now faced the threat that her new husband would go to jail—or worse. On top of that I'd have to tell her that her only son had become totally and permanently deaf.

"Ken, does Sigrid know you're in danger?"

"She knows that, yes."

"Adding the news about Keegan will kill her!"

"You see why I couldn't bear to tell Keegan the truth about Brad? Ignorance can be a great blessing sometimes. But Sigrid has to know in advance, to spare Keegan the sight of her shock. To spare her, too, the way I didn't spare Mary Ann."

"Okay. I want to see her and talk with her, now."

He went to fetch her, asking me to stay put, still afraid I'd somehow slip away. I remembered the man in the flashlight beam, the man with the projector, whom Keegan shot at. We hadn't seen his face. He had dark hair and was Ken's size, and he was agile. That's all I saw.

Ken went in one direction; Cindy came from another, signing almost too fast for me to grasp her impressions of the yacht's kitchen, lounge, and engine room. She'd learned so much—without signs—from our hosts. Behind her strolled two women I hadn't met.

Still giddy from Ken's impassioned explanations, I pulled Cindy around the corner out of their path and sat her down in a deck chair.

"The big wheel . . . all wood and gold . . . the needle points to 'N,' that's North . . . they let me turn the wheel . . ."

"Cindy, look at me. Ken says he and Sigrid always loved each other. Brad tricked her into marrying him. I don't know if it's all true, but Ken says Brad was a crazy man. Maybe Brad committed suicide. . ." On and on went my litany: "Ken says, Ken says."

Her limpid-eyed acceptance of Ken as hero rather than villain made me trust him more. Surely meeting Sigrid would end my bewilderment. A woman married to a man against her will would surely look the part.

Voices floated over to us, comments about the fish

being caught from the sea wall; the two women had stopped by the rail. Cindy's eyes followed mine, and she stood up and stared. Her hand opened, then slowly rose, thumb near her mouth, eyes dancing. "Mother!"

"Whose mother?"

"Keegan's mother! There!"

I shook my head, keeping a good grip on her belt. "No. No accent. Sigrid is Norwegian, remember?"

"Accent?" she spelled.

Dialects, accents, and mispronunciations perplexed her, like when I spelled Rufus' words exactly as I heard them. I'd scarcely glanced at the women. One wore a striped bandanna, slacks, and a boyish shirt. She didn't look much over thirty, and Sigrid was more like forty-three.

"Keegan's nose, Keegan's chin, hair yellow," Cindy ticked items off on her fingers. "Look! Open your blind eyes! Ears don't tell all the truth!"

I looked. The woman's hair was graying a bit at the temples, but her pale face was unlined, and her hips were no wider than mine. The soft voice bore no trace of a Scandinavian accent.

Here came Ken, striding along the deck fast, saying, "Sigrid! I've found you, Darling. I want you to meet some lovely friends of mine."

Cindy's eyes lit up with triumph. "I'm deaf and you're dumb!" she laughed.

"But you're Norwegian!" I cried, the moment Ken turned back to us.

"Yes," the woman smiled. "My parents brought us to America when I was three. Now they've returned to Norway. Ken told you about me?" She was calm, smiling.

Ken took the three of us below, leaving on deck the red-haired woman who'd been with Sigrid—a nurse, he said, named Willo.

We trailed down steep steps to the lounge, then to Ken and Sigrid's cabin "for privacy." Sigrid cleared off chairs for us; she'd been knitting with bright wools.

"Darling, these girls are . . . were on the island with Keegan."

Cindy signed, "Was it HER letter?" I frowned and shook my head at her.

"Keegan?"

Ken had put Sigrid in a chair, but her son's name, like a hypo of adrenalin, brought her to her feet again. She cried, "Do you know my son? Tell me about him. Is he healed, now? Oh, how IS he?"

What could I say? My hands signed her words to Cindy while I snatched a moment to think.

For the first time Sigrid realized that something was odd, that I was talking on my hands, and Cindy had not spoken aloud. Sigrid very slowly sat down again.

"Ken, the little girl is deaf? Oh, you poor, sweet little thing! So pretty, too." She reached out to Cindy, then bethought herself, and turned to me for help. "I'm sorry. It took me by surprise. I don't mean to be tactless." Eyes meltingly on Cindy, she asked her, "Were you born deaf?"

Smart lady. Cindy got the familiar sentence and smiled like the eternal optimist she was. "Yes, my mother had measles," she mouthed and spelled, while I whispered the words to Sigrid.

"Can you go to school? Can you read and write? Can you hear anything at all?"

The usual uninformed questions, but asked in a mother's voice, tenderly. Cindy and I were both young enough to be her daughters, if she could actually be Ken's age.

I had an opening for one of my standard short lectures on deafness, but I only reluctantly launched into it, Cindy watching my hands critically, correcting and adding to my statements. That took up ten minutes. Delay, delay.

Sigrid's questions were the expected ones, though she didn't ask about Braille, thank heavens. Her sympathy, however, was intense and unveiled. Ken's face became even graver.

"Oh, Cindy!" Sigrid cried. "Aren't you lucky to have a sister like Leslie."

"Cindy earns love," I stalled, not able to meet those worshipping eyes. She agonized over Cindy, yet soon we had to hit her with the truth about her own son.

Ken cleared his throat. "Sigrid, I . . . Sigrid, Leslie is Keegan's friend, but not by accident. I brought Leslie to the island. She's there to help Keegan, because he's—"

Ken couldn't say the word. I didn't blame him; I knew who'd have to say it. Even Cindy had her face drawn up in anguish as if she had a toothache.

"Mrs. Howell—"

"Do call me Sigrid, Leslie."

"Sigrid, what we're trying to tell you is that Keegan is . . . Keegan has . . . has lost his . . . hearing."

She sat there waiting for more, for words to modify the last ones, for news about hearing aids, ear surgery, and miracle cures. I remained silent, and her hospital-pale face blanched even whiter.

Cindy got up. She crossed the cabin and put her hands on Sigrid's shoulders. Her mouth trembled too much for any readable words, so she leaned forward and gave Sigrid a soft little kiss on each cheek.

Sigrid hugged Cindy to her, asking over her shoulder, "He's deaf? Is that what you mean?"

Cindy slid down to sit at Sigrid's feet, watching me.

"Deaf like Cindy?"

"No! No!" Cindy shook her head firmly. "Not deaf like ME," she signed. "HE can talk! He does good reading and writing. He's lucky!"

I orally translated that.

Sigrid swallowed a few times. "So he's hard of hearing, then? He had his ears injured in the war. His hearing can be restored, of course. It. . . must be possible to—? Surgery?"

"No, Sigrid," Ken managed to get out, his voice unnaturally low. "He's profoundly deaf. Permanently deaf. It can't be restored. I'm sorry, Darling."

"Oh, Ken, NO!"

"An explosion destroyed the auditory nerves themselves."

She stared straight ahead of her.

"You see how well Cindy gets along," he continued, "and she doesn't choose to talk. I'm sorry, Dearest; I hadn't the guts to tell you, and your doctors said to wait as long as I could. I put the task off on the girls."

"Would it be . . . weak of me . . . to cry?" she stammered.

"Crying's the best thing for it," Ken said. He went over to her bent form to cradle her head against his ribs. She wept hard, her slender shoulders shaking. Tears rose in my eyes and Cindy's.

How would Cindy take this? She thought Keegan was so much luckier than she, but his mother was devastated.

"No, stay!" Ken whispered, when Cindy and I made moves to leave. "She'll want to talk more with you. Won't you, Darling?"

Sigrid revived, saying exactly what I expected.

"At least Keegan's not blind! Some boys come home from war blinded! I should thank God that he's only deaf!" I grimaced at her words.

She gulped and said, "Yes, I have questions. You'll teach Keegan to talk on his hands?"

"He first needed to read signs. He does that, very accurately."

"It's better to read lips, isn't it?"

"Better?" I said. "It's far harder, and pretty exhausting. He'll need to communicate using every possible mode."

Before Keegan's mom ran out of questions—practical, sane questions now—Cindy put in her cheery report: "Leslie loves Keegan. Keegan loves Leslie."

Again she needed no interpreter. Sigrid was startled. "You LOVE him? But of course a girl like you and a deaf man wouldn't—?"

"Keegan hasn't said a word about . . . that," I said, flustered. "That's awfully premature, but mere deafness wouldn't turn me away from Keegan, no."

She surprised me.

"I married a man who was ill, Leslie. It almost ruined my life. I had Keegan, but I wouldn't want to see another girl rush into a commitment . . . out of pity."

"I told Leslie our whole story, Honey," Ken said gently. "She had to know. Keegan fed them all the wrong ideas."

"What a family you must think us!" she cried. "Jealousy, hatred, suicide, and the fear of blackmail for a man kind enough to marry a sick woman deep in debt!"

"Shhhh," Ken laid a finger on her lips. "You're cured now, and I make money enough. What else have I got to spend it on? Men my age are usually putting three kids through college."

"You gave almost half you earned to Brad," Sigrid said, "and now you suddenly have a stepson who . . ."

"Who would be my nephew, no matter whom I married. Sigrid, Keegan will be okay financially, if he sells enough books to pay off the debts. He'll have an island, a house, and his disability pay from the Army."

"He can go back to college," I said, and enjoyed the burst of joy that spread over Sigrid's face. "I'll tell Keegan about Ken and you. If there's evidence, like letters I can show him—"

Cindy punched me. "What about Sigrid's letter that fat man brought?"

"Did you see that attorney, Baker Johnson, while you were in Gainesville?" I asked Sigrid.

"That horrid man? I hope I never see him, unless to testify at his trial! He put a detective on my trail—though, I must admit, he did inadvertently help Ken find me."

I signed to Cindy, "A forged—false—letter!"

Ken stood up. "Let me show the girls their cabin, now. Be right back, Darling."

He bent and touched a kiss to Sigrid's unpainted lips, not just the kiss of a dutiful husband, but of a man who prized and protected her, afraid she'd learn too much, too soon.

He shut himself with us into a snug ship's cabin for two, leaning his back on the door.

"Leslie, what's this about Baker Johnson? I've talked so much you couldn't get a word in edgewise. No more shocks for Sigrid, today, but tell me what's happened since I left."

I told him. I described the visit by Johnson and Rauenbauer, and quoted the letter supposedly written by Sigrid, aided by Cindy's memory.

"Rauenbauer had that old note Sigrid sent to Mary Ann. They copied it, forged a letter from it?" Ken shook his head. "Lord! What Keegan must think of me, now!"

It didn't ease his mind to hear about the ghost that drove away the Deans, the projector with his name on it, and the three thugs who claimed Ken Howell sent them. I threw in the beggar in Gainesville and my feeling we were being watched a few hours ago outside Duane's apartment. Finally we told him Rauenbauer had claimed one of my green and black sedative capsules.

"Then we can't wait'll tomorrow to get there," he said. "We've got to reach the island today. Fast! Johnson's hired man is out there, and Keegan will reach there, soon?"

He wiped his face with a handkerchief. "Wow! What you poor kids have been through! And I added to your troubles by not sending word I found Sigrid. The Deans gone, the food running out . . ."

"There was still lots of food," Cindy corrected him, "And I cook wonderfully!"

"I don't put my name on projectors. Baker dared to hire thugs— Leslie, you warned me not to bring Cindy down into this mess!"

"To help Keegan!" Cindy flared. "I don't care what happens if I can help Keegan!"

She got a hug for that; Ken lifted her off her feet. "I'd hug you, too, Leslie, out of gratitude. But I'll wait to give you a kiss at your wedding, as my . . . my what? Step-daughter-in-law?" He was only half kidding.

"We'll really go to the island, now?" Cindy asked.

"It's after three o'clock, now," I noted.

"We've got to. We'll tow the SIGFORD. This battleship can't get through the channel into the lagoon."

While Cindy and I were still examining our tiny lavatory, double-decker bunks, and table with a railing for rough weather, we felt the engine start. We were on our way north.

We ate sandwiches on deck, our elbows hooked over the rail, watching water churn up from the bow. Over there, the mouth of the Suwanee River slipped past. Twenty miles north, we dropped anchor behind a headland.

"It'll take awhile," Ken told Sigrid. "Maybe I'll spend the night on the island. You're not to worry if I don't come back for you and the girls till tomorrow morning."

"I'm going with you, Ken," I interrupted.

"Nope. I go alone. I've learned my lesson. I won't drag you into it, or Duane, or the Silvens. I'll do my own work, for once."

We managed to get outside Sigrid's ear-shot before I said, "I MUST go with you, Ken! You need me to interpret."

"No!" He shook his head emphatically. "Not after what you gals have suffered. You stay here with Sigrid, both of you. I want you safe."

"I am going WITH you!" My voice was hard. "You're risking your life if you face Keegan alone. He won't give you time to write him notes. Don't make Sigrid a widow a second time!"

"Leslie, I've got some of Sigrid's old letters. We picked out ones that'll clear up Keegan's doubts. I also have the blackmail letters from Brad and the anonymous ones from our dear friend Baker Johnson."

I shut my mouth, but when Ken was halfway down the ladder to board the SIGFORD, I followed him.

"Of course he'll need me as interpreter. See you soon," I said cheerfully to Sigrid, and continued descending.

Ken started to object, but with Sigrid standing there on the deck above us he couldn't do much more than glower. If he told his wife why he wanted to leave me behind, she'd insist on coming along. We both knew that.

When we were down in the SIGFORD, Sigrid called to us, "I promise I won't have another stroke, Ken, if you hurry right back. I will just go quietly crazy!"

We pushed away from the mother ship into the swells, Ken shaking his head at me.

"You're either very brazen or very brave, Leslie!"

"Two sides of the same coin," I told him, knowing only that I had to be where Keegan was—an emotion with many names, but only one course of action.

Back there on the yacht were faces at the rail, Duane's looking troubled—poor neglected Duane. I did not see Cindy. Jim and Jeri Silven waved gaily. Sigrid held her hands clasped in front of her mouth. I remembered her parting kiss for Ken—definitely not a kiss from a woman in love.

"Tell Keegan," I'd heard her ask Ken, "that Brad really wasn't sane; we were all he had." Ken responded, "I won't make Brad look any worse than I must. I sometimes pitied him, too."

Now I could no longer see the SILVEN SEAS tucked behind a headland. I could have gone into the cabin to check my hairdo and lipstick, but unfortunately, I didn't. I stayed on the deck beside Ken, watching the island swell and loom over us.

Had I searched the cabin, we could have turned back in

time. As we plowed through the dark channel of mangroves, out burst Cindy, strutting with audacity.

"I stowed away," she spelled meticulously. "Keegan was MINE, first!"

We couldn't return her to the yacht; too late for that.

Across the lagoon, there sat the MANTA, still moored at the dock. The leaky rowboat on shore indicated that Keegan had already reached home.

"I hope we're in time," Ken muttered, glaring no longer at Cindy, but at that hefty blue cruiser—now loaded with large wooden boxes.

"You girls stay in the boat—both of you. That's an order!" Ken said. "I go alone."

He didn't go, however. Here came Pete from the house down the gravel walk, moving fast, smiling, actually inspired to vocalize.

"Hi, Leslie, Cindy. Is this Ken Howell?" He was chattering so fast I could hardly follow. "Keegan got back an hour ago. He cooked me supper. I'm just leaving. He didn't hear you come. We can't communicate worth a damn!"

Such a lot of words from Pete, and so bland and domestic a homecoming. I grabbed Ken by the arm and suggested a new strategy.

"Why not give me three minutes start on you? You wait. I'll run ahead and talk to Keegan, then you come to the house."

Ken reluctantly agreed to this. When Cindy demanded to accompany me, I said okay. The two of us left Ken and Pete chatting from their boats on opposite sides of the dock. I'd forgotten to introduce Pete, but that didn't seem to matter.

Noise that sounded like Keegan washing dishes drew me toward the kitchen. The livingroom was empty as I trotted through, Cindy in tow. Just let me keep Keegan away from Ken till we could end his hatred of his uncle; of his new step-father.

We bounced into the kitchen, smiling. Keegan was not there.

Someone was there. A man on my side of the doorway grabbed me. On the other side a man grabbed Cindy. We stared at each other past big hands clamped over our mouths. I didn't realize how strong a sick old man could be.

"Don't need to gag the deaf-mute," Rauenbauer told Johnson. The attorney took his hand off Cindy's mouth. She instantly let out a deafening shriek, broken only when she bit his returning hand.

"Damn it! That'll bring Howell!"

He was right. I heard feet come pounding up the front steps. Staight through the living room we saw Ken on the porch, Pete right behind him.

"Leslie! Where are you?"

Pete used a varsity flying tackle to bring Ken down hard on his knees and elbows. Before either man got wind enough to rise, Johnson had hauled Cindy through the living room, yelling, "Don't try anything, Kenneth, or this not-so-mute deafie gets her arm twisted off!"

Cindy was choking with pain and fury, one arm doubled behind her.

Ken let the younger man restrain his arms as they rose. Pete shoved him into the livingroom and hung onto Ken after Cindy and I found ourselves free. I pulled Cindy to me, embracing her so I could spell words secretly under her nose.

"Sorry we'll have to tie you up," Johnson said to Ken. To Pete, "Here. Use my necktie. I detest violence. This is so unfortunate. You should have stayed away, Kenneth. Avoided trouble."

"Where's Keegan?" Ken and I cried with one voice.

"I thought you'd never ask," Johnson smirked, handing over the bright yellow necktie. "He's perfectly safe. When he was supposed to be heading for St. Pete for a day or two, up he pops on a motorcycle, wearing that concealing helmet and slipping past everyone I hired—at considerable expense, Kenneth—to keep him out of danger!"

"Well, Keegan knows who his friends are now, doesn't he?" Ken sneered. "Your barge is full of Keegan's books, right?"

"It is. But you underestimate me. I may talk and walk slow, Kenneth, but I don't think slow. When Keegan came rowing in, he never caught one glimpse of us—of Geoffrey or Pete or myself. Our assistants collared him."

"Those same brutes who broke in a couple of nights ago?" I gasped.

"The same," Johnson said. "Handy helpers to have."

"They said they worked for Ken," I murmured.

"Sayin' that was the only thing they did right. This time we had to come supervise them."

"Where are they?" Ken asked.

Rauenbauer shook his head, motioning for Johnson not to reply, but the fat man continued, confidently and jovially, "They're on the mainland, loading up a truck. The books are all gone, Kenneth, except for this last load. Nothing you can do about it."

I let loose of Cindy, and used those precious minutes to spell into her perspiring palm, "Run. Try to run away. Sneak. Fast."

Pete was starting to tie Ken's hands behind him.

"What've you done with Keegan?" Ken asked. "They didn't rough him up?" As he spoke, his gaze locked on mine, willing me to run. I planted my feet, nodded, and immediately Ken lunged forward, jerking Pete off balance. I gave Cindy a shove toward the door. All three men fought to hold onto Ken, letting Cindy get the front door open and leap through it like a little golden grasshopper. I kicked Rauenbauer in the leg.

"Hell! The brat's got away!" Pete cried.

"Come back, or we'll hurt your sister!" Johnson shouted.

"She can't hear you," I snapped, "Stupid!"

Cindy was out of sight. I'd given her no suggestions, hoping she'd think faster than I. The three men now had only two of us to contend with. They got Ken's hands tied behind him with the strip of cheerful yellow cloth. No one bothered to tie me; they simply blocked my path to the door which they locked in Cindy's wake.

"The little kid can't make trouble. She can't run a boat," Rauenbauer said.

"No, and I've got the SIGFORD's ignition keys," Ken put in quickly. "Let her be."

"Okay," said Johnson, "Lost one, but we'll keep this one. We need only one gal, to insure that the books get safely out of the country."

"What's that?" Ken gasped. "You won't take Leslie—"

"She'll turn up on some street corner, safe and sound, if we meet no interference, Kenneth. She'll be wonderful insurance."

"You'll get no interference," Ken promised.

"Where is Keegan, you monsters?" I cried.

"Keegan's dying," Johnson said, "dying to settle some

scores with you. Don't worry about Leslie, Kenneth; worry about yourself. Considerin' your past encounters, I've a notion how Keegan will greet you."

With Ken tied, Pete could stroll over and slide a hand around my upper arm, pressing close against me. I knew enough not to struggle.

"Keegan had a grandstand seat, all afternoon," Johnson told us. "Our friends tied him to a chair and let him watch them empty the rooms of books, valuable books—"

"Very valuable," Rauenbauer put in. "You've no idea what you had in this house. Fifty thousand was a modest estimate!"

Baker Johnson continued. "Your nephew just wouldn't keep still—verbally or physically. What a violent young man! He never glimpsed the three of us watching while he dragged that chair all over the room. Its legs finally broke off."

"They didn't hurt him?" Ken pleaded.

"No worse than he hurt them, Kenneth. Play rough, and you do get roughed up. Come along. Time to go visit Keegan," Johnson said soothingly.

The five of us trooped past the kitchen and into the Deans' bedroom. I screamed.

Keegan lay spread-eagled on the four-poster bed, his wrists and ankles tied to the four posts. That was horrible enough. What nauseated me and would've maddened Cindy was the sight of Keegan's eyes—his covered eyes. His eyes were taped over with the same pink adhesive tape I'd used to close Ken's knife-slash, my second day here.

Keegan was like a deaf and blind man. He lifted his head and writhed to break free, making the whole bed rattle and shake. I swallowed my tears and my nausea. Neither would help Keegan a bit. I couldn't speak.

Ken spoke for me. "That's torture—to blindfold a deaf person!"

"But we can't have him seeing us, Kenneth," purred Rauenbauer, "and he badly needed a rest. You better save some compassion for yourself. Remember our last day here, when he sat on you, holding a knife to your throat? You ought to be glad he's tied up. . . just like you."

Keegan struggled constantly, calling out, "Where is everybody? What's going on? For god's sake, take this tape off! Let me SEE!"

"Don't worry," Johnson remarked. "We'll soon let him see. See his dear uncle, at least. Let me just find a piece of paper . . ."

"You won't get away with this," Ken cried. "It's brutal. Insane!"

"Not at all insane."

On a legal pad, Johnson began writing, printing words while he talked. "This'll let your nephew know that you've kidnapped his dear mother and had Leslie kidnapped along with the books."

"Who's he supposed to think wrote it?" asked Ken.

"It'll be from my hired men, announcing that they ditched you in order to split your share of the book money. Very simple."

"Sigrid and I are married," Ken said quietly.

"Ummm?" Johnson, without looking up, erased some words and wrote others in their place. "Fine. I never thought you'd move quite that fast. The word 'married' ought to have an interesting effect on Keegan. And if he doesn't kill you, we'll arrange that a lynching party from Okasassa does the job."

"How do you expect to let him loose and not be seen?" Ken demanded.

I did not interrogate them. I just kept staring down at Keegan. Keegan didn't even know people were in the room, gazing at him. His shirt was dark with sweat, and I prayed that the sweat on his face would soak the tape free.

"We'll manage," said Johnson. He was tearing the sheet of paper off the pad. "We'll leave you tied up in this room, cut one of Keegan's hands free, and lock the door. We may have ten minutes lead-time before he can read this note, untie the other three ropes, kill you, and break the door down."

"Hurry up, Baker," Rauenbauer whined. "The light's failing. It'll soon be too dark for me to find the channel out of here."

"Pete knows the way."

"Who's there?" Keegan's voice startled us. "Where's Ken? Where're you meeting that louse? Tell him I'll find him! I'll kill him!"

This didn't improve Ken's color. Sweat streamed down

his face, too. If only I could reach Keegan's hand and spell words into it, but I stood near his sock-clad left foot.

"I would've preferred a simpler plan," Johnson shrugged, "but with all four of you coming back the same day you left, you have to admit we've compensated very well. Instead of losing only books, you'll have Leslie missing for awhile, and probably Kenneth murdered. Neither Keegan nor his mommy will be interested in recovering books. Not with Leslie missing, Sigrid widowed, and Keegan a murderer."

"The girl—? MUST we take her along?" Rauenbauer complained.

"The little deafie would've been easier to handle and easier to persuade the fellas to give up, I admit." Johnson grinned at Pete, "but she has flown."

"Leave Leslie here!" Ken cried. "Let's strike a bargain. I've got a dozen witnesses to the fact that you stole money from Brad. You'll be disbarred for that. Blackmailing me about Brad's death—that's a felony. Leave Leslie behind, and I won't press charges."

"I wouldn't trust you for a minute, and we hold all the cards, Kenneth," Johnson laughed. "You can't press charges against anyone after you're dead!"

Ken thrust out his chin. "Just suppose I survive—?"

"You can't trace used books," Johnson boasted, "and they'll go overseas with gold sheets in them . . ."

"Shut up!" Rauenbauer hissed.

"Keep your shirt on. They can't do one damned thing about it. Gold is awful heavy to smuggle out of the country. Books—thick, age-warped old books—will be ideal. Just a little sugarin' of our profits, Friends."

"You animals!" Ken snapped.

"Fancy you sayin' that!" Baker retorted. "Look at my late, unlamented client. I deserve something for having to deal with a slimy character like Bradford Howell, who'd frame his own baby brother. I didn't think that up! You call ME an animal—that was your own brother who poisoned himself in front of wife, son, and even Betty Coed, remember. What lives in YOUR family tree, huh? If Keegan kills you, it's not some new idea I put into his head, is it? You had the gall to rush into marriage. Okay, you take the consequences. How can a deaf kid run a business, anyway? We're leavin' him half Brad's estate—both house and island—if he doesn't throw it all away by committing homicide!"

"It's growing darker," Rauenbauer reminded him.

"On the other hand, if you don't die, Kenneth, the local sheriff will get some papers tomorrow—" he patted his pocket "—or maybe I'll slip 'em to some citizen of Okasassa and see what happens to you on your next trip through town, huh?"

"Pete," I whispered to the young man who held onto me. "Don't stay mixed up in this. You're not the type! Please help us!"

He grinned. "Hell, Honey, I'm the one who ran the blue movie for you, so to speak. I've been around here lotsa nights. You didn't think one of them old men came rowin' out here to make the ghost for you, did you? Or hauled off and axed your little sand castle? Can you see ole man Rauenbauer playing lumberjack?" He chuckled.

The "ole man" suddenly pleaded, "Tie up the girl and leave her out in the trees. Don't take her along."

Johnson blew up at last. "Look, you academic yellow belly, you're too deep in this to turn moralist! You tried to poison her; you stole her things; you forged our masterpiece. Don't blame me for takin' some precautions."

Johnson held out his note for us to read.

"Ken made your mother marry him. We are letting you have him and splitting his share. We took Leslie. Don't come looking for us and no police, or she'll get what we planned on when we came here last Tuesday night."

"That won't fool Keegan," Ken said. "The grammar alone—"

Johnson stirred the contents of a tray on Margaret's dresser, found a large safety pin, and stuck it in the sheet of paper. "When Keegan reads this, well, I don't reckon he'll be in a mood to parse sentences."

Rauenbauer held onto me while Pete dragged Ken into one corner of the bedroom. He made him kneel in front of the washbowl and tied the ends of the necktie firmly to its drainpipe.

Keegan cried out in shock when Johnson bumped the mattress. The attorney leaned down over him to pin the note to his shirt-front. Flinging his head from side to side, Keegan tried vainly to untape his eyes.

Deep in my throat, I choked on sobs.

"Worry about yourself, Baby; forget the deafie," Pete murmured into my ear, his breath warm. Elbowing Rauenbauer aside, he shook me a little. "Just wait'll tonight . . ."

It was Johnson who went into the kitchen, came back with a knife, and then shooed us out of the Deans' bedroom. I strained back to see over my shoulder—see him fray the rope to Keegan's nearest wrist. Then he threw the knife into the washbasin and slammed and locked the door.

Johnson and Rauenbauer led us, half running, through the livingroom; Pete dragged me along. Down the path the four of us pelted.

Not one sign of Cindy. Pete pitched me into the MANTA, and they all climbed in, Johnson rocking the big boat when he boarded.

"Let's go, Pete, my boy. We'll read what happened in the newspapers!" Johnson said exultantly.

But when Pete turned the key in the ignition, looking nervously over his shoulder at the house, he got only a crackle and pop.

"What the hell?"

I gawked at the boat's instrument panel. It was riven and creased, its wiring exposed, all red and green, like snake's intestines; the fire axe at our feet told us how.

They guessed when and who.

"That filthy little deafie! She busted up my controls!"

"We can't get away!" Rauenbauer shrieked. "Keegan'll see us! Understand everything!

"We got no weapon!" groaned Pete.

"Don't get hysterical," Baker Johnson snapped. "We'll just take the SIGFORD. You can run that, can't you?" He was scrambling back the length of the MANTA.

Pete reached the SIGFORD while I still stood in the larger boat. Rauenbauer gripped a fistful of my hair.

"This boat's okay, but there's no ignition key," said Pete. "Howell said he had the key."

"Jump the ignition," Johnson retorted.

"No time! No tools!"

"Okay. Let me think of a minute," said the attorney, fingertips to brow. "Keegan knows nothing. If we can't leave in the SIGFORD, we'll make him think we just now ARRIVED in it. Wait; listen to me!" Panting, he oozed his bulk up onto the deck.

"Okay. Here's our story: the MANTA's the boat Ken's thieves are using, right? Some boxes are still in it. (We'll have to lose these last books.) We found the SIGFORD over at Okasassa and used it to get here. The thieves ran off when we surprised them, us three friends of Keegan's!"

"Idiot! How are you going to tell a DEAF boy all that?" cried Rauenbauer. "You've ruined us!"

"We write it down, Fool! Find me something to write on. I hear noise up in the house!"

"What about Leslie?" Rauenbauer said, busy keeping me from jumping ship, diving into the lagoon. "She'll tell him everything. She SIGNS!"

"Lock her in the MANTA's cabin."

Rauenbauer shoved, and I catapulted head first into the cabin. Before I got up, the door clicked shut. I threw myself uselessly against it. Portholes no bigger than saucers, salt-caked, let me see the house and dock, and hear the frantic three men, but I was hidden from everyone outside.

What I saw coming from the house lifted my spirits.

Keegan, a rope streaming from each wrist and the knife stuck through his belt, shoved a man ahead of him down the path.

Ken still had his hands bound. He was staggering, stumbling, and blood ran down his chin, but he was alive. He aimed triumphant jeers at Brad's lawyer.

"Whatsamatter? Can't get away? Give up, you freaks! You've had it, now!"

Pete didn't hang around. I saw him leap into the rowboat and start madly rowing. He didn't invite Johnson or Rauenbauer along.

"Where did Ken's men go?" shouted Keegan. "They left five minutes ago! Left Ken behind." He glared at his uncle. "He got hold of my mother. Made her MARRY him!"

My head swam. Keegan was totally wrong, but no one told him so. Ken, even if he could sign, had no hand free. Keegan wasn't enlightened by seeing Ken and Johnson furiously glowering at each other.

Johnson was still rummaging through pockets for writing materials. Rauenbauer started searching Ken—hunting for the ignition key? Ken jerked away, staggering onto the dock, yelling at Keegan, "Sigrid loves me! She's nearby! On a boat! Don't let 'em fool you!"

"Where was the SIGFORD?" asked Keegan, as if he could understand a reply.

"Where's Leslie?" cried Ken.

Rauenbauer located the key and flourished it. He headed for the SIGFORD, Johnson wordlessly following.

The momentary silence was shattered by a gun-shot.

Johnson leaped into a dance like a great performing bear, holding the seat of his pants.

Keegan, hearing nothing, inquired, "What on earth's wrong with you?"

Madly prancing, the attorney yelled, "I'm shot! I'm shot! I'll die! Get me to a doc-tor!" He dropped to his hands and knees, revealing a spreading redness on one great haunch. "Help me! Need a doc-tor!"

Ken laughed. Keegan, spotting the blood, ducked, looking in every direction. "Someone's shooting! Where? I can't hear—!"

Ken stepped backward on the narrow dock, lost his balance, and with his hands still tied behind him, tumbled off. I saw and heard Ken's chin clip the dock before he plummeted into the water, sank, and did not rise.

Keegan had his back to Ken and saw nothing. He was staring at Rauenbauer, who stood with his hands raised over his head, looking in the direction of the shot.

I now saw who'd shot Baker Johnson.

The sniper who rose from behind a potted palm, hefting a rifle, was my little sister Cindy.

Keegan's rifle from the lean-to? She was soaked and muddy, stumbling toward the dock, shouting unintelligibly, freeing a hand to sign, "Help him! In water! Get Ken!"

"Ken! Get Ken!" I screamed, making a duet with Cindy, but if either hearie heard me, he ignored me. Ken Howell was drowning.

A dumbfounded Keegan asked, "YOU shot Johnson?" Then he signed, "He helped Mom!"

"No! Wrong idea!" her hand responded.

Slow down! Slow down for him, Cindy! I silently begged.

Keegan started to take the rifle from Cindy, but she yanked it back, then shoved Keegan to the edge of the dock. She jumped up and down, pointing into the water. Could they see Ken underwater? I couldn't.

"Drowning! Drowning!" A "V" of finger-legs sank into her hand. She grasped herself by the hair, pantomimed pulling someone up, and pointed to the water. She slapped Keegan on the chest, pummeled him. "Save him! Loves your mother! Mother loves him!"

She rushed toward the water as if to dive in herself, and Keegan finally understood. He dragged her back, then, fully dressed, he slid off the dock into the water.

Cindy held the rifle on Rauenbauer, poking at him, gesturing toward the water. When he caught on, he obediently sank to his knees on the dock.

I groaned in relief. Keegan was hauling Ken to the surface—limp, his head lolling. Rauenbauer reached down and gripped Ken's shirt, supporting him while Keegan vaulted onto the dock. The two of them hauled Ken out of the water and stretched him out, his back arched over his bound wrists.

"Help ME! Not HIM!" Johnson cried, writhing on his belly. "I'll bleed to death!"

Cindy gave Johnson a little kick before kneeling over Ken. Keegan knelt too, fingered Ken's throat, pulled his mouth open, pinched nostrils shut, jerked the head back, and blew air into Ken's mouth.

The kiss of life, for a man he wanted dead. Keegan watched his uncle's chest. It did not rise of its own accord. While Cindy held the gun on the other men like a girl guerrila, glowering, Keegan began breathing Ken in earnest, his head rising and dipping, rising and dipping.

Shuddering, thanking God for the swim team and the Army, I watched a true expert perform mouth-to-mouth resuscitation.

Cindy started looking for me, rotating her head. Before Rauenbauer, sitting down with hands again raised, tried to relieve Cindy of that rifle, I must show her where I was. Our side needed a hearing ear, and quickly.

Suddenly I realized how to catch Cindy's attention. I began rushing back and forth, from wall to wall in the cabin. Gradually I overcame the MANTA's inertia. The round-bottomed boat began to rock. I had it rocking vigorously when feet thudded into the stern, and the door clicked open.

I won my freedom, my sister's grinning hug, and possession of the rifle.

"Aim at them," she cautioned me.

Keegan was still pumping up and down over Ken's face, his hands locked over Ken's nose and chin. Keegan didn't see us. It was Rauenbauer who took first advantage of my ears.

"I'm on your side. I didn't do it; any of it! I tried to make them leave you behind; you heard me. I can help you get all the books back. Don't aim that gun at me!"

He was easy to ignore, and Johnson lay sniveling, not going anywhere. Considering the caliber of the rifle and the circumference of him, I doubted he was in any danger. Cindy and I had eyes only for Ken.

Suddenly he choked, and his chest at last heaved. Keegan immediately rolled him face down, slid him to the edge of the dock, and beat him between the shoulder blades. Water cascaded out of Ken's nose and mouth. He gagged and gasped. We felt like cheering, but Keegan's face was still grimly perplexed.

"You saved him! Good!" Cindy signed. "Ken's not bad. We misunderstood."

Keegan drew out the knife from his belt and cut the necktie off his uncle's wrists.

"It was just horrible," Rauenbauer droned on and on—Keegan and Cindy unaware of his recital—"to kidnap you. To blindfold and tie up poor Keegan. I didn't know who was making that ghost. I'm not to blame."

"Wanna bet?" I sneered, without looking around.

Cindy and I hovered over Ken, whose head still dangled just above the water. He drooled water he'd gulped. Keegan stood up and hitched his wet trousers higher on his slim hips. His hand-made birthday shirt had survived it all.

"You can't blame ME!" Rauenbauer cried.

"Oh, shut up and be useful!"

"What'll I do?" he whined.

"Lug your fat friend up to the house," I said, stroking hair out of Ken's wet face. I looked up to see Cindy signing earnestly to Keegan.

"Your mother is beautiful. She's on a big boat out there . . . she loves Ken . . . forever loved him. Ken didn't steal books."

As his pulse grew stronger under my fingertips, Ken's fishy whiteness darkened. Keegan took hold of his ankles and dragged him back from the edge of the dock, so Ken's cheek could rest on the sun-warmed boards.

In two trips we got our casualties to the house, both in shock, but both recovering. Keegan put Ken on the living room couch, and Johnson landed heavily on the Deans' bed. Rauenbauer tied one of his ankles to a bed-post, then deserted his partner, busying himself getting Ken into dry clothes, while Keegan changed in another room.

Cindy and I, drunk with triumph, kept congratulating each other, but Keegan moved like a man in a dream. His untaped eyes stared blankly at the mad world we presented to him, where everything was topsy-turvy—good men evil, evil men good. When I put my hand on his arm, he shook me off, so I attended to Ken, tucking blankets around him. Cindy, however, pursued Keegan, signing until he stood in the doorway and brought her signs to a fluttering fall.

"Leave me alone! I don't understand. I don't know what on earth's happening! Give me time to breathe, will you!"

"Keegan dived in after me? HE pulled me out?" Ken's voice was exultant.

I added, "He also resuscitated you."

Ken's teeth were still chattering as dusk fell on that ninety-degree day. Keegan had walked out the door. I put on all the lamps.

Rauenbauer couldn't do enough for us. It was he who served Ken hot coffee and brought iced tea to Cindy and me. He kept enumerating Baker Johnson's crimes and exonerating himself. Few details were new to Cindy, and fewer to me, but what an eye-opener for Keegan, if he'd believe the old man's speeches.

"I'm going out to get Keegan and force him to listen," Cindy announced. She was gone before I could stop her. Ten minutes later, she dragged Keegan into the house, mercilessly signing to him, "Wrong! You were wrong! Now listen, and be right!"

He'd walked in on another of Rauenbauer's spiels.

"When we came through Okasassa yesterday evening," the man said, "we picked up your mail. Rufus Dean wrote and said his wife was seeing a doctor, and he'd return in a week. Johnson wouldn't give you the letter, of course."

The old man scurried away; I heard angry words from the Deans' bedroom, and back came Rauenbauer with a long envelope. He offered it to Ken, but Ken shook his head no.

Wincing, Rauenbauer had to walk all the way across the room to Keegan. As he passed, I saw that it was addressed to the county sheriff.

"What's this?" Keegan asked, examining the envelope.

Rauenbauer wanted an interpreter. "Tell him it's his father's letter. Blackmail. It says Ken planned to kill him. It's pack-full of lies."

Keegan watched my signing hands from under lowered brows. He didn't open the envelope.

"In Gainesville," said Rauenbauer, "Johnson phoned

Leslie's motel, had her followed, and hired a man to scare her."

"And the capsules?" I prodded.

"Yes, mine, but you didn't take them. They wouldn't have hurt you . . . much. Baker wanted Ken blamed. Baker wanted everyone off the island, but Ken kept bringing more people here, even the child!"

While he caught his breath, I told Keegan about Pete and the projector, and explained the axe in my castle. Keegan had trouble keeping his face stolid. Ken lay silent, one arm thrown across his eyes, choosing not to witness his stepson's acute embarrassment.

"Where's my mother been since Fall?" Keegan quietly asked.

"She went to Norway," began Rauenbauer, and went on to tell the truth. He swore that Johnson, not Ken, sent men to steal books. "Baker ordered Keegan tied to that bed."

Keegan nodded curtly, then turned to Ken.

"Did my mother marry you willingly?"

Ken's arm swung down off his brow. We'd waited a long time for this first interchange between them. Both my hands were poised.

Ken didn't need an interpreter. He raised his right hand and inaccurately but readably spelled, "I love Sigrid. She loves me. Always."

"Ken! You can finger-spell!" I cried. "How'd you learn?"

"In St. Pete, I spotted some deaf people signing. They taught me a little. At least it's a start."

Keegan watched my hands say that, and I watched his face. He concealed his emotions well.

We were neglecting Rauenbauer, who burst into new revelations—our vulture who'd turned stool-pigeon.

"The books are headed to Tampa, to the ship ARCTOA, sailing for Bermuda. They'd already taken several boat-loads to put on a truck parked near Okasassa. They'll be waiting for the last load. Take me to the police, and I'll get your books back."

Strangely, not one of us was moved to thank the man.

I've got to go get Sigrid," Ken said to Rauenbauer, his voice raspy as if his throat hurt. "Hand over the key to the boat."

Keegan snorted, "You can't even stand up! Besides, it's my boat, now. I'm taking this character and the fat one across to the police. Having 'em booked. Toss me the key, Mister."

Rauenbauer tossed Keegan the key.

"I'll go with you." I sprang up.

"Oh, no, you won't!" Keegan retorted.

Keegan glared at me, then at Rauenbauer. "Go get the fat pig; carry him if you have to. I'm not touching him."

Rauenbauer—trying to look more like a cop than a criminal—came marching Johnson into the room, supporting him by the collar and belt. No bullet could have penetrated that much blubber to reach his vitals, but Cindy giggled at the way he walked. On the porch, Keegan picked up his rifle and nudged both of them along.

"If you have trouble, ask for Mrs. McElroy," I said, glad to see Keegan absorb that. He nodded.

"Poor kid," Ken sighed. "He's been acting like a robot, and no wonder. Two hours ago, when I was helplessly watching him read Johnson's note and then work to get the other knots untied, when I couldn't explain a thing, it was the most terrifying experience of my life. Now he's the one who saved my life!"

"Well, Ken," I mused. "He's got so much to forgive himself for, it's best he start by doing you a big favor."

Ken was more damaged than he thought. He'd make no boat trip tonight. He sank into a doze while Cindy and I wandered around putting the house to rights, nibbling snacks, and worrying.

Nine-thirty, and still no sound of the SIGFORD returning. Had Rauenbauer or Johnson snatched the rifle from Keegan and fled? Did Keegan flee rather than return to face Ken? Or had he found the SILVEN SEAS?

That wait was one of the more painful of the summer. I listened, Cindy watched me, and both of us coddled Ken, urging him to drink coffee and then beef bouillon.

Just after eleven I heard the boat came in. I could barely restrain myself from dashing down to the lagoon. Ken would've, had he the strength. But we stayed put.

219

Cindy and I were sitting on the rug by Ken's couch when Keegan walked in. Behind him came a bony-faced, white-haired man carrying a leather bag.

"Doctor Stubbs from Cross City," Keegan said. "That's my uncle. Kenneth Howell, Leslie and Cindy Fallon."

"You the fella had the dunking? Good evenin', ladies."

He came forward, draping a stethoscope around his neck. "I don't generally make house-calls—not to mention island-calls—but the sheriff called and asked me to talk to you tonight, check your condition. After they round up the crooks, they'll come out to take your statements. Nasty business, people gettin' shot and half-drowned. Stealing books. Tsk tsk!"

After listening all over Ken's chest and back, peeling his eyelids open, examining his cut lip, thumping and poking him, Dr. Stubbs gave Ken an envelope of pills.

"I want you to have an xray at Cross City tomorrow, when you can manage the trip."

He motioned Cindy over and gazed at her at close range.

"Did you shoot the fat man?" He held an imaginary rifle and outlined Johnson's shape.

She nodded proudly.

"He hurt your arm?" Again the doctor communicated by illustrative gestures.

She held out her arm, and he examined the bruises.

"Cindy Fallon: bruised," he murmured, and wrote in a small notebook. "Um hmm . . . Kenneth Howell; abrasions on wrists, signs of blows to the jaw . . . Keegan Howell: badly chafed wrists and ankles, and bruises everywhere else . . . Were you hurt, Leslie?"

"No. Just dragged around a bit."

"Let me see." His warm, immaculate fingers peeled up my sleeves. "My, you girls bruise easily. It checks with what I was told. Two men were booked. I've just removed the bullet Cindy put into Mr. Johnson, and since we have the rifle, I think there'll be no trouble for you folks. An Okasassa resident, a Mrs. McElroy, vouched for you."

He gave Ken his card. "Come by after the xray. Here's antibiotic salve, for all those chafed limbs."

Efficiently, crisply, the doctor finished up. He left with Keegan, who'd ferry him back to the mainland. We three shook our heads in wonderment.

"Do you realize how difficult it is to get doctors to make house-calls? And Keegan did it, deaf!"

"Look what Cindy did, deaf!" Ken added, affectionately mussing her hair.

"I taught her to shoot. With no father around, I had to play dad. I taught her things a father teaches a son."

Keegan returned promptly, his eyes glittering.

"They're in jail. Rauenbauer didn't want to go behind bars, but he's in the Cross City jail, too. Johnson won't sit down comfortably for awhile. The sheriff sent men after the boxes of books. The ship won't sail till they get there."

"You had no . . . trouble?" I asked.

"They wrote me notes. I speech-read a little—I hope. Mrs. McElroy showed up, and she could actually finger-spell. Guess I can thank you for that."

Keegan had a big manila envelope in his hand. I glanced at Ken, who nodded. That particular envelope held letters from Sigrid that Ken left for him in the SIGFORD's cabin.

"Thank you for the doctor," Ken spelled with unbearable slowness. Cindy sat down beside him to start correcting his finger-spelling, her lips pursed like a grammarian intent on breaking a student of "ain't."

"I want to see my mother. Now," said Keegan.

"She's not strong," Ken said, dropping his hand wearily and letting me interpret. "She'll have gone to bed long before this. Let's go get her in the morning—either you or I can go."

"You must eat," Cindy told Keegan.

"I'll make out," he said.

He headed for the stairs with the two envelopes, then paused. He turned.

"Need a hand?" he said huskily to Ken.

"I can walk," Ken replied, edging off the couch.

Then I saw his face change. He said, "Yeah, I'd sure appreciate a little help."

I stood at the foot of the stairs, watching the two men ascend—the uncle and nephew, the step-father and step-son. No way for me to interpret, when Ken murmured to Keegan, "Thank you. Thank you for everything, Son."

I wondered if Keegan speechread that last word.

Tomorrow began for me before sunrise—more Keegan's day than Sigrid's.

Awakened in the dark by a tap on my door, I let the visitor—presumably male—wait while I tunneled into my shift. Cindy wouldn't have bothered to knock.

It was Ken, in a blue bathrobe, tilted sideways to lean on my door frame.

"Hate to awaken you, Leslie, but I'm worried about Keegan. I keep waking up with aches and nightmares, and each time I can hear the kid pacing, pacing overhead. His room's right above mine. It's gone on all night. He's read those letters, and it's really hit him."

"Oh, poor Keegan.!"

"I'd better not approach him right now, and Cindy hasn't a gentle enough touch. I know it's more of my meddling, but will you go up and talk with him?"

"Sometimes meddling isn't a bad idea," I said.

I dressed and went upstairs. When I got Keegan's attention and gained admission to his room, I saw behind him letters in Sigrid's staccato handwriting. They were spread out on the desk under the student lamp. Their contents, I wagered, would scorch anyone's eyes to tears.

Keegan ought to cry, but a pacing man does not cry.

Keegan was fully dressed, and his bed had not been opened.

"Come outside," I said. "It's going to be a beautiful sunrise." I made the sign I loved, finger-and-thumb circle of sun rising beyond the horizon of my left arm. "Come outdoors with me."

From the front porch we saw the first pinkness of dawn behind the black wall of mangroves.

"You look very weary," I signed. "Did you not sleep at all?"

He shook his head, staring fixedly at the next day as it moved upon him. We walked together beside the lagoon, until he grimaced up at the windows above. He led me down the path to the solitude of the Gulf beach.

"Wasn't Cindy wonderful?" I sought a safe topic.

"Yes."

"I taught her to shoot. She shoots better than I do."

He interrupted me. "Cindy's almost grown up, Leslie. She's grown, even though she's deaf." His expression was grave.

Many visitors would soon impinge upon our solitude—the sheriff, Sigrid, Duane, the Silvens—so I grabbed this last chance.

"Keegan," I said, "I care a great deal about you. You and I, shall we . . . somehow . . . be together, after this?"

He watched my moving hands, his eyes slitted sideways.

"Don't draw away, Keegan! Everything's still the same between us, isn't it?"

"I've learned something, Leslie. I read my mom's letters . . . got a real education in one night. One thing I learned is what happens when two people are badly mismatched."

"Your father and mother? But you're no Brad Howell! You know that! Your father was sick and weak and neurotic. You're sane and healthy—"

"And deaf."

"Keegan! You can't think so little of yourself!"

"I don't think little of myself, Leslie," he said.

"Those thugs . . . they humiliated you. I wish you HAD shot them!"

"I've been thinking a lot about them. Yeah, they'd scorn a deaf guy, but I'm also a damn Yankee, I'm college-educated, I'll have money, and I had you. They were jealous, too; very jealous. They didn't destroy my self-image, Leslie."

He was miles ahead of me; I gaped.

"And go easy on my father. I always knew he was a neurotic. Now I realize he was psychotic. But also clever. He wanted Mom, and he got her. A smart move. Cruel and selfish, but very clever. Mom's the one who acted stupid. She married on the rebound, foolishly. Like you. I bet you'd marry me—also on the rebound."

"On the rebound? That's absurd! On the rebound from

whom? DUANE?"

"On the rebound from Cindy."

"What?" my hands and voice shrieked. "How ridiculous! That's insane! CINDY?"

"She's grown up. She'll need you less and less. So you must get yourself a replacement—a deaf replacement."

I was tongue- and hand-tied with astonishment, and my astonishment was changing to rage. I wanted to slap that cynical, piquant face.

"You're crazy! You're insulting!"

"Look at yourself, Leslie. You baby Cindy, try to keep her dependent. You think you're her guide to life. You've made her your whole life. You didn't marry last year, because your fiance was leery of Cindy."

"He ran off with another girl!"

"Cindy says you were getting impatient with him long before that. You let someone take him away from you."

"Cindy says that? She talks to you about things like THAT?"

"What's more interesting? You taught me to communicate with her, remember? Don't you expect us to gossip—in your absence? You and I often discuss HER."

"But when did you two talk . . . so much, alone?"

"Sometimes she'd slip down to my room and march right in for a chat."

"In your bedroom?" I squeaked. "At night?"

Keegan let out a rather humorless laugh. "Hey, I never laid a hand on her! I'm no cradle-robber. A kid who looks about eleven is no temptation at all! YOU, on the other hand—" He allowed himself a sardonic grin.

"How often," he said, "does your little sister meet a person who knew the big, wide world, but also knows how it feels to be deaf? A friend who really appreciates—and respects—her? Cindy chafes under that heavy wing of yours, Mother Hen. Better ease up, or she'll peck the hand that feeds her."

"I never knew she felt that way!"

"Because she hid it. She's capable of subtlety, Leslie. She thinks you have a right to treat her any way you want because she lost you your father."

"WHAT? Cindy thinks WHAT?" I got nauseated, the beach spinning around me.

224

"It's true, isn't it? Your dad moved out because of her deafness. It took her a while to figure it all out, and some detective work—"

"How? She can't overhear anyone—"

"Cindy hasn't the heart to tell you this, but I believe she wants me to." He cleared his throat. "Okay. Cindy got into family papers, letters. I can't blame her. If you can't hear, you have to read, to get the facts. If only I'd come across letters like the ones I've read tonight—back years ago!"

"How could Cindy understand—?"

"She told me she took some letters to kids at her school who could read well. She got explanations from them."

"Oh my God!"

"She realizes your father acted irresponsibly, but it still is obvious her deafness broke up the family. She wants to compensate you for that."

"Compensate me?"

"She lets you go on thinking she's a perfect little marvel, a genius at intuition, and other esoteric 'deaf' arts. You overestimate her. And then you turn around and underestimate her emotional maturity. She puts up with it, because she wants to fill the hole your father left in your life."

"But I thought I was playing daddy to HER!"

"You were. You are. But YOU need a father, too, just as I needed a saner father. Cindy and I discussed it a lot, discussed parents and kids. Take Ken, for instance. Cindy says Ken is about your father's age. She likes him—which used to infuriate me—and she wanted you to marry Ken, to get a father AND a husband. Before my mother reappeared, that is."

"And SHE planned to marry you, I suppose?" I tried to keep sarcasm out of my voice and keep my eyebrows level.

"She realizes she and I are too different. Then, when she saw you getting infatuated with me—now just wait—" he held up a hand "—and me falling for you, Cindy gracefully stepped aside. She wants you to have everything you want. She's got a helluva generous heart, your baby sister."

"Oh, Keegan!" I was fighting tears.

225

"Cindy's very intelligent, but she's intellectually stunted. She lost those crucial first six years of learning. She'll be lucky if she learns to master the newspaper. She won't make it to Gallaudet College, not with all you can do for her. Not even if you keep her with you constantly, like Helen Keller and Annie Sullivan.

"And she doesn't want that. She wants to break free. You have to let her go, let her enjoy the deaf community, which—as I understand it—you can commute into but not fully share. In a couple years, she can make it on her own."

"I'm sure she'll do wonderfully."

"You say that, but you feel awfully superior to her. You know you do, and you should. You can hear."

"But I love her! I do truly love her!"

"Sure. You've got a loving nature. But this talk about loving her more than you would a hearing sister—that's nonsense! A hearing sister who knows about current events, fads, fashions, sports, movies, who shares the same sort of friends—you think you wouldn't enjoy her more? You could chat without having to stare at each other all the time, while you do other things with both hands. You could talk on the phone without using a teletypewriter. Leslie, wake up! You can love Cindy without making her into a miracle-child, which she isn't. She's neither a child nor miraculous!"

"Why are you hurting me like this?" I cried, ignoring the splendid sunrise, bright as many rainbows.

"Because you're trying, in a very feminine and subtle way, to propose marriage to me."

I was appalled, my fingers and toes curling up, fried in his brutal perception, his cruel honesty.

"I'm very lucky to have you here. You and Cindy. It was insane to misjudge you; I've suffered agonies of remorse. Cindy's lucky that her sister's devoted to her. But you do it . . . you did it because it fulfilled you, made you feel needed and important . . . and superior. You know that, Leslie. Admit it. You don't need Cindy or me to pour out gratitude upon you, in addition to all THAT profit."

"Oh, I HATE you!"

"Good. You react violently, because it's true. You want to marry me, and that might be too tempting a deal. Just

226

stop and think. You would not—" his words fell like heavy stones on me—"You wouldn't be nearly so eager to marry me if . . . I . . . were . . . not . . . deaf."

Tears streamed down my cheeks—scalding tears on flaming skin.

"I'm not a guy you like a lot who just happens to be deaf. You want me not in spite of my deafness but because of it. That's an insult to me, Leslie. How much will you like me when all this is out in the open?"

"I thought YOU needed self-respect," I cried, my fingers tangling in my haste, "and you destroy all of mine!"

"It hurts me to hurt you. I care about you very much."

"What can I doooo?" (the last word a lonely coyote-wail through unheard lips).

"For starters, don't give me an unfair advantage over Duane. He's nuts about you; it's obvious. Don't reject him just because he's able to hear. Lord, Leslie, you're like the whites who had to prove their broad-mindedness when integration started. They HAD to date black kids, whether they preferred them or not. Black guys and gals felt they had to go with whites. Now it's saner; you love whom you love, not a color, not a handicap, but a PERSON!"

"I'll go away. I'll leave, today. Cindy can stay. She can teach you."

"Over-reaction! Cindy can't hear. You're more valuable to me now. You know that. As my tutor. My interpreter, or at most, my friend."

"You don't want . . . anymore . . . to . . . touch me?"

He threw his head back and hoarsely laughed. "Oh, Leslie, you idiot! I'd give my right arm to carry you up into those trees, and make love to you all day! But that's desire, hungry desire, that I've felt since I met you. That's not the same as your picking me up like a cross to bear for a lifetime! I've held back because you're a decent girl who wants desire and love and marriage all together. Take one, take all."

I stood gaping at him. Not one word about his agony over Ken, Brad, and Sigrid. He was already beyond that, was constructing his future. And destroying me . . . and mine.

Keegan wasn't finished.

"I doubt that I have enough to offer you to make up for my deafness."

"You DO! Oh, Keegan, you have so much to offer—"

"Stop idealizing me! Cindy and I are not marvels! We're handicapped. Wake up! You can help us deaf people without being our saviour—The Miracle Worker. I told you we are NOT little miracles!"

He started back toward the house. "I need an hour's sleep," he explained. "I haven't lain down all night."

I would not go with him. I planted myself on the beach, gasping for air. Soon my resolve weakened. Before he reached the front porch, I'd nearly caught up with him, running so fast the wind dried my tears. Then I hesitated. I stood watcing him spread the fragile yellow netting of the Mexican "matrimonio" hammock for two. He lay down in it, his bare feet as high as his head. He did not see me. From the steps I watched his body relax, his muscles releasing in little spasms.

Keegan Howell—the man I wanted to spend the rest of my life sleeping beside—now saw his father, his mother, and his uncle in the bald light of day. He saw me, too; saw what I was. And I looked worst of all.

I crept past him into the house and found Ken in the shadows of the living room, a mug of coffee steaming on his knee.

"Where's Keegan?"

"In the hammock."

"Did he talk it out? Did he tell you how he felt?"

"Not really."

"He didn't?" Ken exclaimed. "What did he talk about?"

"About Cindy . . . and about himself. And me."

"You and he— I hope something good is developing between you two," he said, closely watching my face.

"You'd better hurry. Go get Sigrid, if you want to surprise Keegan. He's asleep."

Ken gulped his coffee, arose, retrieved the SIGFORD's key from the livingroom table, and then stood in the doorway, gazing down at the hammock. Suspended in mid-air, eyes closed, Keegan would never suspect that anyone stood there discussing him.

I asked Ken, "Did you tell Sigrid anything about Keegan's attempts on your life?"

His reply came instantaneously. "Of course not! For her sake as well as his . . . and mine. Leslie, what I want is a loving wife and son. I've never had that, and I want it desperately. If only Keegan were in fact my own son . . . ."

He shook his head. "I used to come into his room when he was a child, sleeping peacefully like that," he said, his dark eyes soft. "That's the only time I could get near him. One time Brad caught me and said, 'You'll never get HIM!' He knew, hard as we tried to hide it, that Sigrid and I loved each other. All he had for his own was his son. I didn't turn Keegan against him while he was alive. I'm glad of that."

When Ken was gone, I roused Cindy and stayed away while she made herself breakfast.

I found myself vowing that I never wanted to see either Cindy or Keegan again. Cindy's happy prettiness stung my eyes, and I hid my drooping mouth from her "What's wrong?" signs. I hated them both and hated myself for hating them. I was angry and wretched, grieving for my murdered self-image.

So I was a big hypocrite campaigning against hypocrisy in others. A parasite upon the deaf while fighting for their rights. I wanted to disappear, to leave them both and see how they got along without my ears. I kept re-examining the past. Surely I wasn't jealous when Cindy taught Keegan to sign. I felt very proud of her. I'd never expected her to confide family secrets to Keegan, though. To talk to him like an equal.

I shouldn't have taken this job. I shook my head miserably. No. It was the right job. I was a paid tutor, and ought to do only what I was paid to do, not give way to emotion. No. I should've indulged my desires. Why not roll on the sand with Keegan as Beryl once did—give him a language and companionship and physical relief as well?

"Marriage" was the bad word.

No it wasn't. Ken and Sigrid's marriage was a miracle, happening after twenty years of his faithfulness (in his fashion), and her loyalty both to Brad and to him. I was the one who could never marry the man I loved.

"Let's look at this, Leslie," I told myself. "Grow up ten years in one hour."

Suppose I'd come here as a model, and Ken was my age.

Suppose we fell in love. Would I plunge into marriage to him? Had a younger Ken proposed, I would've thought it over at length. I'd have show him to Cindy (always my touchstone), and had him meet Mom and my stepfather. I'd give thought to my further education and career. We'd have to discuss kids, and religion and politics . . .

Keegan was right. Damn him, he was right! Hateful Leslie was, at only twenty-one, a possessive mother. A manipulator worse than Ken ever was, with a stranglehold on her sister-child. Cindy would soon break free, but a wife could sink her talons into a young husband, suck him dry. . . . Yeah, Keegan would be lucky to marry a hearing, signing, interpreting, wife—if she were not me. Not me. I'd failed the test of Cindy, so I wasn't the girl for Keegan.

When Cindy sauntered into the room, licking jelly off her fingers, I sent her out on the porch to awaken Keegan. It was getting late. She performed that task with ecstatic dispatch, swinging him slowly until he roused. What I felt was real, honest-to-goodness, crass and vile jealousy.

He didn't talk to either of us; he got ready for company.

In fresh clothes, his hair still wet from the shower, his eyes darting but seeing nothing, Keegan began pacing again, up and down the porch. I kept out of his way.

How does a man prepare to meet a mother he feared was dead? A mother who loves the man he hated? Add to that the horror that he'd never again hear a word she said.

Ken returned in another half hour, by now strong enough to help from the SIGFORD his blonde, slender bride. She was no longer in boyish slacks but wore a thin green dress that the wind whipped around her knees. She came up the path alone, a smile readied for her son.

Keegan stood on the porch, feet apart, legs braced. I stayed just inside the front door, and Ken remained on the dock near the boat, trying to look busy.

Keegan waited for Sigrid to climb the steps, and when she reached the porch, her hands clasping and unclasping like pink flowers, he stepped forward and folded her in his arms. They didn't need words. She was crying.

"It's all right. It's all right, Mom," he finally said.

"I'm all right. And you're so beautiful. Never more beautiful"

Much smaller than he, even in clogs, she straightened her back and looked up into his face. No attempt to burst into speech. Her hands glided up his sleeves, to his neck, over his ears, and stopped; her transfixed face collapsed again, and she put her forehead on his shoulder and sobbed.

Keegan rocked her gently. "Cry, then. It'll make you feel better. But don't pity me, Mom. I've had a very happy life, up to now. You made sure of that, you and Ken. You were the ones to suffer. Let me enjoy your happiness now."

He walked her into the house, an arm around her shoulders.

"Leslie? Your hands?"

My hands were ready. She didn't take her eyes off Keegan.

"You know everything, now? You forgive me?"

"Does anyone need forgiveness more than I do?" he asked.

". . . After all this, all Brad's lies, can you ever trust my husband?"

"My step-father," he said. Then, with a touch of bitter humor, "It's step-mothers that are supposed to be the wicked ones, not step-fathers. But it'll take time, Mom. Long conditioning . . . Mom, why didn't you leave Dad? I'd have understood, eventually."

"It would've been murder," she said through my fingers. "As Brad finally proved, suicide was always a possibility. And if he'd chosen to live, he had no relatives to care for him. You couldn't go to school and nurse him; he couldn't live with Ken. He had no friends. Then too, if I'd been free, I would have married Ken. Picture that."

"I guess so. You'd have lost me . . . for a time."

"We've all suffered, Keegan. Can we begin again? Can I invite my . . . my new husband into your house, and all three of us start over?"

Keegan turned his head and looked out the door at Ken, who sat on the dock, staring into the water. From up here he appeared very small and young.

"He told me you saved his life, Keegan."

"He did?"

"He said those vile men tied you both up, and when he fell off the dock, you saved him. Saved me from being a widow once again."

"Shhhh, Mother," he said, and he held her close for a moment.

Sigrid suddenly turned and was facing me, her eyes alight. "I have an idea for a . . . for a wedding present. Let's get Ken. Cindy?"

Cindy, I found, had been spying on the visual half of this conversation from the far corner of the living room. Sigrid called her husband up to the house.

The moment he arrived, she said, "I want a wedding present, Ken. I want Cindy to give us the sign language. Like she taught Keegan, teach us! I can't even spell letters. I want to talk to my . . . to our son!"

Seeing this on my fingers, Keegan tried to control his face, but failed; he turned and pushed through the door into the kitchen.

"I'll get us coffee," said Ken, but I offered to do so. I found Keegan still in the kitchen, staring at nothing.

"I've nothing to give them," he said. "The house is Mom's, already. Dad willed everything to me just to hurt her and foil Ken, but he won't succeed. It's theirs."

"Can you give them your love? Both of them?"

"Mom's lovable; that's easy. All I feel for Ken is awe. And amazement. It'll take time. I'm gonna see if I can get into summer school, second term at U of F. I've gotta get out of here."

He got out. He went right out the back door.

Sigrid didn't know Keegan's new habit of disappearing, which Ken knew only too well. I made coffee, served it, and the four of us discussed the island, the house, and wintertime in Norway. When I complimented Ken on his lovely photographs of me playing in the sand, he seemed very grateful.

Sigrid kept looking past me expectantly for her son, and to distract her, I took her up to my bedroom, formerly hers, offering to move out immediately.

She objected. "You keep this room. I don't want my princess-room now. I want to bunk with my husband."

I blushed at my naivete.

Ken brought their baggage upstairs, and Cindy charged

in to present Sigrid with a bouquet of pink and white hibiscus and oleanders. Sigrid, unable to ask Cindy anything directly, thanked my sister and asked us, "Where is Keegan?"

"Be patient. He's doing some repair-work on his attitudes. He'll be just fine."

The sheriff hadn't yet arrived to question us when I heard faint pounding and—nerves taut—rushed outside. Keegan was in the stern of the SIGFORD, chiseling off the wooden letters of the boat's name. The D, R, and O were already floating in the water behind the boat. It was inexplicable, almost appalling.

He did something else now. The hammering done, he was using a paint can and brush. Changing the name.

I couldn't bear·it. I retreated into the house, back to the kitchen, where Sigrid was washing our cups while Ken dried. It seemed like half an hour, but the kitchen clock ticked off only ten minutes before Keegan's shadow fell across the doorway. He motioned us to follow him. The four of us rushed after him like puppets yanked by strings.

He pointed to the dock. We hurried down the path, gazing at the stern of the SIGFORD—the former SIGFORD. The S and I and G remained, and the F was painted into an R. It was, however, not renamed "SIGRID."

Cindy, of course, understood first. She gave a little hop.

"S-I-G-R-E-N," she spelled. "Sigrid and Ken!"

Keegan reached into his pocket and handed a key not to his mother, but to his step-father.

"MY wedding gift," he said huskily.

Sigrid grabbed her son in a quick, fierce embrace. When she released him, Ken grabbed his hand, but Keegan didn't shake hands with him. He carried Ken's hand to Sigrid and placed her right palm on Ken's. That sorta made the sign for marriage.

When I murmured that explanation, Ken smiled broadly. He dragged from Keegan a twisted half-smile in return. But Ken did not try to hug him. He was learning some patience.

After the sheriff's brief visit, in which he told us everything that had happened, and we nodded assent, we ate Cindy's lunch of thawed hotdogs filled with cheese. Then the newlyweds left in the boat for the coast. Ken needed his precautionary chest xray. Cindy wanted to go along, so they took her.

I was doing the dishes, plummeting to earth again—to hell—after the exultation of the reunion of mother and son. I heard footsteps, turned and put my back against the sink.

Keegan came in and stared silently at me.

"What do you want me to do?" I finally said.

"Anything you like."

"But I like you. I used to love you."

"No, you didn't. You loved my deafness."

"KEEGAN!"

"And after all this, I'd be surprised if you ever wanted to see me again."

Without another word, without looking back, he walked out the door.

I slammed dishes into the rack unrinsed, dripping salt tears into the suds. My work was done. Ill-done. I was the one who had no gift to give to anyone. In Gainesville, he could easily find a member of the Registry of Interpreters for the Deaf to help him out with lectures. Maybe there'd be other deaf students there, and surely hard-of-hearing ones. He could go to Gallaudet College if things got too rough at Florida.

I swept today's sand out of the kitchen with ferocious strokes. Damn it, Keegan. I DO love you, under this aching anger that feels like hatred. I love your elfin brows, your wit, your delicious mouth with its brutal words, your wisdom, your tanned, bruised body, your grace, your facile hands.

Ironic, isn't it, Keegan? I'm ready to argue that you're not like your weak father, that you're fully worthy of me, and I find that I'm unworthy of you.

I was wrong, wrong, wrong. Wrong with Cindy, wrong for you. The suffering savior of the deaf was just feeding her own ego. I flayed Ken, Rauenbauer, and even Duane for denigrating the deaf, while I, myself— Keegan now saw me naked of my pretensions, but Cindy had seen me years ago. Back then, I claimed I couldn't play in the school band because I should be home with my poor little deaf sister. In fact, we couldn't afford the clarinet and the uniform. Oh, yes, Leslie! Examples are legion!

"But I love him. I LOVE Keegan," I cried to the copper bottoms of the pots and pans on the wall. "I want to hate him, but I can't!"

Soon I was running back down the path to the beach, running because otherwise I would want to pour a bottle of whiskey down my throat, and whiskey burns.

I walked up and down on the hard-packed, shell-studded sand, pacing as Keegan had paced all night, praying for his wisdom to come upon ME and tell me what to do.

Victorian heroines, disgraced and abandoned, drowned themselves. I considered turning ninety degrees west and walking out into the warm water. . . thereby ruining a honeymoon, devastating Keegan and Cindy, destroying as Brad Howell had destroyed lives.

No, the unselfish thing was to act natural, smile, be neutral and detached, and clear out as soon as possible. Go back to Ohio and seriously reconsider my career. Go not to the professors who gave me A's and had me report on congenital deafness and the new signs—no, go to the Toledo deaf club members and ask, "Am I fit to teach deaf kids? Can I treat it as a career and not as my soul's aalvation?

What would they reply, if they dared be as frank with me as Keegan was?

For what seemed hours I paced, with no interest in the sun's course across the hot, blue sky. I walked on gorgeous shells and did not pick them up. My heart interfered with my breathing.

Deaf to everything but the thud of my heart and the surf beside me, blind to everything but the sand, I found myself looking down at a pair of feet that were not mine.

Keegan didn't say anything, just studied my face. I'd managed to get my chin up. My hands were lead weights I couldn't have raised to sign if my life depended on it. They hung there, dragging down my shoulders.

"Leslie, look at me."

I didn't want to.

"You ought to hate me by now, for all that," he said.

There was more? I said nothing. What would he do with me, now?

"I told the truth," he said, "But your worst enemy wouldn't have laid all that on you all at once, so brutally. How are to taking it? Want to hit me?"

I shook my bent head.

"It feels far worse to be pitied than to be struck in anger."

I thought of Cindy striking him for the blasphemy of "deaf-mute," of the jeering thugs toying with him.

"Go on. I deserve it."

Permitting myself a rush of indignant fury and hurt, I swung my hand suddenly across his face, stinging moisture into his eyes. He scarcely flinched.

He laid his palms on my cheeks, again raising my face to his. "If all I said hasn't made you hit me any harder that that, then maybe there IS more than I saw, Leslie. I had to find out. I had to unload all of it on you, hard, and see if you retained any interest in me. See if it was just a shallow, girlish fantasy."

"Oh, it isn't," my lips said, and he read that.

"People can do wonderful deeds for the wrong motives," he said. "For foolish motives. I might have been a murderer, and certainly would still be a miserable recluse, if you hadn't come. And stayed. And endured."

"Cindy did it."

"Unh huh, there you go again! Yes, Cindy helped. But look at me. I helped make my mother's life a hell, and I almost killed Ken. More than once. I'm a fine one to give you a tongue-lashing. I did it only to find out if there'd be anything left in you—for me."

His solmenity was almost unbearable. My hands caught hold of his. I tried to break free.

"Leslie, listen. There's no cure for my kind of deafness. We know that. But pretend. 'If I could hear, if suddenly, right now, I could hear as well as you can, would you still look at me . . . with that love in your eyes?"

He cautioned me, "No, don't give me a quick answer. Think about it. Imagine it. Be sure that you know."

I imagined it. I shut out his face and imagined Keegan a normal, hearing man. It was torture. A great bubble of grateful joy swelled inside me, and as quickly burst when my eyes flew open to see his gaze directed at my parted lips, waiting to read my words.

He wasn't restored. He'd never be. Life with Keegan

would mean sharing his suffering—daily pain, little taunts and big misunderstandings. Discrimination against him, other people's fears, confusion and loneliness. Year after year, Keegan's wife would watch him fight to live normally amid all the well-intentioned humiliations of the hearing world. It would be like marrying a man with leukemia, facing his physical torture, with remission (for Keegan, those times when he'd fit into the deaf world), and then relapses (when deaf people did not accept his hearing-man's personality, and when he was back in the hearing world that he could no longer hear).

I thought of Sigrid's vastly informed warning, of Cindy's preference that I marry a man like Ken. I remembered Keegan's words that had flayed me raw.

I thought for a long time, and Keegan stood twelve inches from me and waited, watching the thoughts parade across my face.

Then very softly, with tiny, hesitant gestures, I said, "We could . . . try? Just try?"

"Your wisdom grows." Gentle words. "People can always try. Yes. No one has the whole answer, neither you nor I."

A sob came up in my throat like a cough, and he pulled me to him, to rest my face in the curve of his strong, swimmer's neck.

"Second term starts in two weeks over at the University. Do you think they'd have any courses you'd need? Cindy said you're already a registered interpreter. I can think of someone who might possibly need an interpreter. A paid interpreter."

I nodded, hanging onto him in the salt wind that flapped our pants legs about our ankles.

"Hoooy!"

Cindy's cry, and we saw her at the tree-line, hands flung out, held motionless by something she saw in our faces. Keegan finally motioned with his head, and she came down the sand, fascinated horror in her eyes. Keegan understood.

"I told her, yes." He signed quickly. "And she still loves you. And me. Both of us."

Cindy was now the one embarrassed before her sister. She put her little blonde head down and charged, burying her hot face in my shirtfront.

237

I felt a more intense love well up in me than I had ever known. I held her and kissed her platinum hair. We needed no signs.

Keegan had taken from his pocket a pad and pen. He wrote something, and turned Cindy around to give a note to her.

It said, "Why not let Cindy give you your first lesson in signs? Don't worry about us. Leslie and I are taking a long walk. See you around sunset. Keegan."

"We have a lot more to talk about," Keegan told Cindy.

Abruptly, she stuck the note back at him. "Take to who?"

"You know who," he said.

"Write who."

He snapped the pen point down again, pressed the note on his palm, then looked over at me. His blue eyes left me hanging between a smile and a fresh burst of tears. He was thinking. Struggling with something, under Cindy's hopeful gaze.

He sighed, wrote, and gave the note back to her. She read it, smiled happily at him, and flashed the note at me before she turned to dash back up the beach toward home.

Keegan had added a salutation to his note. It now began, "Dear Ma and Pa—"

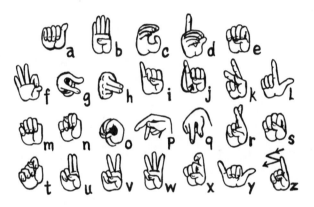

Appendix

Information about deafness and sign language is obtainable from the following resources:

NATIONAL ASSOCIATION OF THE DEAF, (NAD) 814 Thayer Avenue, Silver Spring, Maryland 20910, (301) 587-1788.

Publishes the DEAF AMERICAN magazine and the BROADCAST-ER newspaper monthly. Publishes and distributes sign-language texts, cards, and films, and materials on all aspects of deafness and the lives of deaf people. Bookstore catalog available, and information.

(JUNIOR NAD, c/o Gallaudet College, 7th and Florida, N.E., Washington, D.C. 20002)

AMERICAN SOCIETY FOR DEAF CHILDREN, 814 Thayer Avenue, Silver Spring, Maryland 20910, (301) 585-5400

Publishes a bimonthly newsletter, the ENDEAVOR, and advises parents and the public on issues relevant to parents of the deaf.

GALLAUDET COLLEGE, 7th and Florida, N.E., Washington, D.C. 20002. Liberal Arts College for the deaf, Graduate School, research programs.

Sign Language Programs; Public Information service with brochures on many topics; Kendall School and the Model Secondary School for the Deaf serve pre-school to pre-college-age students. Bookstore catalog available.

NATIONAL TECHNICAL INSTITUTE FOR THE DEAF, One Lomb Memorial Drive, Rochester, New York 14623.

Affiliated with the Rochester Institute of Technology. Deaf students integrated with hearing. Interpreters and other programs for the deaf.

REGISTRY OF INTERPRETERS FOR THE DEAF, (RID) 8719 Colesville, Suite 310, Silverspring, MD 20910, (301) 279-0555.

Certifies interpreters and publishes a directory listing them.

NATIONAL CENTER FOR LAW AND THE DEAF, Florida Avenue at 7th, N.E., Washington, D.C. 20002, (202) 651-5000.

Distributes materials and advises upon civil rights and civil and criminal prosecution involving deaf people.

TELECOMMUNICATIONS FOR THE DEAF, INC., (TDI) 814 Thayer Ave., Silver Spring, MD 20910, (301) 589-3786, 589-3043 (TDD).
Coordinates acquisition and distribution of surplus teletypewriters to deaf people, publishes a newsletter and a directory of numbers.

NATIONAL THEATER OF THE DEAF, (NTD) 305 Great Neck Road, Waterford, Connecticut 06385.
Touring company offering traditional and original dramas on stage and on television; signs and voice narration both used.

AMERICAN HUMANE ASSOC. HEARING DOG PROGRAM, 5351 S. Roslyn St., Englewood, CO 80111, (303) 779-1400, 770-5599 (TDD).